URBAN PUBLIC POLICY

Issues in Policy History
General Editor: Donald T. Critchlow

URBAN
PUBLIC
POLICY

Historical Modes
and Methods

Edited by
Martin V. Melosi

The Pennsylvania State University Press
University Park, Pennsylvania

This work was originally published as a special issue of *Journal of Policy History* (vol. 5, no. 1, 1993). This is its first separate paperback publication.

Library of Congress Cataloging-in-Publication Data

Urban public policy : historical modes and methods / edited by Martin V. Melosi.

      p.   cm.
   "This work was originally published as a special issue of Journal
of policy history (vol. 5, no. 1, 1993)"—T.p. verso.
   Includes bibliographical references.
   ISBN 0-271-01093-2 (paper)
   1. Urban policy—United States—History—20th century. 2. City planning—
United States—History—20th century. I. Melosi, Martin V., 1947- .
   HT123.U763 1993
   307.76'0973—dc20   93-15358
                                                             CIP

Contents

Editor's Preface

The Los Angeles riots that occurred in May 1992 catapulted the problems of the city back on the policy agenda. The cauldron of social problems of the city, as the riots showed, offers no simple solutions. Indeed, urban policy includes a range of policy issues involving welfare, housing, job training, education, drug control, and the environment. The myriad local, state, and federal agencies only further complicate formulating and implementing coherent policies for the city.

This volume, while not offering specific proposals to remedy the problems of the city, provides a broad historical context for discussing contemporary urban policy. The essays address issues related to public housing, poverty, transportation, and the environment. In doing so, the authors discuss larger themes in urban policy as well as provide case studies of how policies have been implemented over time in specific cities. Of particular interest, two of the essays discuss the role of the historian in shaping urban policy and the importance of historical preservation in urban planning.

This volume therefore provides a context for looking at urban policy in different ways and for arriving at new prescriptions for relieving the ills of the American city.

Donald T. Critchlow
General Editor

MARTIN V. MELOSI

Introduction

Social scientists Lawrence J. R. Herson and John M. Bolland describe the connection between the city as government and the city as an urban place in terms of "rules that direct and constrain behavior on behalf of the collective good; services that make collective living possible; and money—raised through taxes—that pays the people who enforce the rules and provide city services."[1]

Such a definition assumes a somewhat mechanistic view in establishing urban policy, that is, government simply responding to perceived public needs. Historian Terrence McDonald has been an outspoken critic of the so-called "functionalist" analysis of cities which makes the assumption that social institutions such as urban government and urban political regimes "persist and develop because they fulfill certain functions, either for urban society as a whole or for diverse subgroups of that society."[2] McDonald is not attacking functionalism per se. "The problem with a functionalist framework," he concludes, "is not that it is necessarily wrong, but that its assumptions (e.g., that functions are fulfilled) are frequently unexamined, and that its framework (i.e., that some variables influence some other variables) is unclear."[3] McDonald's criticism is a valuable cautionary note for examining urban public policy and for avoiding the view of local government "as a process that was automatic, rather conflict-free, and perhaps even wholly beneficent."[4]

But urban public policy is not derived solely from the local government process. In the twentieth century in particular, cities are parts of regional networks and are also tethered to state and federal governments by a host of laws, policies, and programs that directly affect local decision-making.

Can urban policy history help to make sense of city actions? According to Seymour J. Mandelbaum, "Far from caring too little about history, all the participants in the policy community care too much about it to leave it to any group of specialists or to wait for the development of a scholarly consensus."[5] Alas, this may be true. However, the complexities of urban public policy are such that the ability of historical research to examine long-trend lines, to offer carefully crafted analogies, and to provide historical perspective gives urban policy history value. The problem becomes not producing useful studies, but finding ways to get them into the hands of policymakers.

This volume does not offer answers to that problem directly, but it does demonstrate the broad range of historical research being conducted in the area of urban policy history and some vital contemporary issues to be confronted in cities throughout the country.

In "Five Downtown Strategies: Policy Discourse and Downtown Planning Since 1945," Carl Abbott argues that downtown policy has been characterized by "sharp discontinuities" and the repeated implementation of policies "that take off at right angles to those of the previous decade." His argument is in fundamental disagreement with Bernard Frieden and Lynne Sagalyn's study, *Downtown, Inc: How America Rebuilds Cities* (1989), which assumes "unidirectional development" from urban renewal through downtown malls and festival markets.

Paul George Lewis's "Housing and American Privatism: The Origins and Evolution of Subsidized Home-Ownership Policy" sets the Section 235 home-ownership program established in the 1968 omnibus housing legislation in a broad political and analytical context. Lewis argues that although the program was intended to encourage home ownership among low- and moderate-income families, it ultimately was retargeted toward higher income groups. Essentially, federal subsidy payments and guarantees to lenders and developers ultimately undermined its "redistributive vision."

"Chicago Influences on the War on Poverty," by Noel A. Cazenave, states that the basic models of social enterprise and community action employed in the controversial Community Action Program of the War on Poverty in the 1960s were used in Chicago twenty years earlier. Focusing on two case studies—Hasseltine Byrd Taylor's report on the Chicago Area Project and the Council of Social Agencies of Chicago's study of Saul Alinsky's Back of the Yards Neighborhood Council—Cazenave raises questions about "the congruence of the utilization of social science experts and the encouragement of democratic participation in public-policy formation and implementation in a modern democracy."

Sy Adler addresses some key issues about industry-government relations with respect to urban transportation in "The Evolution of Federal Transit Policy." Adler is interested in the "dynamics of municipalizing a failing private industry." As he argues in his study, transit policy was captured by "central business district activists in cities across the country seeking to enhance the locational advantages of their place in the face of increasingly intense competition from suburban business centers." Compare his conclusions with Abbott's thesis about downtown development.

My selection, "Down in the Dumps: Is There a Garbage Crisis in America?" questions the casual use of the term "crisis" to define solid waste collection and disposal problems in contemporary American cities. Through examining the significant elements of the solid waste system in a historical context, I conclude that the solid waste problem is too complex simply to regard it as a crisis: "Much of what has come to be considered the 'garbage crisis' is not the product of immediate past practices or present inaction, but a series of chronic problems, interrelated in such a way as to defy a simple solution."

Harold Platt is interested in cities within a regional context. "World War I and the Birth of American Regionalism" stresses that historians "have all but ignored the subject of society at war as a causal factor in the formation of public policy" and have given short shrift to city planners' use of technology as a "source of influence" in the generation of policy. The study examines the impacts of World War I on two conflicting groups of planners—"Progressive reform idealists," who would eventually form the core of the Regional Planning Association of America, and practicing city engineers. For both groups, the regional power grid became the "ideal metaphor of regional planning" and the single most powerful tool for achieving their goals.

The last two pieces address issues within the history profession vis-à-vis the policy process. In "City as Artifact: Heritage Preservation in Comparative Perspective," Alan Mayne pillories the history profession, "which has remained ambivalent about involvement with either preservation practice or with history making as a public activity." His vehicle for discussion is a comparison of American and Australian historic preservation practices. In his conclusion, Mayne calls for historians to act: "Empowerment is not an intellectual exercise for armchair socialists. It requires historians to participate fully in the public policy arena: not just conducting historical research, but sitting on committees, collecting signatures, and raising donations." More interested in method than motivation, Seymour J. Mandelbaum's "Reading Old Plans" muses about the value in reading formal planning texts. On a broader plane, Mandelbaum is concerned with ways of thinking about historical documents—especially those that offer insights about the three-dimensional world. "The identity I invent," he concludes, "need not capture exactly the perspective of any particular reader—as if that were even possible—but it must be embedded in authentic practices and prejudices, in knowledge and passion, in flesh and in blood."

The essays in this volume are intended to provide readers with fresh insights on a range of important urban themes. The contributors have produced new research not only in the hope of carrying forward a dialogue on their topics of interest but also in pursuing new modes and methods of exploring urban policy history. Yet more work remains to be done on an even wider range of topics. And more attention needs to be given to ways to encourage the use of history in the policy-making environment.

University of Houston

Notes

1. Lawrence J. R. Herson and John M. Bolland, *The Urban Web: Politics, Policy, and Theory* (Chicago, 1990), 7.

2. Terrence J. McDonald, *The Parameters of Urban Fiscal Policy: Socioeconomic Change and Political Culture in San Francisco, 1860–1906* (Berkeley and Los Angeles, 1986), 2–3.

3. Ibid., 3.

4. Ibid., 12–13.

5. Seymour J. Mandelbaum, "Urban Pasts and Urban Policies," *Journal of Urban History* 6 (August 1980): 454.

CARL ABBOTT

Five Downtown Strategies: Policy Discourse and Downtown Planning Since 1945

Americans have planned for their downtowns within a continually changing framework of images and assumptions about the nature of central business districts. During each decade since World War II, discussion of downtown problems and possibilities has been dominated by a distinct set of assumptions that has conditioned academic research, federal policy, and local planning. From decade to decade, experts on downtowns have chosen different themes as central to the interpretation of downtown growth, change, and policy needs. As the understanding of the situation has changed, so have the preferred planning solutions and public interventions.

This argument about the importance of understanding the history of "downtown" as an intellectual construct can be contrasted with three major approaches that have dominated the analysis of downtown planning and policy in the United States over the last half century.

A number of writers have analyzed downtown policy as an expression of interest-group or class politics. In this interpretation, downtown is one of several arenas in which different groups contest for control of urban land patterns. Most common, the battle for downtown is seen as a one-sided contest between the city's large corporations, banks, and land owners on one side and small businesses and low-income residents on the other. Influential examples include Clarence Stone's work on Atlanta, Arnold Hirsch's study of Chicago, Chester Hartman's work on San Francisco, and Chris Silver's history of Richmond. Gerald Suttles's recent examination of contemporary Chicago in *The Man-Made City* recycles the same approach with sympathy for the goals of gentrification and land conversion rather than the more common concern with the social costs of downtown redevelopment. A comparative analysis of six current downtown plans by Norman Krumholz and Dennis Keating implicitly places the documents in the context of group politics by testing their balance between economic development and social equity.[1]

Other analysts have adopted a structure-driven model in which downtown development and redevelopment programs are seen as rational responses to specific socioeconomic circumstances and problems. A pure structural model is organized around a dynamic of challenge and response. Changes external to the policy system, such as new technologies, immigration, or the regional readjustment of economic activity, create problems that call forth policy solutions. In turn, altered circumstances may give rise to new problems that call forth new solutions. This model assumes that policies are logically situated between problems and programs, although policies may have unintended as well as intended consequences.[2]

A detailed recent application of the structural approach is Jon Teaford's *The Rough Road to Urban Renaissance*, which examines revitalization policy in twelve northern cities and finds a series of partial successes that lead repeatedly to more complex problems. Teaford treats downtown planning and urban renewal as elements in comprehensive revitalization programs that have also included annexation, public housing, industrial development, and transportation. He finds a broad shift from optimism to pessimism and diminished expectations during the 1960s. Nevertheless, city leaders are seen as fighting gamely against a shifting set of problems, winning occasional battles but neither winning nor losing the larger war.[3]

A third approach follows a teleological model that traces the roots of present successes. Bernard Frieden and Lynne Sagalyn, for example, are modern equivalents of the Whig historians who celebrated the progress of liberty in the growth of the English Constitution. Their study, *Downtown, Inc.: How America Rebuilds Its Cities*, essentially follows a structural model written as the story of progress. A single clear problem is identified in the 1940s and 1950s. Politicians and planners then work through trial and error toward an increasingly effective solution, moving from urban renewal to festival markets and downtown malls. There is room for detours but not for the blind alleys that Teaford describes.[4]

Without rejecting these three approaches to the history of downtown policy, this article offers a supplementary perspective. I believe that many scholars and planners have shared an underlying assumption that "downtown" is a singular knowable entity—a basic category of urban analysis. In this common conception, academic and applied research presumably illuminate more and more aspects of this knowable entity, allowing the fine tuning of plans and policies. My emphasis, in contrast, is on "downtown" as a constructed concept whose meaning or understanding has undergone surprisingly rapid changes. As the structural model argues, these mutable understandings have certainly been rooted in the changing social and economic structure of American cities, and they have certainly proved of varying use to different groups and interests. However, they have also had lives of their own as intellectual constructs, with the thematic understanding of one decade defined in part as a reaction against earlier ideas. In turn, these ideas about downtowns can be seen as filtered reflections of broader trends in political thought or cultural expression.

This article explores these changing ideas by examining the contents and assumptions of a variety of formal and informal texts. One obvious set of sources is academic and professional analysis of downtowns by geographers, planners, and real estate specialists. The discussion is also based on my understanding of implementation efforts and programs, from urban renewal to the pursuit of amenity projects. Situated between the analysis and the programs have been formal downtown plans and planning processes that have tried to link theory and practice. Chronologically parallel shifts in content and emphasis among the three sorts of texts help to substantiate the assumption that public action about central business districts has been rooted in a partially autonomous realm of changing ideas.

The shift from one thematic understanding to another has not been unidirectional. Downtown policy has been characterized by sharp discontinuities and the repeated implementation of policies at right angles to those of the previous decade. The changing themes and recommended solutions can be summarized as a set of ideal types. No single city has exactly matched the sequence, and thematic elements from one policy era have carried over into the following decades. Nevertheless, the historian can define five successive themes and related policies.

- 1945–55: The downtown as the *unitary center* of the American metropolis required improved access through highway improvements and downtown ring roads.
- 1955–65: Downtown understood as a *failing real estate market* appeared to require the land assembly and clearance associated with the urban renewal program.
- 1965–75: Downtown as a *federation of subdistricts* called for community conservation, historic preservation, and "human scale" planning.
- 1975–85: Downtown as a *set of individual experiences* required regulation of private design and public assistance for cultural facilities, retail markets, open space, and other amenities.

- 1985–: Viewed as a *command post* in the global economy, downtown has required planning for expanded office districts and supporting facilities.

Downtown as the Unitary Center of the Metropolitan Area: 1945–55

Thinking about American downtowns during the first half of the twentieth century was shaped by the idea of the unified metropolitan community. Although the metropolitan area concept was developed in the early twentieth century, it gained broad popularity with the definition of the easily grasped Standard Metropolitan Area for the 1950 census.[5] The idea assumed the existence of a dominant central city, which was itself structured around a downtown core. Academic analysis of downtowns therefore operated within the framework of Ernest Burgess's zonal model and Homer Hoyt's sectoral model of urban land use, both of which posited that cities were organized around unitary centers.[6]

Building on work from the 1920s and 1930s, experts in the postwar decade analyzed land values to identify the precise center of central business districts (CBDs) and the gradient of real estate values away from that center. John Rannels utilized a detailed survey of central Philadelphia land uses to define the "center of gravity" and degree of dispersion of CBD activities.[7] Other researchers tried to define "downtown" as distinguished from its surrounding blocks of deteriorated or transitional uses. Raymond Murphy, James Vance, and Bart Epstein epitomized the research effort with an elaborate analytical definition of the downtown based on building heights and the percentage of total floor space on each block that was devoted to a carefully limited list of "central business uses." Their standardized definition was intended to allow easy comparisons among downtown areas taken as units.[8]

Related studies of commuting and shopping patterns found that the golden age of the 1920s, when downtowns were *the* place to go, was alive and well after World War II. Gerald Breese found that total daytime population in downtown Chicago in 1946 matched the previous peak of 1929. Sociologist Donald Foley documented a strong upward trend in the number of people entering the CBDs of small and mid-sized metropolitan areas between 1926 and 1950 and concluded that there was little substance to the notion that suburban dispersion was undermining central business districts.[9] Most planning projections of downtown land-use needs assumed a straight-line continuation of past relationships between metropolitan growth and size and the roles and size of the central business district.[10]

Business and marketing literature agreed on the strength of downtown as an office and retail center. C. T. Jonassen's analyses of shopper preferences in Columbus, Seattle, and Houston found that downtowns held a significant edge over struggling suburban shopping centers. "The advantages now enjoyed by the central business district," he concluded, "are not easily alterable, for they are rooted in the ecological structure of American cities and in their cultural and social system." Downtowns, said J. D. Carroll, were the "only focus" and the "only sites" for essential urban activities. The sole requirement was successful treatment of traffic congestion and parking.[11] Whatever the changes in metropolitan areas, concluded the Central Business District Council of the Urban Land Institute in 1954, "downtown continues to hold its position as the gathering place of America—the center of business and finance, the center of shopping on its most lavish scale, the center for theaters and for culture."[12]

The assumption that everyone still wanted to get downtown defined the logical focus of planning activity as the improvement of access and circulation. Downtown itself was taken as a given—as a unique and essential element within a metropolitan structure. The postwar development plans that dozens of cities prepared in 1943, 1944, and 1945 offered broadly inclusive programs for capital investment with little special targeting for downtown.[13] The last generation of classic master plans during the 1940s gave little explicit attention to the downtown itself as a special problem. Instead, the typical proposal was for the opening of new circumferential highways closely bordering the downtown, to improve access and set off surrounding residential areas. Also prominent were proposals for civic centers as metropolitan foci, a recycling of a key idea from the City Beautiful–era century that assumed the natural centering of the metropolis.[14]

Two points stand out in a set of major comprehensive plans prepared in the mid- and late 1940s for Washington, D.C., Richmond, Dallas, and Cincinnati.[15] The first is that few of the planners considered the CBD to be seriously at risk. The plans tended to give greatest attention to housing, neighborhood identity, and neighborhood conservation. In turn, neighborhoods were to be linked together into a single metropolitan community by transportation improvements and by their common relation to the downtown. For example, Cincinnati's *Metropolitan Master Plan* of 1948 acknowledged the "close relationship between the Central Business District and each community" but did not see the CBD itself as requiring attention. The Dallas plan ran to fourteen volumes, none focused specifically on downtown.[16]

When downtown did need attention, the solution was improved access through peripheral freeways. Harlan Bartholomew wanted to use the 1946 *Master Plan for Richmond* to promote the vision of a tightly centralized city, in part by expanding the central business district and tying it to neighborhoods by a set of highways and widened boulevards. As Chris Silver has noted, the new or improved roads would define the boundaries for an expanded business core. The result, said the document, would be "continued stability and protection of values within the central business district." Elsewhere in the South, Nashville cleared the back slopes of its Capitol Hill in 1954 to provide space for a park, parking lots, and the James Robertson Parkway to loop traffic around the back side of the CBD and across the Cumberland River on a new Victory Memorial Bridge.[17]

The National Capital Park and Planning Commission offered a similar prescription in its 1950 plan for the Washington region. Its proposal for an inner highway loop drawing a one-mile circle around the White House and the retail-office core was the work of Harland Bartholomew in his role as chief consultant to the NCPPC. The idea was seconded by the influential Washington architect Louis Justement, who had made a similar proposal in a 1946 book, *New Cities for Old*. It was supported as well by the transportation subcommittee of the Committee of 100, a local good planning/good government organization.[18]

Victor Gruen's highly publicized plan for downtown Fort Worth is a climax of thinking about a unitary downtown. An architect with experience in shopping center design, Gruen proposed a grand scheme to isolate the core of Fort Worth within a ring of six grand parking garages served by a highway loop. With its streets freed from automobiles, downtown Fort Worth could recapitulate the suburban shopping mall. Had Fort Worth acted on the plan, it would have given physical expression to Gruen's valuation of freeway loops and ring roads as "defense lines" and "fortification systems" around the downtown. It would also have expressed his understanding of the "metropolitan core" as the "heart of the city."[19]

Downtown as a Failing Business Center: 1955–65

In January 1955, J. Ross McKeever summarized the real estate trends of the past year for the readers of *Urban Land*, the trade journal of the real estate development industry. He left no doubt that downtown was "the functional heart of a metropolitan area" and the "focal point of community life." Two years later, Baltimore developer James Rouse told the same readership that downtowns were in serious trouble. They were physically obsolete and could not effectively reach the growing suburban market. Planners so far had dealt only with symptoms rather than sources of downtown problems. Only drastic action could assure the *rebirth* of the central business district. [20]

The contrast between the two views demonstrates the rapid emergence during the mid-1950s of a new understanding of downtown as a declining activity center and failing real estate market. By the early 1960s, most Americans understood downtown as a district in crisis because of the relative or absolute decline of its attractiveness to shoppers, theatergoers, and service businesses. The 1958 Census of Business played an important role by documenting the shift of retailing and personal services to suburban locations. The 1960 Census of Population administered an additional shock by showing that many central cities had fallen far short of their expected populations. [21] With these "heralded indicators of decadence" as background, scholars analyzed the decline of downtown business in a group of studies that examined 1948–58 data and appeared in a cluster between 1960 and 1964. As in the previous decade, however, most of these studies continued to treat downtowns as economic units, comparing aggregated data on sales and employment. [22]

One local response was to organize a business group devoted specifically to upgrading the competitiveness of downtown. Unlike areawide chambers of commerce or the ubiquitous postwar planning committees of the 1940s, these downtown groups battled for a share of the retail and service market rather than working for aggregate economic development. Examples can be found in Denver and Cincinnati, San Diego, Portland, and Richmond. The Committee for Downtown Baltimore grew out of the Retail Merchants Association in 1954. The Minneapolis Downtown Council appeared in 1955, the same year that the Indianapolis Civic Progress Association incorporated "to enhance the attractiveness and utility of the central downtown area." "Downtown in St. Louis, Inc." organized in 1958 to engage in a "crusade" to renew downtown. [23]

The later 1950s and early 1960s also brought a round of focused downtown plans that worried explicitly about the future of the central business district. City planners now expressed the new understanding that downtown could easily lose its logical and organic predominance. Cleveland planners in 1959 worried that the future vitality of their downtown was threatened by suburbanization and blight as well as traffic. Dallas's revision of Bartholomew's master plan included a separate report on the "Dallas Central District" (1961). Cincinnati's *Central Business District*

Plan (1958), *Central Business District and Riverfront Report* (1961), and *Plan for Downtown Cincinnati* (1964) noted the shortfall of new private investment, proposed new zoning, and called for redevelopment of blighted land.[24]

As Cincinnatians and Clevelanders realized, the most obvious policy response to downtown business decline was urban renewal. Amendments in 1954 and 1959 transformed the Housing Act of 1949 into a downtown renewal program. Urban renewal advocates assumed that downtown could be made competitive by underwriting the real estate market and adding in public projects as attractors. The preferred target was underutilized or "blighted" land just beyond the retail and office core. The nearly universal results were peripheral clearance projects and construction of public facilities. Renewal in cities such as New Haven, Pittsburgh, Philadelphia, and Washington was abundantly documented in newspapers, magazines, and books such as Jeanne Lowe's *Cities in a Race with Time* (1967).[25] The underlying impulse, as many critics were to point out, was to impose the universal rationalism of modern design on large segments of American downtowns.

Academic research in the later 1950s supported the renewal strategy by emphasizing the distinction between an intensively used downtown core and a less intensively used "frame." The idea of a frame was a more limited restatement of the historic "zone in transition." Downtown frames were hodge-podge zones of warehouses, light industry, cheap housing, transportation terminals, auto dealers, and public institutions such as hospitals. The idea evolved in applied work in Seattle and Cincinnati and was elaborated in detail by Edgar Horwood and Ronald Boyce in 1959.[26] Ernest Jurkat presented a similar concept with different terminology when he defined a "belt" zone in cities like St. Louis that roughly matched the functions of the frame.[27] The analysis justified land clearance in downtown fringe areas to protect and enhance the core.

Plans in Oakland and Baltimore were good summaries of the new views. A reviewer for the *Journal of the American Institute of Planners* called Baltimore's *Plan for the Central Business District* the "prototype of the comprehensive CBD plan." Increases in private and public offices partially balanced the projected declines in retail, wholesale, and industrial uses. Downtown not only needed new facilities such as parking garages but also required much broader replanning of land uses to support a selected set of region-serving functions. The centerpiece for implementation was the Charles Center redevelopment project to remake the downtown core. Oakland's *Central District Plan* in 1966 distinguished among a core, inner ring, and peripheral ring, each of which called for a different set of public interventions.[28]

Downtown as a Federation of Everyday Environments: 1965–75

The massive land clearances of the 1950s fueled a reaction against urban renewal in the early 1960s from both the conservative and liberal sides of the political spectrum. The former emphasized the economic failures of urban renewal and its inability to improve on the private market in land and housing. The latter described its unwanted social impacts and the destruction of viable lower-income communities.[29] One of the perhaps unexpected side effects was the redefinition of downtown as a set of distinct functional subdistricts, each of which appeared to foster a different sort of activity and each of which needed particularized treatment.

This new vision or image drew on the work of Herbert Gans, Jane Jacobs, and Kevin Lynch, all of whom suggested that downtowns had to be experienced on the relatively small scale of individual buildings, blocks, and districts.[30] The contrast between older and newer views can be read in a comparison of Gruen's 1955 plan for Fort Worth and his plan for Boston from the early 1960s. In the latter he identified a dozen and a half "pedestrial nuclei, each devoted to a variety of land uses, with an emphasis, however, on those which have developed historically." Seven of the nuclei were in the "so called CBD" and eleven just outside.[31] The transition can also be seen in a comparison of 1961 statements by Jacobs and Charles Abrams. Drawing their sense of the American city from New York, both Jacobs and Abrams hoped to achieve vibrant, active downtown districts. Abrams also reaffirmed the idea of downtown as a single unit, asserting that "a downtown area is a cohesive unit which lives or dies as a whole." Jacobs, in contrast, treated downtown as a set of intertwined activity centers. In the best-selling *Death and Life of Great American Cities*, she wrote about diversity, subdistricts, and concentrated "pools of use." "Every city primary use," she wrote, "needs its intimate matrix of 'profane' city to work to best advantage. The courts building in San Francisco needs one kind of matrix with its secondary diversity. The opera needs another kind."[32]

Academics participated in the new understanding of downtowns as multiple centers with behavioral studies of user subareas and efforts to define the social and economic geography of downtowns. Common products of the 1960s were studies of retail clustering and the mapping of functional subdistricts for cities such as Dallas, New Orleans, and Chicago.[33] University of Washington researchers found that downtown Seattle was composed of "user subsystems" and activity nodes that should be delineated before the city undertook any new plans and projects.[34] Historical geographers such as David Ward and Martyn Bowden supplemented the current mapping efforts by studying the historical coalescence of downtown out of a variety of functional subareas.[35]

It is clear that subarea analysis was in the air by the later 1960s. In 1963, consultant Donald Monson had responded to the concerns of the Central Association of Seattle with a *Comprehensive Plan for the Central Business District.* Monson's proposal was Gruenesque, ignoring the constraints of the city's steep hills to propose a ring highway defining a unitary downtown, fringe parking garages, and pedestrianized shopping streets. Seven years later, the Central Association's own annual report stated that downtown Seattle was best understood in terms of a "system of functional zones, each with a distinct character that, when integrated into the whole, make up the central nervous system of our metropolitan community." Each of the six districts "has its own role to play and potential to fulfill" in the expected development of Seattle as a headquarters city.[36]

Omaha's formal plans also displayed the changing policy orientations of the three postwar decades. As Janet Daly has shown, the "Omaha Plan" of 1956 scarcely recognized downtown as a problem and emphasized infrastructure investment. Ten years later, the *Central Omaha Plan* (1966) recognized special downtown needs but placed its faith in interstate highways and urban renewal. The next seven years, however, brought a generational transition in civic leadership and a willingness to focus on the multiple experiences that downtown had to offer. A new central business district plan in 1973 divided downtown Omaha into eight "neighborhoods" or functional areas. Planners hoped that a variety of functions and attractions would pull residents back downtown, and that each identifiable district would strengthen the others.[37]

The story was the same in Portland. Urban renewal planners in 1957–60 envisioned a compact downtown defined by a freeway loop and peripheral parking lots. The local downtown business lobby supported the proposals in the hope that property values could be stabilized in a small, limited-function business district. A decade later, a new generation of business leaders, politicians, and citizens redefined downtown Portland around the theme of variety. The citizen advisory committee that wrote the planning guidelines for the new Downtown Plan of 1972 divided the core into twenty-one districts on the basis of current uses, opportunities for redevelopment, and visual coherence. The plan inventoried current uses for each area and focused on possibilities for new housing, secondary retail centers, pedestrian circulation, public transit, and waterfront open space. Previous plans for downtown Portland had offered bird's-eye views in which tiny automobiles coursed along looping highways between toy houses and skyscrapers. The 1972 plan depicted downtown Portland as a sequence of sidewalk scenes. Retired men played chess in the park, students munched junk food near Portland State University, shoppers strolled a transit mall, and children played around a new foundation.[38]

By the early 1970s, the subdistricted downtown was as much a staple of planning documents as the unitary downtown had been in 1950. Indeed, subarea analysis remained a standard for downtown description into the 1990s. After 1975, however, it became accepted background rather than an exciting discovery.[39] A sampling of downtown plans from 1976 to 1986 shows that Dallas and Atlanta each identified three districts. Dayton identified seven, Washington seven (or perhaps ten), Richmond eight, and Oakland eleven. Denver found six districts in its core and four more in a surrounding transition zone. Seattle built its downtown plan on eleven "areas of varied character."[40]

Downtown as a Set of Individual Experiences: 1975–85

As American cities recovered from the severe real estate recession of 1973–74, planners and policymakers reevaluated their discovery of the multiple downtown. Subdistrict analysis identified a wider range of development opportunities than a unitary analysis. At the same time, its recognition of residential groups and secondary business clusters built in a bias in favor of conservation and enhancement rather than redevelopment.

The desire to stimulate downtown business and investment brought a renewed interest in downtowns as consciously manipulated artifacts. In this newest understanding, downtown was less a set of distinct social environments than a collection of opportunities for individual experiences. Downtown areas were increasingly seen as environments to be consciously designed in the interest of enjoyment and tourism. This conception of downtown as a theme park accepted its loss of primacy within the metropolitan community. It was to be reconstructed to serve tourists, conventioneers, and occasional visitors on safari from the suburbs. It also accepted that suburban "outer cities" were emerging as co-equals to downtown and then borrowed some of the ideas of the consciously designed suburban environment. If direct retail competition with suburban malls was a failure, planners asked, why not emphasize specialized entertainment and shopping. The results were downtowns conceived as museums, cultural centers, amenity districts, and amusement parks.

An obvious reflection of the new understanding was a flood of interest in the academic and professional literature on the economic role of the arts and on the recovery of physical amenities, especially along waterfronts. Books and articles on the arts as contributors to urban development policy peaked in the early 1980s.[41] Beginning in the early 1970s, William H. Whyte examined the environmental determinants of individual responses to parks, plazas, sidewalks, and other downtown public spaces. He helped to popularize a view of downtown as a series of personal experiences and choices.[42] A number of educational programs and public-interest lobbying groups with an interest in the promotion of enjoyable downtowns also emerged or expanded during the late 1970s and early 1980s. Examples include the Main Street program of the National Trust for Historic Preservation, the Waterfront Center, and Partners for Livable Places.

Although usually read as cultural criticism rather than policy analysis, Robert Venturi, Denise Scott Brown, and Stephen Izenour's manifesto, Learning from Las Vegas (1972), documents the same emerging understanding of downtowns. The result of a Yale architecture seminar, the book defined Las Vegas as the populist alternative to the carefully ordered and centered city. The city's "downtown" is its commercial strip, a new main street of activity nodes that are connected by automobiles and announced by huge signs. The purpose of commercial Las Vegas is to present a series of surfaces. It is a city whose business district is explicitly designed as a sequence of fragmented and individualized experiences.[43]

In rejecting the necessity and value of a unitary downtown, Learning from Las Vegas was an early example of the postmodern turn in Western culture. Postmodernism emerged in art, architecture, and literature as a reaction against the austerity, universalism, or formalism of mid-twentieth-century culture. Given its name in the early 1970s, its emergence as a set of linked ideas or artistic preferences has been dated variously to the early 1960s by Fredric Jameson and Charles Jencks and to the 1970s by David Harvey. Jane Jacobs, Robert Venturi, and the advocacy planning movement have all earned a place as early examples of the political side of postmodernism, with its emphasis on popular culture and open pluralism.[44] The revaluation of subdistricts as primary to the functioning of downtowns clearly expressed the same ideas.

Likewise, the elevation of downtown as a stage set in the mid-1970s fit with an increasing emphasis on the inherent value of the unexpected.

The self-consciously theatrical design of the show-off buildings that characterized postmodernism by the later 1970s depended on juxtaposition of styles, jumbling of spaces, and playful use of historical allusion. City centers themselves were increasingly presented as open theaters of individualism. Jonathan Raban's *Soft City* (1974), offered by David Harvey as one of the first postmodern treatments of the city, depicted London as an "encyclopedia" or "emporium of styles." In Raban's version, living in the city was an art in itself, making the physical setting a stage or canvas for its inhabitants.[45] In practical application, the new aesthetic meant downtown plans that emphasized design values and aimed for special attractions to appeal to the maturing baby boomers who would soon find themselves caricatured as "yuppies."

Boston and Baltimore are easily identified as pioneers of the American downtown as artifact. In the later 1960s and early 1970s, efforts to promote new downtown retail centers had produced some prominent failures as well as profitable developments. Baltimore's Inner Harbor redevelopment program and Boston's initial efforts in the Fanueil Hall/Waterfront area dated to the same problematic years of the late 1960s. However, they bore fruit between 1976 and 1981 with attractive new open space and spectacularly successful retail complexes that were quickly dubbed "festival markets." Frieden and Sagalyn have documented more than one hundred comparable projects between 1970 and 1988, most of them since the late 1970s, when the Boston and Baltimore examples encouraged city governments to become active partners.[46]

Many of these festival market projects are open to Harvey's critical description of "an architecture of spectacle, with its sense of surface glitter and transitory participatory pleasure." A climax product of the species is Horton Plaza in San Diego, first planned in the 1970s and opened in 1987. The "Plaza" is a contrived environment that draws visitors into a mildly but deliberately confusing shopping mall. The interior spaces offer multiple levels, bridges, passageways, and curving corridors. They are programmed with safely interesting activities. They are decked out in painful pseudo-Mediterranean pastels. They are explicitly presented as a "fun" alternative to the "gray" office towers of downtown San Diego.[47]

Festival markets were part of a long shopping list of amenity projects for the 1980s. Exhibition space in major convention cities doubled between 1975 and 1990. Cities added performing arts centers, arts districts, waterfront redevelopment, downtown open space, historic districts, rehabilitated hotels, and museum/aquarium complexes.[48] San Antonio's roster of projects for the 1980s included the River Center festival market, an expanded convention center, a domed stadium, a restored theater, a new art museum in an adapted historic building, a luxury hotel, and a transit mall. Most of the projects on the standard list aimed at the creation of low-end service jobs to replace the lost manufacturing and warehousing jobs that were no longer located on the downtown fringe.

In formal planning, the emphasis shifted significantly to design control, preservation planning, fine-tuning of floor-area ratios, amenities bonuses, and similar approaches that treated downtowns as visual experiences. Federal allowance of accelerated depreciation for historic buildings in 1976 and investment tax credits after 1981 encouraged a boom in the designation of buildings and downtown districts. The interest built on the earlier thematic understanding of downtown as a set of subareas. It took off when the designation of historic districts also appeared to meet the newly perceived need to turn downtown into a collection of stage sets.[49]

Downtown planners by the early 1980s tended to see the task of downtown planning as promoting and linking groups of experiences from which visitors could pick and choose.[50] New Orleans's Growth Management Program (1975) used historic districts and incentive zoning for pedestrian amenities. The innovative *Time for Springfield* [Massachusetts] plan of 1978 emphasized recycling historical structures, open space, cultural facilities, reclamation of the Connecticut riverfront, and aggressive programming of public festivals. Chicago's 1981 *Comprehensive Plan* mentioned leisure-time activities first, cultural institutions second, offices third, and manufacturing last. A privately commissioned Central Area Plan (1984) envisioned central Chicago as a complementary mix of housing, retailing, tourism, cultural facilities, new offices, and old landmarks. Milwaukee's *Downtown Goals and Policies* (1985) stressed pedestrian linkages among hotels, a convention center, retailers, and cultural attractions; it placed design review and improved lakefront access near the top of implementation measures. Richmond's *Downtown Plan* (1984) similarly emphasized the need to maintain an attractive environment, to cluster amenities, to expand cultural activities, and to tie together the downtown subdistricts. It placed marketing, public relations, advertising, and special events on the same level with financial assistance and transportation in the implementation program. "A more alive Downtown," said the plan, "means more culture and leisure time offerings, special shopping opportunities and other uniquely urban qualities which add to the quality of life in Richmond. Bit by bit it all results in an improved national image, a better local identity, and an increased sense of pride in one's city."[51]

The new directions of aesthetic planning were anticipated in New York's extensive design overlay districts and reached a climax in the San Francisco *Downtown Plan* of 1985. New York first used special zoning districts in 1968 to protect the special character of the Manhattan theater district. By the early 1980s it had adopted thirty such districts to preserve design values.[52] San Francisco's heralded plan responded to a downtown development boom that doubled office space between 1965 and 1983. The 1985 document was presented as a growth management plan, but it built on the city's *Urban Design Plan* of 1971. Although the plan claimed to aim at maintaining San Francisco's predominance as a world commercial city, it gave nearly half its space to issues such as protecting solar access, increasing open space, requiring the preservation of 271 historic buildings, and promoting an interesting skyline through design review of new buildings by a panel of experts.[53]

Downtown as Command Post: 1985–

Since the late nineteenth century, skyscrapers filled with executives and typists have been the essential symbol for downtowns. After spending the 1970s arm and arm with pedestrians, by the mid-1980s experts had rediscovered downtown's continuing importance as a transaction center. The recognition was triggered by the continued downtown building boom that ran from the mid-1970s to the end of the 1980s, dwarfing the earlier booms of the 1920s and the urban renewal era and bringing newspaper stories that headlined "U.S. Downtowns: No Longer Downtrodden."[54] In the thirty largest metropolitan areas, office construction in the first half of the 1980s ran at twice the rate of the 1970s, which had in turn outpaced the 1960s by 50 percent.[55] The boom hit more than New York, Boston, and Los Angeles. Less glamorous cities like Louisville added three million square feet of office space and Cleveland added six million.[56]

The office boom held out the hope that downtowns could tap into the global service economy at the high end of managerial, professional, finance, and consulting jobs as well as at the low end of entertainment and personal services. It substantially re-created an understanding of downtowns as unique centers. In this case, however, they were seen less as the unitary center of an individual metropolis than as centralized nodes of activity within national and global networks. This newest understanding sees downtown as floating freely in global economic space, just as the high-rise office towers of Atlanta or Houston float above their surrounding parking fields with little connection to nearby neighborhoods. Indeed, the decision by the Department of Commerce that the 1987 Census of Retailing would cease to report data for central business districts was an official declaration that general retailing for the metropolitan market is no longer viewed as an important downtown function. Landscape critic J. B. Jackson agrees that the urban center has lost its role in daily life, transformed instead into "an impressive symbol of remote power and unattainable wealth." The downtown as command post is "dedicated to power and money and technology, not to traditional human activities or institutions."[57]

One academic response in the last decade has been a large literature on the restructuring of economic space within the globalized economy. Much of this literature is Marxist in approach, with downtowns as the most visible expressions of the structure of economic power. As John Friedmann and Goetz Wolff have put it, world cities are increasingly divided between worker "ghettoes" and capitalists in their office tower "citadels."[58] Traditional geographers and economists explain the emergence of the high-rise downtown in terms of the continuing value of central locations for face-to-face contact and the quick exchange of sensitive or specialized information—what Gail Garfield Schwartz calls "off-the-record information [which] cannot be transmitted on any way except in person."[59] Writers such as Richard Child Hill and Joe Feagin in the mid-1980s analyzed the public policies that promote high-rise downtowns as the "corporate center" strategy.[60]

A second academic and professional response has been a new interest in the politics of real estate development and deal making. Paul Peterson's City Limits set a theme for the 1980s by arguing that economic development is the primary and proper role for local government. Urban policy specialists have zeroed in on cases such as the North Loop project in Chicago as examples of the political complexities of contemporary development. The downtown development case studies in the Urban Land Institute's Cities Reborn are matched by such university press books as Downtown, Inc.[61] The 1980s saw a new academic interest in real estate development curricula that span the interests of planning programs and business schools. Traditional regulatory planning is now matched by the newer subdiscipline of development planning, whose practitioners mobilize public resources to encourage growth on a project-by-project basis.[62]

In formal planning, the 1980s brought a renewed attention to accommodating the perceived needs for downtown growth, at least in the form of office space. Philadelphia's extensively analyzed downtown plan of 1988 is characterized as an "economic development plan" whose first goal is to "achieve significant economic growth" by developing the "enormous potential" of the "office-based information and service economy."[63] New plans for Denver (1986) and Cleveland (1988) aim to reinforce downtowns as financial and administrative centers. The plans accept a vision of quaternary- and quinary-sector growth and propose ways to capture much of the new economic activity within the city core. New York City pointed the growth of its mid-Manhattan business core westward to Seventh and Eighth avenues and beyond to the proposed Lincoln West project.[64] Springfield's *Visions 1989* replaced the 1979 goal of enriching individual experiences with a strategy aimed at securing office expansion spilling over from Boston and New York. Planners in San Francisco, Portland, Seattle, and Chicago accepted the desirability of new office towers and debated whether to direct such growth upward through amenity bonuses and higher floor-area ratios or outward by rezoning and redeveloping the downtown frame.[65] The operative question was not "whether" but "where."

The emphasis on the networked downtown suggests the continued strength of the generalizing forces of modernization. The current idea of downtown as command post affirms the essential characteristics of modernism—abstraction, deracination, universalism. It calls for architecture and planning in which the function of information exchange overrides complexities and variations in form. The rise of this newest interpretation implies that the postmodern themes of the 1970s and 1980s are ordinary turns in an ongoing discourse. Postmodernism as seen from downtown is part of a continuing dialogue rather than an epochal rewriting of a century-old understanding of urban development.

The primary texts of downtown policy show that we think differently about cities now than we did in earlier decades. Not only do we know more and different things, but we fit this knowledge together around different understandings and assumptions that seem too obvious to articulate. We already know to be careful in projecting economic and demographic trends. We need to exercise the same caution about intellectual trends, for accepted preferences in planning ideas can change with nearly the speed of artistic or architectural fashion. New understandings are as likely to reject or ignore the recent past as to amplify its particular themes. Only by taking the historian's backward step can we see how far and how quickly those understandings have moved.[66]

An obvious lesson for policymakers is that our mutable understanding of downtown has built contradictions into its planning goals and physical fabric. Downtowns show an unresolved tension between the goals of the current and previous decades. At the street level, for example, they are structured as a grab bag of individual choices. Above the street they are utilized intensely by the corporate sector. The contemporary mixed-use development, with its lower-floor shops, restaurants, and theaters and upper-level offices, is a tangible manifestation of the tension. At the same time, the office expansion agenda can clash directly with the earlier understanding of downtown as a coalition of subareas. Office development planning offers little place to districts that do not contribute to the explicit corporate center strategy. Given these contradictions, policymakers should not be surprised that the legitimation of subdistricts and the promotion of amenities created constituencies that may challenge the plans of the 1990s. Seattle is a case in point of popular resistance to plans with a tight focus on control functions. Many residents in the late 1980s came to view downtown development and the preservation of a downtown usable by average citizens as competing goals. In 1989 they voted a symbolic limit on downtown development when it appeared that the new *Land Use and Transportation Plan for Downtown Seattle* (1985) failed to protect either the appearance of downtown or the livability of close-in neighborhoods.[67]

The challenge in Seattle and other cities such as San Francisco suggests that planners and policymakers need to turn their attention to the characteristics that make downtown different from other nodes in the transactional grid. Whether we call them outer cities or outtowns or edge cities, peripheral office clusters can house many transactional functions as effectively as established downtowns. Nevertheless, downtown continues to offer the urban advantages of variety and intensity in ways not possible on the edge. Indeed, the one advantage of core over periphery is its social inclusiveness. Downtown is certainly a natural home for plugged-in executives, but it can also be an effective setting for integrating old minorities, new minorities, and majority society. It remains the one part of the metropolis that most effectively generates new ideas by bringing together the greatest range of groups and individuals. The idea of a socially inclusive downtown could logically recombine the old idea of a unitary center with the mid-1960s vision of downtown as the home to distinct groups and communities. Such a reconstructed understanding of downtown as everybody's neighborhood would also reaffirm the belief in cities as single metropolitan systems that offer comparable sets of opportunities to all their citizens.

Portland State University

Notes

1. Clarence Stone, *Economic Growth and Neighborhood Discontent: System Bias in the Urban Renewal Program of Atlanta* (Chapel Hill, N.C., 1976); Arnold Hirsch, *Making the*

Second Ghetto: Race and Housing in Chicago, 1940–1960 (New York, 1983); Chester Hartman, *The Transformation of San Francisco* (Totowa, N.J., 1984); Christopher Silver, *Twentieth-Century Richmond: Planning, Politics, and Race* (Knoxville, 1984); Gerald Suttles, *The Man-Made City* (Chicago, 1990); Norman Krumholz and W. Dennis Keating, "Downtown Plans of the 1980s: The Case for More Equity in the 1990s," *Journal of the American Planning Association* 57 (Spring 1991): 136–52.

2. Terrrence McDonald, *The Parameters of Urban Fiscal Policy: Socioeconomic Change and Political Culture in San Francisco, 1860–1906* (Berkeley, 1986), 1–18, criticizes the structural-functional approach for leaving out human agency and the political process and for assuming that what did happen was what had to happen.

3. Jon C. Teaford, *The Rough Road to Renaissance: Urban Revitalization in America, 1940–1985* (Baltimore, 1990).

4. Bernard Frieden and Lynne Sagalyn, *Downtown, Inc.: How America Rebuilds Its Cities* (Cambridge, Mass., 1989).

5. Robert C. Klove, "The Definition of Standard Metropolitan Areas," *Economic Geography* 28 (April 1952): 95–104; Kenneth Fox, *Metropolitan America: Urban Life and Urban Policy in the United States, 1940–1980* (Jackson, Miss., 1986), 24–30.

6. E. W. Burgess, "The Growth of the City," in Robert E. Park, ed., *The City* (Chicago, 1925); Homer Hoyt, *The Structure and Growth of Residential Neighborhoods in American Cities* (Washington, D.C., 1939).

7. Richard M. Hurd, *Principles of City Land Values* (New York, 1924); Calvin F. Schmid, "Land Values as an Ecological Index," *Research Studies of the State College of Washington* 9 (March 1941): 16–36; John Rannells, *The Core of the City: A Pilot Study of Changing Land Uses in Central Business Districts* (New York, 1956).

8. Raymond Murphy and James E. Vance, Jr., "Delimiting the CBD," *Economic Geography* 30 (July 1954): 189–222, and "A Comparative Study of Nine Central Business Districts," *Economic Geography* 30 (October 1954): 301–36; Raymond Murphy, James E. Vance, Jr., and Bart Epstein, "Internal Structure of the CBD," *Economic Geography* 31 (January 1955): 18–46; George W. Hartman, "The Central Business District: A Study in Urban Geography," *Economic Geography* 26 (October 1950): 237–44. The Census Bureau first reported retail sales data for CBDs in 1954 (including 1948 data in the reporting).

9. Gerald Breese, *The Daytime Population of the Central Business District of Chicago* (Chicago, 1949); Donald L. Foley, "The Daily Movement of Population into Central Business Districts," *American Sociological Review* 17 (October 1952): 538–43.

10. See the studies inventoried in Shirley Weiss, *The Central Business District in Transition* (Chapel Hill, N.C., 1957), 27–36.

11. C. T. Jonassen, *The Shopping Center Versus Downtown: A Motivation Research on Shopping Habits and Attitudes in Three Cities* (Columbus, Oh., 1955), 100; J. D. Carroll, Jr., "The Future of the Central Business District," *Public Management* 35 (July 1953): 150–53.

12. Hal Burton, *The City Fights Back* (New York, 1954), 208, 257–60; Richard Nelson and Frederick Aschman, *Conservation and Rehabilitation of Major Shopping Districts*, Urban Land Institute Technical Bulletin No. 22 (Washington, D.C., 1954), 5; "People's Attitudes Toward Downtown Providence," *Urban Land* 15 (November 1956): 8.

13. Carl Abbott, *The New Urban America: Growth and Politics in Sunbelt Cities* (Chapel Hill, N.C., 1987), 113–22; Gerald Nash, "Planning for the Postwar City: The Urban West in World War II," *Arizona and the West* 27 (Summer 1985), 99–112; Teaford, *Rough Road to Renaissance*, 36–42.

14. For example, see June Manning Thomas, "Attacking Economic Blight in Postwar Detroit," and Dwight Hoover, "City Planning in Middletown, U.S.A.: Muncie, Indiana, 1920–1990," in *Proceedings of the Third National Conference on City Planning History* (Hilliard, Oh., 1990), 165–84 and 198–218.

15. The plans are summarized and analyzed in the following: Howard Gillette, Jr., "A National Workshop for Urban Policy: The Metropolitanization of Washington, 1946–

1968," *The Public Historian* 7 (Winter 1985): 7–27; Robert B. Fairbanks, "Metropolitan Planning and Downtown Redevelopment: The Cincinnati and Dallas Experiences," *Planning Perspectives* 2 (September 1987): 237–53; Robert B. Fairbanks and Zane Miller, "The Martial Metropolis: Housing, Planning, and Race in Cincinnati, 1940–1955," in Roger Lotchin, ed., *The Martial Metropolis: U.S. Cities in War and Peace* (New York, 1984), 191–222; Silver, *Twentieth-Century Richmond*. Involved in developing the plans were an overlapping group of consultants and specialists: Harland Bartholomew for Dallas, Richmond, and Washington; Sherwood Reeder for Cincinnati and Richmond; Tracy Augur for Cincinnati and Washington; and Ladislas Segoe for Cincinnati and Richmond.

16. On the Dallas plan, see also E. A. Wood, "A City Looks to the Future: Dallas Believes in City Planning," *Southwest Review* 29 (Spring 1944): 310–11.

17. Silver, *Twentieth-Century Richmond*, 84; Robert James Parks, "Grasping on the Coattails of Progress: City Planning in Nashville, Tennessee, 1932–1962" (M.A. thesis, Vanderbilt University, 1971), 125–33; Don Doyle, *Nashville since the 1920s* (Knoxville, 1985), 121–29.

18. Gillette, "National Workshop"; Louis Justement, *New Cities for Old* (New York, 1946), 95–144. Tracy Augur was the chair of the transportation subcommittee.

19. Victor Gruen, *The Heart of Our Cities* (New York, 1964), 47, 218–19, 225, 305; Howard Gillette, Jr., "The Evolution of the Planned Shopping Center in Suburb and City," *Journal of the American Planning Association* 51 (Autumn 1985): 454–56; "Typical Downtown Transformed," *Architectural Forum* 103 (May 1956): 146–55.

20. J. Ross McKeever, "A View of the Year," *Urban Land* 14 (January 1955): 4; James W. Rouse, "Will Downtown Face Up to Its Future?" *Urban Land* 16 (February 1957): 1, 3–5.

21. Teaford, *Rough Road to Renaissance*, 123.

22. Ronald R. Boyce and W. A. V. Clark, "Selected Spatial Variables and Central Business District Retail Sales," *Papers of the Regional Science Association* 11 (1963): 167–94; George Sternlieb, "The Future of Retailing in the Downtown Core," *Journal of the American Institute of Planners* 29 (May 1963): 102–11; Lorne Russwurm, "The Central Business District Retail Sales Mix, 1948–58," *Annals of the Association of American Geographers* 54 (December 1964): 524–36.

23. Teaford, *Rough Road to Renaissance*, 48–50; Robert Barrows, "Indianapolis: Silver Buckle on the Rust Belt," in Richard Bernard, ed., *Snowbelt Cities: Metropolitan Politics in the Northeast and Midwest since World War II* (Bloomington, 1990), 144; Clyde Browning, "Recent Studies of Central Business Districts," *Journal of the American Institute of Planners* 27 (February 1961): 82.

24. Cleveland City Planning Commission, *Downtown Cleveland 1975: The Downtown General Plan* (Cleveland, 1959); Jayne Merkel, "Mid-Century Planning in Cincinnati: The 1948 Cincinnati Metropolitan Master Plan and the 1964 Plan for Downtown Cincinnati," in *Proceedings of Third National Conference on City Planning History*, 452–78; Fairbanks, "Cincinnati and Dallas." See also a discussion of the Central Minneapolis Plan (1960) in Alan Altshuler, *The City Planning Process* (Ithaca, N.Y., 1965).

25. Jeanne Lowe, *Cities in a Race with Time: Progress and Poverty in America's Renewing Cities* (New York, 1967); Leo Adde, *Nine Cities: The Anatomy of Downtown Renewal* (Washington, D.C., 1969); Abbott, *New Urban America*, 146–69.

26. Edgar W. Horwood and Ronald R. Boyce, *Studies of the Central Business District and Urban Freeway Development* (Seattle, 1959); Browning, "Recent Studies," 82–83; Larry Smith, "Space for the CBD's Functions," *Journal of the American Institute of Planners* 27 (February 1961): 35–42.

27. Jurkat's work is cited in John Rannells, "Approaches to Analysis," *Journal of the American Institute of Planners* 27 (February 1961): 23.

28. City of Oakland, *Central District Plan* (Oakland, Calif., 1966); Browning, "Recent Studies," 85–86; Shirley Weiss and Walter Thabit, "The Central Business District Plan for Downtown Baltimore," *Journal of the American Institute of Planners* 27 (February 1961): 88–

91. See also Real Estate Research Corporation, *Economic Survey and Market Analysis of Downtown Denver* (Chicago, 1962).

29. Martin Anderson, *The Federal Bulldozer* (Cambridge, Mass., 1964); Herbert Gans, "The Failure of Urban Renewal," *Commentary* 40 (April 1965): 29–37; James Q. Wilson, ed., *Urban Renewal: The Record and the Controversy* (Cambridge, Mass., 1966); Scott Greer, *Urban Renewal and American Cities: The Dilemma of Democratic Intervention* (Indianapolis, 1965).

30. Jane Jacobs, *The Death and Life of Great American Cities* (New York, 1961); Herbert Gans, *The Urban Villagers* (Glencoe, Ill., 1962); Kevin Lynch, *The Image of the City* (Cambridge, Mass., 1960).

31. Gruen, *Heart of Our Cities*, 321–25.

32. Charles Abrams, "Downtown Decay and Revival," *Journal of the American Institute of Planners* 27 (February 1961): 6; Jacobs, *Death and Life*, 168, 174.

33. A. Getis and J. M. Getis, "Retail Store Spatial Affinities," *Urban Studies* 5 (1960): 317–32; W. G. Hardwick, *Vancouver* (Don Mills, Ontario, 1974); Brian Berry, *The Geography of Market Centers and Retail Distribution* (Englewood Cliffs, N.J., 1967); Dennis Conway et al., "The Dallas–Fort Worth Region," in John S. Adams, ed., *Contemporary Metropolitan America* (Cambridge, Mass., 1976), 4:17; Peirce Lewis, "New Orleans—The Making of an Urban Landscape," in Adams, *Contemporary Urban America*, 2:193.

34. Arthur L. Grey, David L. Bonsteel, Gary H. Winkel, and Roger A. Parker, "People and Downtowns: Use, Attitudes, Settings," 1970 study excerpted in *Downtown Mall Annual and Urban Design Report*, vol. 4 (New York, 1978), 55–72. See also Frederick P. Stutz, "Adjustment and Mobility of the Elderly Poor Amid Downtown Renewal," *Geographical Review* 66 (October 1976): 391–400.

35. Martyn J. Bowden, "Downtown through Time: Delineation, Expansion, and Internal Growth," *Economic Geography* 47 (April 1971): 121–35, and "Growth of Central Districts in Large Cities," in Leo Schnore, ed., *The New Urban History* (Princeton, N.J., 1975), 75–109; David Ward, "The Industrial Revolution and the Emergence of Boston's Central Business District," *Economic Geography* 42 (April 1966): 152–71.

36. Central Association of Seattle, "Discussion Guide: Seattle Central Business District Plan" (1963) and "The Emerging Downtown: 1970," in Downtown Seattle Development Association Papers, Box 8, University of Washington Manuscripts Department.

37. Janet Daly, "The Changing Image of the City: Planning for Downtown Omaha, 1945–1973" (Ph.D. dissertation, University of Pittsburgh, 1987).

38. Carl Abbott, *Portland: Politics, Planning, and Growth in a Twentieth-Century City* (Lincoln, Nebr., 1983), 207–28, and "Urban Design in Portland, Oregon, as Policy and Process, 1960–1989," *Planning Perspectives* 6 (1991): 1–18.

39. The neighborhood movement of 1965–80 paralleled this era of downtown analysis with its revaluation of small-scale and everyday environments. Many cities had institutionalized and routinized neighborhood participation by the 1980s.

40. Dallas Department of Planning and Development, *Central Business District: Past Planning and Current Issues* (Dallas, 1982); Central Atlanta Progress, *Central Area Study II* (Atlanta, 1988); Dayton Department of Planning, *Downtown Dayton* (Dayton, 1976); Government of the District of Columbia, *A Living Downtown for Washington, D.C.: Planning Concepts* (Washington, D.C., 1981); Mayor's Downtown Plan Committee, *Downtown D.C.: Recommendations for the Downtown Plan* (Washington, D.C., 1982); Richmond City Planning Commission, *Downtown Plan* (Richmond, 1984); *Oakland Central District Development Program: Initial Planning and Management Concepts* (Oakland, 1984); Denver Partnership, Inc., and Denver Planning Office, *Downtown Area Plan* (Denver, 1986); City of Seattle, *Land Use and Transportation Plan for Downtown Seattle* (Seattle, 1985).

41. Sharon Zukin, *Loft Living: Culture and Capital in Urban Change* (Baltimore, 1982); William Hendon and Douglas Shaw, "The Arts and Urban Development," in Gary Gappert, ed., *The Future of Winter Cities* (Beverly Hills, Calif., 1987), 209–17; J. A.

Whitt, "Mozart in the Metropolis: The Arts Coalition and the Urban Growth Machine," *Urban Affairs Quarterly* 23 (September 1987): 15–36; Harold Snedcof, *Cultural Facilities in Mixed-Use Development* (Washington, D.C., 1985).

42. William H. Whyte, *The Social Life of Small Urban Spaces* (Washington, D.C., 1980) and *City: Rediscovering the Center* (New York, 1988).

43. Robert Venturi, Denise Scott Brown, and Stephen Izenour, *Learning from Las Vegas* (Cambridge, Mass., 1972).

44. Fredric Jameson, "Postmodernism, or the Cultural Logic of Late Capitalism," *New Left Review*, no. 146 (July–August 1984): 53–92; Charles Jencks, *Post-Modernism: The New Classicism in Art and Architecture* (New York, 1987); David Harvey, *The Condition of Postmodernity: An Enquiry into the Origins of Cultural Change* (London, 1989).

45. Jonathan Raban, *Soft City* (London, 1974); Harvey, *Condition of Postmodernity*, 3–6.

46. Laurence A. Alexander, "Introduction," in *A New Concept: The Downtown Shopping Center* (New York, 1975), 2–3. Frieden and Sagalyn, *Downtown, Inc.*, 365–67, list seventy-five major projects. Eleven opened in 1971–75, twenty-seven opened in 1976–80, and thirty-seven opened in 1981–85.

47. Harvey, *Condition of Postmodernity*, 91; Frieden and Sagalyn, *Downtown, Inc.*, 191–97; "Horton Plaza, San Diego, California," Urban Land Institute Project File 16 (1986).

48. Tony Wrenn, *Urban Waterfront Development* (Washington, D.C., 1983); Robert McNulty, *The Economics of Amenity* (Washington, D.C., 1985).

49. Dennis Gale, *Washington, D.C.: Inner-City Revitalization and Minority Suburbanization* (Philadelphia, 1987), 41.

50. Nicholas Falk, "Baltimore and Lowell: Two American Approaches," *Built Environment* 12 (1986): 145–52; Peter Hall, *Cities of Tomorrow: An Intellectual History of Urban Planning and Design in the Twentieth Century* (London, 1988), 347–51. For positive evaluations, see John Fondersmith, "Downtown 2040," *The Futurist* 22 (March–April 1988): 9–17, and Wayne Attoe and Donn Logan, *American Urban Architecture: Catalysts in the Development of Cities* (Berkeley, 1989).

51. Jane S. Brooks and Alma H. Young, "Revitalizing the Central Business District in the Face of Decline: The Case of New Orleans, 1970–1990," Working Paper No. 5, Division of Urban Research and Policy Studies, University of New Orleans (1991); James C. O'Connell, "The Role of Marketing in Urban Plans: The Case of Springfield, Massachusetts," paper presented at Fourth National Conference on City Planning History, Richmond, November 1991; Suttles, *Man-Made City*, 34–38; Milwaukee Department of City Development, *Downtown Goals and Policies, 1985* (Milwaukee, 1985); Richmond, *Downtown Plan*, 131, 135.

52. Jonathan Barnett, *Urban Design as Public Policy* (New York, 1974) and *An Introduction to Urban Design* (New York, 1982), 77–124; Kenneth Halpern, *Downtown USA: Urban Design in Nine American Cities* (New York, 1978); Raquel Ramati, *How to Save Your Own Street* (New York, 1981).

53. San Francisco Department of City Planning, *Downtown Plan* (San Francisco, 1985); Krumholz and Keating, "Downtown Plans"; Allan Jacobs, *Making City Planning Work* (Chicago, 1978); Barnett, *Introduction to Urban Design*, 125–36. Charles Jencks, *Post-Modernism*, 247–49, describes San Francisco's plan as "standard Post-Modern theory."

54. William E. Schmidt, "U. S. Downtowns: No Longer Downtrodden," *New York Times*, 11 October 1987, 1, 28:2.

55. Frieden and Sagalyn, *Downtown, Inc.*, 265.

56. Rachelle Levitt, ed., *Cities Reborn* (Washington, D.C., 1987), 67; Thomas Campbell, "Cleveland: The Struggle for Stability," in Bernard, *Snowbelt Cities*, 131.

57. John B. Jackson, "The Sunbelt City: The Modern City, the Strip, and the Civic Center," in *The Southern Landscape Tradition in Texas* (Fort Worth, 1980), 32–33.

58. Robert Cohen, "The Changing Transactional Economy and Its Spatial Implications," *Ekistics* 46 (January–February 1979): 7–14; John Friedmann and Goetz Wolff,

"World City Formation: An Agenda for Research and Action," *International Journal of Urban and Regional Research* 6 (1982): 309–43; Susan Fainstein, Norman Fainstein, and Alex Schwartz, "Economic Shifts and Land Use in the Global City: New York, 1940–87," in Robert Beauregard, ed., *Atop the Urban Hierarchy* (Totowa, N.J., 1989), 45–85.

59. Gail Garfield Schwartz, *Where's Main Street, U.S.A.?* (Westport, Conn., 1984); Allen Pred, *City-Systems in Advanced Economies* (New York, 1977); J. Thomas Black, "The Changing Economic Role of Central Cities and Suburbs," in Arthur Solomon, ed., *The Prospective City* (Cambridge, Mass., 1980), 80–123. Jurgen Friedrichs and Allen Goodman, *The Changing Downtown: A Comparative Study of Baltimore and Hamburg* (New York, 1987), emphasize the growth of the tertiary sector and the expansion of downtown office space.

60. Richard Child Hill, "Crisis in the Motor City," in Norman Fainstein and Susan Fainstein, eds., *Restructuring the City: The Political Economy of Urban Development* (New York, 1983), 80–125; Joe R. Feagin, "The Corporate Center Strategy: The State in Central Cities," *Urban Affairs Quarterly* 21 (1986): 617–28; James Simmie, "Planning Theory and Practice: An Analysis of the San Francisco Downtown Plan," *Cities* 4 (1987): 304–24.

61. Paul Peterson, *City Limits* (Chicago, 1981); Terry Lassar, ed., *City Deal Making* (Washington, D.C., 1990); Bernarrd J. Frieden, "Center City Transformed: Planners as Developers," *Journal of the American Planning Association* 56 (Autumn 1990): 423–38; Gregory Squires, ed., *Unequal Partnerships: The Political Economy of Urban Redevelopment in Postwar America* (New Brunswick, N.J., 1989); Suttles, *Man-Made City*; Larry Bennett, "Beyond Urban Renewal: Chicago's North Loop Redevelopment Project," *Urban Affairs Quarterly* 22 (December 1986): 242–57.

62. Hall, *Cities of Tomorrow*, 347–51.

63. Philadelphia City Planning Commission, *Plan for Center City* (Philadelphia, 1988), 15–16; Madeline L. Cohen, "The 1963 and the 1988 Plans for Philadelphia's Center City: A Problem of Differing Planning Philosophies," Working Paper No. 202, Society for American City and Regional Planning History, 1990; Seymour Mandelbaum, "Reading Plans," *Journal of the American Planning Association* 56 (Summer 1990): 350–56; Krumholz and Keating, "Downtown Plans," 146–47.

64. H. V. Savitch, *Post-Industrial Cities: Politics and Planning in New York, Paris, and London* (Princeton, N.J., 1988), 52–69; Susan Fainstein and Norman Fainstein, "Economic Restructuring and the Politics of Land Use Planning in New York City," *Journal of the American Planning Association* 53 (Spring 1987): 237–48.

65. O'Connell, "Marketing in Urban Plans"; San Francisco, *Downtown Plan;* Portland Bureau of Planning, *Central City Plan* (Portland, 1988); Seattle, *Land Use and Transportation Plan.*

66. This article is not the first to find major turning points in ideas about downtowns. Janet Daly examined the period from 1945 to 1973 and found a basic change of attitudes in the late 1960s. Robert Fairbanks and Zane Miller have put the divide in the late 1950s, fitting the change within a larger argument about a shift of American political culture from the remnants of republicanism to consumer liberalism and the promotion of individual self-fulfillment. See Daly, "Planning for Downtown Omaha"; Zane Miller, "History and the Politics of Community Change in Cincinnati," *The Public Historian* 5 (Fall 1983): 17–35; Zane Miller and Bruce Tucker, "Cincinnati: The New Urban Politics," in Bernard, *Snowbelt Cities*, 91; Robert B. Fairbanks, *Making Better Citizens: Housing Reform and the Community Development Strategy in Cincinnati* (Urbana, Ill., 1989).

67. For example, see the preservation/development tensions described for San Francisco, Seattle, and other cities in Richard Collins, Elizabeth Waters, and A. Bruce Dotson, *America's Downtowns: Growth, Politics, and Preservation* (Washington, D.C., 1991).

PAUL GEORGE LEWIS

Housing and American Privatism: The Origins and Evolution of Subsidized Home-Ownership Policy

In the late 1980s, congressional investigations revealed patterns of influence peddling, lack of oversight, and poorly targeted expenditures at the U.S. Department of Housing and Urban Development, criticizing both the content and administration of various federal housing initiatives. Some commentators have concluded that the dogged preference for a private-sector strategy and the privatization of public activities in the Reagan administration—goals pursued while the agency suffered dramatic budget cuts—are at the root of recent HUD embarrassment.[1]

A closer examination of federal involvement in urban housing reveals a longer history of privatism in the pursuit of public goals, with roots much deeper, and consequences far more profound, than those uncovered in recent investigations. This article will grapple with some of the structural obstacles to the national goal of decent housing by examining the emergence and evolution of one significant federal program, the Section 235 home-ownership assistance plan.

Enacted in the Housing and Urban Development Act of 1968, Section 235 was a Great Society effort to encourage home ownership among low- and moderate-income families. As such, the venture represented an unprecedented incursion by the federal government into local private housing markets. Ultimately, however, lenders and developers—not the poor—received federal subsidy payments and guarantees, and the program's distributive aspects overwhelmed its redistributive possibilities.

Section 235 made social goals dependent on effective and honest private actions. Those goals proved elusive when profit-seeking became the program's major raison d'être. As such, Section 235 illustrates the frailty of many federal urban policies, which were often as much captive of and paralyzed by business goals as were policies in the classic "private city."[2]

The Political Context of the 1968 Act

Existing Federal Housing Policies

Viewed in context, the 1968 Housing and Urban Development Act was an attempt by the Johnson administration and Congress to address the flaws and inadequacies of existing federal housing policies, as well as to respond to urban social turmoil. Aside from a few experimental and modestly funded subsidy programs, the federal approach to urban housing had consisted of two basic modes of action through the mid-1960s: home mortgage insurance under Federal Housing Administration (FHA) programs, and the financing of public housing projects.

The FHA, founded in 1934 as an emergency agency in the Depression atmosphere of anxiety over the housing and banking industries, proved to be one of the most significant New Deal programs. The FHA decisively influenced spatial socioeconomic patterns in the United States for decades.[3] Founded to protect the private credit market and provide jobs, and continually attentive to that goal, the FHA responded to the growing postwar housing market of the white middle classes, guaranteeing long-term loans for millions of new suburban homes.

The same three-decade period saw the federal government pursue, at modest authorization levels, the subsidization of public housing units for the poor and ill-housed. Operated after 1937 by local public agencies, these means-tested rental units also had their roots in emergency legislation, having grown out of job-creation initiatives of the Public Works Administration.

These two sometimes contradictory "streams" of federal housing policy—FHA mortgage insurance and public housing—were central to the development of the urban crisis of the 1960s, and academic and elite opinion by then had caught up with the programs' shortcomings. Both policies exacerbated socioeconomic and racial concentration and segregation, which the Kerner Commission on Civil Disorders found at the root of urban rioting in the 1960s. Public housing had become a target of criticism for the concentration of social misery it frequently engendered in high-rise city projects. Combined with an expanded slum clearance program in the 1949 Housing Act, which had proclaimed the goal of "a decent home and suitable living environment for every American family," public housing instead came to be associated with the indiscriminate federal bulldozer and "Negro removal" of the urban renewal programs.

Meanwhile, the legacy of the FHA's racially discriminatory guidelines for mortgage insurance had become well known by 1968.[4] By reifying and abetting the trends toward suburban single-family detached housing, moreover, the FHA had produced a back-door "national urban policy" in a country thought to be without one. By 1970 America boasted more than ten times as many government-insured (generally middle-class) homes as there were subsidized housing units.[5] Federal expenditure on mortgage insurance and income-tax deductions for home owners was overwhelmingly greater than public housing and urban redevelopment programs.[6] Overall, federal policy served mainly to facilitate the private housing industry—the real determinant of the lion's share of the nation's shelter. While thirty-five federal housing programs operated over the thirty years prior to 1968, privatism was "the essential and basic factor in America's housing."[7]

Meanwhile, the poor, the elderly, and minorities, while spending increasingly larger proportions of their incomes on shelter in the 1960s, were not party to the rapid growth in home ownership.[8] By 1968, the United States met only one-tenth of its estimated need for subsidized housing,[9] and housing production as a percentage of GNP began falling ominously.[10] Riots in the inner cities, meanwhile, presented a new challenge. Alarmed policymakers associated bad housing with "antisocial" behavior, an attitude dating back at least to the settlement-house movement of the late nineteenth century. The Kerner Commission's widely read report recommended large-scale construction of assisted housing as one possible solution.[11] Affordable housing was in short supply in urban areas, and racial disorders catalyzed the response.

Housing Policy and the Johnson Presidency

Under these pressures, the Kennedy and Johnson administrations successfully presented major housing bills to Congress in 1961, 1964, and 1967. Also, significant fair housing initiatives joined urban renewal and subsidy programs on the federal law books for the first time.

Section 235, however, was shaped not only by the legacy of existing legislation, but by the Johnson administration's unique approach to domestic policy. Lyndon B. Johnson was an opportunist without a coherent overall plan for new social legislation.[12] Instead, Johnson sought "big" programs to establish his own credentials as a leader after John F. Kennedy's assassination. In the process he often showed his mastery of political symbolism, and was effective at packaging his legislation in grand rhetoric, even hyperbole, to achieve his legislative victories.[13] Johnson also frequently turned to the idea men who filled his inherited cabinet. The "issue networks" widely believed to characterize today's national policy-making mushroomed during this period.[14]

President Johnson and his advisers were motivated by a desire to give all Americans the rights and opportunities that citizenship promised. Unlike some of the architects of the New Deal, they maintained a unitary, rather than a class-based, conception of society. Richard Neustadt's characterization of the Great Society is prescient; he sees it as an effort to "outflank group conflict, override class structure, and improve the lot of everyone in America."[15]

One political tool Johnson used to build consensus and a sense of purpose was presidential task forces, composed largely of political outsiders. In 1964, one such task force, headed by urbanist Robert Wood, recommended the creation of an executive agency that could integrate human resource and social service goals with bricks-and-mortar programs like urban renewal. On the other hand, the head of the Housing and Home Financing Agency, Robert Weaver, recommended simply upgrading his agency to cabinet status. This option suggested continued emphasis on the urban built environment rather than on its social environment, since the HHFA primarily pursued traditional physical policies through the FHA.

Johnson waffled and Congress was seemingly uninterested in specifying a role. Ultimately both approved the more comprehensive vision uniting various aspects of federal urban policy under HUD. However, Weaver (America's first black cabinet member) was appointed as secretary in January 1966, and the existing HHFA, attuned as it was to the housing industry, was folded into HUD.[16] For new home-ownership initiatives aimed at social goals, this would mean implementation by the FHA bureaucracy, with its long-standing orientation against the inner city and "bad-risk" customers.

In 1967, with a diminished congressional majority and a growing popular unease over urban unrest and the "solutions" that had been proposed, LBJ convened the President's Committee on Urban Housing. He instructed its members to "find a way to harness the productive power of America—which has proved it can master space and create unmatched abundance in the market place" in order to provide decent housing for slum dwellers.[17]

In accordance with this business-oriented charge, Johnson appointed a committee dominated by a private-enterprise perspective. Its membership included twelve business leaders (mainly CEOs, though a few members had urban redevelopment credentials), three labor leaders, and only three individuals from academe or public service—the groups that had predominanted in earlier Johnson task forces. Dubbed the Kaiser Committee after its chairman, businessman Edgar Kaiser, the committee's goals were product-oriented rather than human-oriented: to seek rapidly accelerated production and rehabilitation and widespread private participation in federal housing programs.

Although the Kaiser Committee did not offer its final report until December 1968, its input was crucial for many planks of the HUD Act of 1968. The committee's conclusions stressed that private enterprise, working in conjunction with continued federal assistance, "can best provide the muscle, the talent and the major effort—when there are opportunities to earn reasonable profits and to function at maximum efficiency." Moreover, "the programs which work best—such as the FHA mortgage insurance programs—are those that channel the forces of existing economic institutions into productive areas."[18] While the committee saw dispersal and deconcentration of the central-city poor as one goal, it offered no real political guidance on this front.

In February 1968, President Johnson addressed Congress to announce the proposed Section 235 program. Quoting the Kaiser Committee at times, he used much the same rhetoric, invoking "the genius of American business," and arguing that "the real job belongs to local government and the private sector. . . . What is needed is a new partnership between business and government."[19]

The idea of subsidized home ownership had had a gestation period in the Washington policy community. A pilot program in the St. Louis area had been deemed a qualified success, and the earlier Wood task force also had considered it as a potential option. Charles Percy (R-Ill.) had campaigned for a Senate seat on his plan for a "National Home Ownership Foundation." Upon election, he and Republican congressional colleagues pushed the plan in the 1967 session, but the congressional Banking and Commerce committees, which oversaw urban affairs, decided to wait for a White House initiative.

Thus the Johnson administration was pressed into action both by circumstances and politics. In response, the Section 235 home-ownership program became a prominent component of the monumental 280-page, seventeen-title Housing and Urban Development Act of 1968. The Act also contained the second Model Cities authorization, the "New Towns" proposal, and expanded several existing programs. Like many domestic priorities, the Johnson administration approached housing policy piecemeal, and through a multiplicity of new policies, rather than overhauling the logic of federal intervention. Nevertheless, the administration presented the omnibus act to Congress in a rhetoric of innovation and new solutions.

As noted earlier, Johnson's political strategy of forging consensus involved proclaiming bold goals that could find wide support. In the case of the 1968 omnibus housing bill, this tactic involved a stated aim of a properly housed nation in ten years. Johnson articulated the first *specific* national housing goal: 26 million new units by 1978, 6 million of those to be in some way federally subsidized. But he provided no real direction for the *location* of the new housing, or for the implementation of a "suitable living environment."[20]

The Mechanics of Subsidized Home Ownership

Section 235 amended the 1934 Housing Act so as to unite the two methods of housing assistance that characterized federal policy since that earlier era—home mortgage insurance and subsidized shelter for the poor. In a tightening federal fiscal environment, Section 235's designers sought to use a share of federal funds to induce a massive housing effort on the part of private lenders and developers. The program's advocates hoped that Section 235 would encourage low- and moderate-income homeownership much as the FHA's prior commitments had allowed such opportunities to be safely opened up to the middle classes. Charles Haar, then HUD's Assistant Secretary for Metropolitan Development, told an academic housing conference that for all of the FHA's limitations, it "effectively tapped latent energies to loosen up a congealed society." He stressed that the 1968 HUD Act could create a similar synergy through "its extensive provisions for a limited partnership between national government and private enterprise."[21] Congressional backers of the bill would also defend 235 for this provision of "leverage"—a multiplier effect for federal dollars.

With an emphasis on housing production, 80 percent of all 235 authorizations were reserved for newly built homes of "modest but adequate quality." The FHA was to approve builders' plans for these homes before construction and set a figure for each unit's mortgage. "If a builder is efficient, this price should include a fair profit."[22] These new housing units were to be allocated largely in sizable residential tracts constructed by major developers, who were considered most viable for the new program.[23]

As a temporary provision to supply housing rapidly for as many families as possible, the remaining 20 percent of authorizations could be used for extensively rehabilitated structures. For this "existing home" provision, the FHA was to inspect and appraise relatively inexpensive structures whose seller had applied for 235 status for the unit.

After FHA inspected and appraised the new or rehabilitated unit, and the buyer's mortgage application was approved, he or she could make a downpayment of as little as two hundred dollars. The buyer was expected to pay 20 percent of adjusted monthly family income toward the installments. The government would pay the monthly remainder due on a normal market-rate mortgage, up to a maximum subsidy payment. This maximum was calculated as the difference between 20 percent of the family's income and what the payment would be with a mortgage interest rate of one percent.[24]

From a financial standpoint, public intervention on behalf of Section 235 families was thus to consist of two steps. The first was mortgage insurance from a new FHA high-risk fund, making lenders willing to advance mortgage loans to these applicants. The usual restrictions for FHA insurance were waived, although successful beneficiaries still had to show themselves to be reasonably creditworthy and have some regular income source. (FHA, primarily a financial agency, had long prided itself on surpluses in its mortgage insurance fund.) The second financial step was the effective subsidization of interest rates down to the one percent threshold. The HUD Secretary was to contract with lenders to pay the required portion.

The legislation did not fundamentally alter the demand side of the housing market (for instance, through a voucher approach), nor did it create a second, "social market" for housing (as had public housing in the rental market since the 1930s and public broadcasting in the communications market in 1968). Section 235 did attempt to underwrite the *risks* of low- and moderate-income home ownership. It also helped the home-building and lending industries to expand their markets safely. In the language of fiscal sociologist James O'Connor, one might say that it served the "accumulation" and "legitimation" goals of the state at the same time.[25] That is, Section 235 helped expand private markets and, as will be shown below, was seen by some legislators as promoting the social peace in American cities.

The Rhetoric of the Legislative Debate

The 1968 housing bill emerged from the House and Senate banking committees with solid support for Section 235.[26] Floor debate (in May

1968 in the Senate, July in the House) touched on many points of the long and complicated omnibus legislation. Not surprisingly, Section 235—in many ways the bill's centerpiece, listed as the first section of the legislation—drew a particularly large share of attention.

From the start, legislative debate made it clear that Section 235 found wide bipartisan favor and would eventually pass. Nevertheless, this bipartisanship by no means signaled a unanimity of purpose. Members of Congress advanced at least three quite different rationales for subsidized home ownership. These three justifications, as reflected in lawmakers' rhetoric, expose the variety of goals and visions for the program with which HUD would have to wrestle in implementing 235.

The floor debate illustrates the uncertainties over what a "Great Society" should mean. As delineated below, two congressional visions of Section 235 among its proponents focused on ideas of equity, differing mainly on the scope of the program: Was it to be a social benefit or a safety net? A third vision centered around the issues of race, behavior, and civil disorders.

Fulfilling the American Dream?

Many northern Democrats, such as Representatives Joseph Minish (N.J.) and Charles Wilson (Calif.), saw the bill as an important milestone of federal social legislation. In the waning days of optimism over the Great Society, these New Deal Democrats represented the liberal true believers. Wilson saw 235 as "facing up to the magnitude of the housing and urban problem,"[27] while Minish intoned that "homeownership—and all that it connotes—is a vital part of the broad American ambition. This is an urge that is deep in our roots and our heritage."[28]

This was the inclusive, Johnsonian vision of public policy. Less concerned about administrative details, these legislators were simply eager to see the bill help everyone—but particularly the "working people," who were still at the heart of Democratic support, and the home builders, a resourceful congressional pressure group. They echoed the goal of home ownership that had long represented the fair fruits of an affluent society to many in the traditional Democratic rank and file.

Minimum Funding for Maximum Results?

This inclusive vision of home ownership was challenged by a proposed amendment in the House offered in the name of equity and fiscal restraint. It sought to limit the recipient base to those at 130 percent or less of the income qualification levels for public housing. (The initial bill gave the Secretary of HUD very broad discretion over the families and income levels to be served by 235.)

Representative John B. Anderson (R-Ill.), who offered the income-limiting amendment, noted the problem of rising expectations among America's poor, and argued:

> [I]f these poor families are not going to be reached it is cruel and dishonest to masquerade behind a label. . . . We are not talking about very much low-income housing. We are talking about a lot of moderate-income housing. . . . This is a bill that ought to be written for the poor people of this country, not for the Home Builders Association or any other group.[29]

Representative William Brock III (R-Tenn.) concurred: "I never cease to be amazed at the argument of people who talk so much in their districts about helping the poor only to come on the floor and oppose an amendment which would require that Federal funds go to the people we are supposed to be helping."[30]

In response to this argument, Representative Leonor Sullivan (D-Mo.), noted that the very poor had been unable to handle the financial responsibilities in the earlier home-ownership experiment in her St. Louis area district. She argued that 235 ought to be targeted at higher income levels. And Representative Henry Reuss (D-Wis.) maintained that "unless you beam it at moderate-income people . . . you are beaming it at nobody, because a pauper cannot own a home. It does not make economic sense."[31] Nevertheless, the House approved Anderson's amendment 271–137, defeating the old-time New Dealers.[32]

This second group of congressmen, led in the House by Anderson and Brock, seemed to view home-ownership subsidies as limited and *leveraged* expenditures for maximum equitable results, rather than as a vague quality-of-life program. Representative Chalmers Wylie (R-Ohio), for example, approved of the bill because government acted only as a catalyst to what he thought would be an undoubtably successful private-market reaction, noting that "the Federal Government is not in the investment business."[33] In the Senate, similarly, Jacob Javits (R-N.Y.) said Section 235 would exert "maximum leverage in drawing private mortgage money into serving the disadvantaged population."[34] Senator John Sparkman (D-Ala.) argued that the great federal housing laws had always been privately oriented, geared "toward helping our people to achieve the goal."[35] Though they differed on income eligibility standards, most congressmen saw an increased and stabilized capital pool for producer groups—that is, enhanced private production—as the solution to this public problem.

Changing Behaviors?

April 1968 had seen riots in Washington and Baltimore, with the Poor People's Movement encampment also moving into the capital city that year. For those concerned with racial and class tensions in the nation's cities, and frightened by unrest in their own community, Section 235 represented one palatable policy approach in a puzzling political era. The Kaiser Committee had acknowledged "knotty sociological relations between rundown housing, human behavior, environmental conditions of total neighborhoods, and the disadvantaged life of the poor," concluding that "good neighbors are properly protective citizens."[36]

The perceived association between housing problems, property rights, and social unrest also played itself out in the congressional debates. Senator Javits reminded his colleagues that the Kerner Commission on Civil Disorders had reported more structures destroyed by urban renewal than built by subsidized housing programs, concluding, "If we have learned anything in recent years through antipoverty efforts, it is that we must couple assistance programs with elements that provide motivation and dignity if we are to achieve an end to poverty and degradation in this society."[37]

While numerous members of Congress tried to forge a causal link between bad housing and antisocial behavior, Representative Reuss's language was the most explicit: "We think a man who owns his home is not likely to burn it down." This group saw 235 as "a way to make slum families stable and responsible." Pragmatic capitalists, these legislators were willing to allow an unprecedented federal incursion into local markets and land use because, as Representative Frank Thompson (D-N.J.) noted, "the times are enough to make radicals of us all."[38]

Finally, a small opposition composed of conservative Republicans and southern Democrats disagreed on the desirability of any home-ownership program. They were wary of expensive programs, welfare statism, and "the new association between housing and the racial question."[39] But this contingent was sufficiently small that the bill breezed through the Senate by a 67 to 4 vote, and the House by 295 to 114. In conference committee, the main discrepancy between the chambers was the income-eligibility limit, and the figure was finally adjusted to 135 percent of the public housing income ceiling. But 20 percent of funds were reserved for more "flexible" use by HUD.

Implementing Section 235: Trials and Outcomes

If Congress in its floor debates revealed ambiguity over the justification of low-income home ownership and the direction the program should take, Section 235's implementation was no less confused. The program's administrative pitfalls have been chronicled extensively.[40] These and other prominent facets of the history of Section 235 show how the unresolved dilemmas of its enactment were reflected in subsequent problems in its operation.

The Production Imperative

President Richard M. Nixon chose former Michigan governor George Romney to head HUD in the initial period of 235 implementation. By all accounts, Romney took the 1968 housing-production goal seriously.[41] By the end of March 1969, HUD had exhausted its entire fiscal-year budgetary contract authority for Section 235 ($25 million), and it held further applications that would require another $40 million in funding.[42]

Section 235 did initially spur a large-scale building effort and significantly influenced the level of housing activity in a slow market. The program accounted for six percent of all housing starts in 1971, when it was the biggest government housing subsidy program. This amounted to 125,000 new and 15,000 rehabilitated homes in that year alone.[43] In one county in Washington, 80 percent of all real estate sales in 1970 were 235 homes.[44]

In the unstable economy of the early 1970s, however, the 235 boom also helped aggravate serious inflation in the housing market. Perhaps a more fundamental problem was that underfunding made the program an inequitable one, as FHA was forced to ration homes to only a portion of its qualified applicants. Ironically, one argument that had been made on behalf of 235 at its founding was that Congress had continually cut other housing appropriations, and that 235 could overcome this problem through its multiplier effects on housing starts.[45] Expenditures on subsidized housing did indeed accelerate sharply during the Nixon administration's first term. But Republican strategists feared a program that was too successful, one that might disturb or transform their electoral base in the suburbs.[46]

Administrative Antipathy

During this period, the FHA proved to be uniquely unsuited to serve the housing needs of the poor. As noted earlier, the FHA's history reveals an organization of limited goals, with an orientation toward suburbia and financial soundness. When the FHA suddenly was given charge over a social program promoting home ownership for the disadvantaged and resuscitation of city neighborhoods, it showed itself to be unprepared for such an about-face.

The sad fact was that the departmentalization of federal housing and urban initiatives under HUD was by itself not sufficient to establish an equitable federal urban policy.[47] While the FHA had been folded into HUD, its privatist ethos—reflected in its employees' behavior—was scarcely altered. The FHA's inspectorships often remained patronage positions, and its officials followed the familiar bureaucratic career pattern of shuttling between the private and public sectors. Despite the Fair Housing requirements of federal housing programs after the 1968 Civil Rights Act, the FHA remained attuned to the segregative practices that had profitably served the real estate industry. Under Section 235, inspectors approved deteriorating homes with bloated prices in segregated neighborhoods.[48]

Secretary Romney complained in 1971 that the FHA was being asked to change from a credit-oriented to a consumer-oriented organization more or less instantly, and under conditions of a national credit shortage.[49] He found the 1968 housing programs, including Section 235, "poorly conceived and . . . uncautiously developed."[50] The whole array of fifty federal subsidy programs was proving too complex for successful administration, and Congress was in general hardly supportive of the overloaded HUD.[51]

Other Unforeseen Challenges of Low-Income Home Ownership

Section 235 quickly encountered a litany of problems, technical and social, reflecting the tensions of this brand of low-income home ownership. For example, some purchasers soon found that the 20 percent monthly contribution, when limited by the maximum subsidy to an effective one percent interest rate, would actually amount to as much as 49 percent of their monthly family income.[52]

As some in Congress warned, moreover, income limitations meant that families in precarious financial positions were admitted to the program. In stressing traditional American virtues of home ownership, few legislators had considered that single-parent, welfare-dependent households would represent many in the targeted income group. Congress passed a related program designed to provide home-ownership counseling, but did not fund it.[53] New home owners, unprepared to face the maintenance and repair costs of their Section 235 homes, simply abandoned the dwellings in many cases, leading to one of the government's many unanticipated program costs.

Furthermore, 235 served to continue and even reinforce the problem of dual housing markets and suburban exclusion. Consider, for example, the disparities in the proportion of welfare families purchasing *new* (primarily suburban) 235 homes (1.5 percent), as opposed to those buying *existing* (primarily city) 235 homes (15 percent). Given the emphasis on new housing starts, constraints created by the availability and cost of land meant that new Section 235 homes were built overwhelmingly outside the old central cities. This drew a sharp exclusionary response from suburbs, with local forces turning to litigation and municipal referenda to resist subsidized housing.[54]

The existing homes served older and bigger families and a higher proportion of single-parent households. In cities, blacks represented the primary market for the 235 units, which were located predominantly—in some cities exclusively—in segregated or changing neighborhoods. The program gave real estate brokers tremendous discretion in determining where existing 235 houses would be located, and many brokers saw novice 235 buyers as an "easy sell."[55]

The 1968 Act did not adequately address the issue of spatial equity in subsidized housing. Political pressure on the new Republican administration, moreover, boded against a sustained emphasis on integration. Later legislation created new obstacles, mandating that local governments approve the siting of subsidized housing.[56] Thus, even new 235 developments were very often set in low-income, minority suburbs, or in bleak unincorporated areas. Of the latter, Michael Danielson wrote in 1976, "Lacking public transportation, community and commercial facilities, and other amenities, the only thing these areas tend to attract is more subsidized housing."[57]

The Public-Private Scandal

Reports of payoffs by speculators to FHA inspectors in several cities soon led to a series of investigations of Section 235's administration. A 1970 Senate report found evidence that "some FHA appraisers have allowed blatantly defective homes to be sold to lower income families."[58] A congressional staff report in 1971 warned that through the FHA, HUD "may be well on its way toward insuring itself into a national housing scandal. . . . FHA has allowed real estate speculation of the worst type to go on in the 235 program and has virtually turned its back to these practices."[59]

In many cases FHA inspectors allowed thoroughly inadequate "rehabilitated" homes to be sold to novice low-income purchasers, particularly minorities, with real estate speculators reaping windfall profits. Fraudulently inflating purchase prices, these investors frequently had the cooperation of FHA personnel in this implementation "nightmare."[60]

Some homes were condemned by local building-safety officials within months of purchase. A Spokane survey found that 101 of 113 respondents who purchased rehabilitated housing did not believe the house was worth what they had paid. After emergency reinspections by top HUD officials, Secretary Romney agreed that speculators' rehabilitation of homes had "typically left a great deal to be desired." In fact, the scandal was not limited to the existing home program. New 235 homes were found to be "instant slums" in towns in Washington and Missouri, as some builders used the cheapest materials and standards possible. An internal HUD audit in December 1971 found 26 percent of new and 43 percent of existing 235 homes substandard or uninhabitable.

Soon after the critical 1971 congressional staff report and hearing, Romney ordered a temporary moratorium in the existing-home portion of the program in certain regions. Meanwhile HUD began referring some FHA appraisers to the FBI for investigation. More than a thousand criminal indictments of FHA staff, real estate operators, and bankers followed. Most were convicted.[61]

Problems developed among consumers as well as producers. Public housing tenants who had been delinquent on their rents were in some cases approved for 235 home ownership. Massive defaults on mortgages ensued, especially in central cities. Forced to acquire properties once they became abandoned or uninhabitable, "HUD became the nation's biggest slumlord."[62] The department owned at least five thousand former 235 houses in Detroit alone by 1975.[63]

Subsidized home ownership, which was intended to remove the stigma of economic integration, added to it through scandal. Cushing Dolbeare notes that successes in such programs are invisible, while failures tend to be permanent and very apparent.[64] Municipalities responded to the bad publicity by reinforcing zoning, building-code, and environmental constraints on affordable homes.[65]

Romney left HUD in the scandals' aftermath. In January 1973, as part of the unprecedented executive impoundments of congressional appropriations, President Nixon—whose support for Section 235 was ambiguous at best—imposed a moratorium on the program. The courts ultimately judged Nixon's impoundments illegal, and a judicial order in August 1975 forced HUD to obligate the unused balance of the Section 235 appropriations to be made available for use.[66]

Section 235 Under Ford and Carter

The Ford administration restarted Section 235 in 1975, but with rule changes that opened its subsidies to a more middle-income clientele. The previous income ceiling—135 percent of the public housing limit—was changed to 80 percent of the median area income. Congress raised this ceiling to 95 percent of the area median for a family of four in the Housing Authorization Act of 1976. By 1978, the average income of families assisted under 235 had jumped from $8,085 to $11,532.

The Carter administration reversed its comparatively generous national urban policy in mid-course, trying to accommodate the country's new mood of fiscal restraint and increasing social conservatism.[67] It sought to come to terms with the extreme fluctuations that had been plaguing the mortgage market in the early and mid-1970s—despite the supposed stabilizing effects of federal entry into the market. This instability pushed the Carter administration toward an emphasis on middle-income housing and the vitality of the banking industry.[68]

In this context, what might be called the "middle classification" of the 235 program continued. By the close of the decade, the average family income under the program was above $13,500, and the median downpayment was up to $1,917. Fewer than 45 percent of 235 homes were being located in "urban" places, and less than one percent were now classified as "center city." Consequently, only 7.7 percent of 1979 mortgagors were black, with 11 percent Hispanic and 79 percent white.[69] Supposedly "radical," Section 235 followed in the footsteps of other housing programs that had become "directed mainly to the upper band of the below-average income groups."[70]

The price of continuing various federal housing subsidies became politically untenable in a stagflationary economy. The costs of subsidized housing construction and maintenance rose much more quickly than the income of the poor, and ever-greater public subsidization and spending was required. In the 1970s, home-owner income doubled in the general population, while the costs of homes tripled.[71] In the case of Section 235, by 1978 HUD had had to acquire over 15 percent of the prerevision 235 homes, "often in barely salvageable condition."[72] Reeling from past errors, and buffeted by high market interest rates, the government administered strong medicine, radically trimming Section 235 appropriations. The patient has not recovered.

The End of Liberalism?

Theodore Lowi asserted in 1979 that even Republican administrations find it nearly impossible to sidestep or fundamentally change the confused internal-group liberal legislation and administration of federal programs.[73] But Lowi wrote of the Nixon experience. The Reagan administration promised, and to some extent delivered, fundamental changes in the relationship between the national government and states, localities, and private enterprise.[74] Housing was a major target of federal cutbacks, and the case of Section 235 is instructive.

By 1988, low-income housing programs had a budget 75 percent less than their 1981 levels. Reagan and a submissive Congress eliminated the lion's share of housing subsidies, leaving states and localities to try to pick up the slack.[75] The Reagan years saw HUD's budget drop from 4.5 to 1.3 percent of total U.S. budget authority. Under Secretary Samuel Pierce, the department effectively dropped from cabinet-level visibility, later to regain attention only sporadically through revelations of Pierce-era scandals. The lack of a directed and sustained attention to housing policy was seen by 1989 as "leav[ing] the entire effort in disarray."[76] In short, federal housing policy barely existed. Meanwhile, the burdens of housing costs were as difficult to bear as ever. The percentage of income that poor people spent on housing had been drifting upward for two decades.

In the case of Section 235, legislative and administrative alterations in the 1980s resulted in an increasingly middle-class-oriented, untargeted program with little impact on the ill-housed of the inner cities. The subsidy ceiling of one percent effective annual interest rate was administratively overriden by HUD to an effective four to eight percent floor, mainly because HUD did not want to "attract a buyer who really [could not] afford the costs of homeownership."[77] The minimum downpayment, once two hundred dollars, was adjusted to three to six percent of the home's purchase price after the 1975 restart of the program, which easily could push the figure into thousands of dollars. Searching for ways to limit its expenditure commitment, Congress enacted a new "subsidy recapture" provision in 1980,[78] and a 1983 amendment limited federal subsidy agreements to ten-year terms. Having long since lost sight of the original income targeting of the program, HUD did away with the limit on family assets. The purchaser's required monthly contribution of 20 percent of family income was lifted to 28 percent.

Despite these changes, HUD still experienced a ten percent default rate on Section 235 homes in the late 1980s. The Department spent nearly $38.7 million on the acquisition of foreclosed 235 properties in FY 1990 alone.

As funds were appropriated far more slowly in its revised form, the "new" (i.e., post-1975) Section 235 program had subsidized just 123,182 units by October 1990, as compared to the 458,323 subsidized under the original phase of the program (1969–73).[78] Congress passed the HUD

Reform Act in 1989, addressing ethics and financial disclosure problems, after scandals surfaced in different HUD subsidy programs. The same legislation extended 235 through September 1991 and permitted HUD-insured refinancing of certain 235 homes.[80]

State, Market, and Urban Housing: Home Ownership as Social Policy

Section 235, like U.S. policy in general, has been hamstrung by the lack of recognition among federal policymakers of the deep and complex social, economic, and political roots of the urban housing crisis. Subsidized home ownership, designed as a revolutionary program to help radically increase the U.S. housing supply, ultimately became an incremental addition to the confusing array of poorly targeted, multiple-goal federal programs. It did little to reverse fundamental problems in the overall housing sector, actually reinforcing segregation and speculation in many cases.

Noting that the "eradication of urban blight, in itself, will not eliminate city slums,"[81] the Kaiser Committee recommended a creative new building program rather than supporting the bulldozer legacy of urban renewal. Nevertheless, Congress enacted what was essentially another bricks-and-mortar program under 235 rather than a human-centered reform.

The disbursement of subsidies and guaranteed investments to the housing and lending industries helped change the tenor of "subsidized home ownership" from a redistributive social program—which would improve the lot of America's ill-housed—to an inequitable transfer program based on the particularistic criteria of local zoning regulations, the profit motives of large-scale builders, the ingenuity of speculators, and the moral fiber of FHA inspectors. Rather than pull masses of poor people out of poverty, the program made cheap houses available to a portion of successful applicants and subsidized a small number of private-sector actors.[82]

Given its legislative origins, the fate of Section 235 was not surprising. To settle for a private agenda for a public-policy problem, given the FHA's existing biases, virtually guaranteed the problems that would plague the implementation of the program. Lawmakers have depended too heavily upon private-sector and local interests to exercise automatically the means to achieve national urban goals. Housing-production subsidies have been called "upside-down federalism, where the federal government makes the little decisions and the communities and private firms make the big ones."[83] Washington specified minor financial details, but not a locational or urban-development policy per se.

In a market society, it is hardly unreasonable that private entities sometimes be deployed for public ends. But in the absence of clear national standards, rules, and priorities, private enrichment may emerge as the only unambiguous objective. The 1968 Act did not establish housing as a right, leaving its ultimate human aims vague. President Johnson and some congressional supporters sought a consensual, if unclear, way to distribute the benefits of American middle-class life to more people. Other lawmakers saw 235 as a strict, means-tested program—an incremental addition to a piecemeal welfare system—or as a means of behavior modification.

Congress, moreover, dealt with housing in committees primarily devoted to banking and currency—a legacy of the roots of federal urban policy in FHA, which had been intended to stabilize credit markets. Through the entire process of designing a subsidized home-ownership policy, only one side of the equation was consulted—production. While the Kaiser Committee had representatives from business, labor, and government, both its report and the legislative debates show a lack of effort at determining the housing desires and ambitions of the affected population itself—except by reading motives into urban violence. HUD's emphasis on numerical production goals undoubtedly diluted product quality while giving short shrift to consumer desires.

It is not clear that the ownership of homes ought to be a goal of federal policy.[84] If there is to be such a goal, policymakers must address the degree of universalism the policy requires. In the case of home ownership, targeting benefits to the "most deserving" poor is an extraordinarily risky financial venture. This dilemma represents what Henry Aaron calls "the brutal choice of housing assistance."[85]

Section 235 illustrates certain pitfalls in the way key actors in the American state perceive problems and possible courses of action. In the case of housing needs, a key shortcoming lies in government's inability to concentrate resources. The federal government is hindered as much by the problematic division of labor between state and market as by its own revenue constraints. The Section 235 plan led to scandal and cutbacks because government chose the wrong mechanism to transfer resources— marginal alterations of the existing market. Americans have not looked fondly upon direct redistribution or socialized housing, but attempts to redistribute through markets, without altering the underlying income characteristics of the population, can be neither efficient nor equitable.

Some policy analysts feel that supply-side housing policies such as 235 simply cannot work.[86] But a more damning explanation for the frustration of much federal housing policy may be its very attempt to assume normal economic relations of supply-and-demand curves. Blair Badcock argues that demand-side approaches also take socially constructed housing markets more or less as givens, and their focus on the individual behavior of a housing consumer provides a very atomistic picture, "deflecting attention from the structures that bound that behavior."[87] In his view, assumptions about "housing choice" in behavioral models are little more than ideological indulgence. Michael Peter Smith notes that housing and labor markets are far from perfectly efficient, arguing that "in reality, distortions, disequilibrium, and imperfections characterize economic life in contemporary American society. Secrecy, high information costs, and socially structured accessibility to information about jobs, products, and services abound. Monopoly and oligopoly are common. Workers are attached to people, places, and cultures."[88] Given this realization, housing policies that simply seek to expand or tinker with the existing market at the margins will not often solve fundamental problems.

Some critics read different, unstated goals into the federal government's repeated intrusions into housing supply. They emphasize the state's role in bolstering profits among housing capitalists.[89] However, one need not hypothesize dire conspiracy theories or power elites to challenge "neutral" market ecology studies of metropolitan areas. As recent urban literature increasingly demonstrates, sociopolitical structures and spatial structures are registered in one another and need to be theorized jointly; cities are a "socially produced form, resulting from the interplay between the state, capital, and space."[90]

Viewed in this light, the seemingly consensual localism, privatism, and incrementalism characteristic of the American national state result in a jerry-built urban social policy, which is in turn reflected in an inequitable urban form. Existing private markets represent a privileged status quo in the policy-making process.[91] This "mobilization of bias" in the U.S. political system, to use E. E. Schattschneider's term, is buoyed by such factors as weak and ideologically ambiguous national parties, the local orientation of House members, our received "classless" political-economic ethos, and other factors too complex to consider here; in recent years the constraint of large national budget deficits has also been a factor. In sum, these political patterns bode ill for any sustained, national, truly "public" program that would address directly the life chances and housing options of poor people.

Meanwhile, policymakers agonize over homelessness and housing unaffordability, continuing testimony to the inadequacy of Section 235 and its programmatic brethren. Survey data reveal that a substantial majority of the U.S. population views these problems as a governmental responsibility.[92] The United States cannot long avoid resolving the public role in addressing the housing dilemma.

Princeton University

Acknowledgments

Thanks are extended to Michael Danielson and Martin Melosi for their careful critiques of successive versions of this paper.

Notes

1. Jeff Gerth, "Risks to H.U.D. Rose after Its Shift of Responsibility to Private Sector," *New York Times*, 31 July 1989; comments of Hon. Marge Roukema (R-N.J.), *Congressional Record*, 14 November 1989, H8611.

2. Sam Bass Warner, Jr., pioneered the interpretation of urban governance in terms of the usurpation of the public agenda by a private perspective. See *The Private City* (Philadelphia, 1968). For later perspectives on structural limits to urban policy, given the state-market division of labor in the United States, see Martin Shefter, *Political Crisis/Fiscal Crisis* (New York, 1985); and Stephen Elkin, "Twentieth-Century Urban Regimes," *Journal of Urban Affairs* 7:2 (1985): 11–28.

3. An excellent overview of the FHA experience is Kenneth Jackson, *Crabgrass Frontier* (New York, 1985), chap. 11. See also Charles Abrams, "New Roles for Private Enterprise in Housing," in *Cooperation of the Public and Private Sectors in Housing*, Princeton University Conference 88 (Princeton, 1968), 66–74.

4. Until 1949, the FHA favored white home buyers by officially recognizing racial and ethnic "stability" as a sound credit policy. Even a court decision overturning the FHA's policy of requiring racially restrictive covenants did not change its general orientation favoring white exclusionary suburbs. FHA credit was gradually expanded to reach those somewhat lower on the economic ladder by the early 1960s, but declining central-city areas remained effectively redlined. Jackson, *Crabgrass Frontier*; Abrams, "New Roles for Private Enterprise," 67. Calvin Bradford demonstrated how later changes in FHA credit guidelines, meant to provide more credit possibilities in minority areas, served only to subsidize exploitative dual housing markets. See Bradford, "Financing Home Ownership: The Federal Role in Neighborhood Decline," *Urban Affairs Quarterly* 14:3 (1979): 313–35.

5. Frank Thompson, Jr., "The Congressional Politics of Housing," in *Cooperation of the Public and Private Sectors*, 86; Michael Danielson, *The Politics of Exclusion* (New York, 1976), 203.

6. Kenneth Fox, *Metropolitan America* (Jackson, Miss., 1986), 91; U.S. Congress, Congressional Budget Office, *Federal Housing Policy: Current Programs and Recurring Issues* (Washington, D.C., 1978), 1.

7. Richard Davies, "One-Third of a Nation: The Dilemmas of America's Housing, 1607–1970," in Jerome Finster, ed., *The National Archives and Urban Research* (Athens, Oh., 1974), 44. See also President's Committee on Urban Housing, *A Decent Home* (Washington, D.C., 1968), 11.

8. Carl Abbott, *Urban America in the Modern Age* (Arlington Heights, Ill., 1987), 66; Chester Hartman, *Housing and Social Policy* (Englewood Cliffs, N.J., 1975), 10–11.

9. President's Committee, *A Decent Home,* 53.

10. Morton Schussheim, "Toward New Housing Policy," Committee for Economic Development, Supplementary Paper 29, 53–55.

11. United States, Kerner Commission (National Advisory Commission on Civil Disorders), *Report* (New York, 1968).

12. In this sense the Great Society was by no means politically revolutionary. See Bernard Firestone and Robert Vogt, eds., *Lyndon Baines Johnson and the Uses of Power* (New York, 1988), chap. 6 and throughout; and Paul Conklin, *Big Daddy from the Pedernales* (Boston, 1986).

13. HUD Secretary Robert Weaver recalled, "As I look back, I am confident that if there had not been some of that hyperbole, if there hadn't been some goals that were accused of being unrealistic at the time, people would not have thought big, and if they didn't think big they couldn't think like Lyndon Johnson throughout and they wouldn't have gotten the legislation." Firestone and Vogt, *Lyndon Baines Johnson,* 99.

14. Hugh Heclo delineates the role of insulated, professionalized issue networks in policy-making, and the resulting increases in the number of legislative proposals, in "Issue Networks and the Executive Establishment," in Anthony King, ed., *The New American Political System* (Washington, D.C., 1978), 87–124. Consider Sargent Shriver's description of his role in developing the War on Poverty as "scrounging around in the private sector, the public sector, in any sector I could find an idea, to put into this legislation." Quoted in Firestone and Vogt, *Lyndon Baines Johnson,* 93–94.

15. Richard Neustadt, *Presidential Power,* rev. ed. (New York, 1980), 184–85.

16. The story of HUD's origins is in Marlan Blissett, "Untangling the Mess: The Administrative Legacy of President Johnson," in Firestone and Vogt, eds., *Lyndon Baines Johnson,* 65–71; and Royce Hanson, *The Evolution of National Urban Policy 1970–1980* (Washington, D.C., 1982), 2–3.

17. President's Committee, *A Decent Home,* 1.

18. Ibid., 1, 54. One might also argue that these "most successful" programs were the ones that had been the most generously funded.

19. *Congressional Record* (Washington, D.C., 1968), 4043, 4044–45.

20. See Hartman, *Housing and Social Policy,* 15.

21. Charles M. Haar, " 'Public' and 'Private,' " in *Cooperation of the Public and Private Sectors,* 22.

22. President's Committee, *A Decent Home,* 66, 79.

23. The National Association of Home Builders, long a powerful Washington lobby, was widely reported to have had a large hand in drafting the legislation. See Hartman, *Housing and Social Policy,* 137. Its former president, Leon Weiner, sat on the Kaiser Committee.

24. This amounted to a typical monthly federal subsidy of $40 to $70 in 1968. Household income was to be recertified every two years.

25. James O'Connor, *The Fiscal Crisis of the State* (New York, 1973).

26. Following a typical strategy, Johnson, secured particularly enthusiastic committee sponsorship by giving key congressional players a stake in his legislative program. These included Senator Percy and Representative William Widnall, Republican sponsors of the original home-ownership proposal; the southern committee chairmen in each chamber, Senator John Sparkman and Representative Wright Patman; and Representative Leonor Sullivan, whose St. Louis district had hosted the pilot program. This ensued a core of active on-floor lobbyists for the bill.

27. *Congressional Record,* 20305.

28. Ibid., 20555.

29. Ibid., 20306.

30. Ibid., 20307.

31. Ibid.

32. Brock proposed another amendment to raise the required proportion of monthly income to be paid toward the mortgage from 20 percent to 25 percent. It was rejected.

33. *Congressional Record*, 21850.

34. Ibid., 15239.

35. Ibid., 14944.

36. President's Committee, *A Decent Home*, 2.

37. *Congressional Record*, 15240.

38. Quoted respectively in ibid., 20307; M. Carter McFarland, *Federal Government and Urban Problems* (Boulder, Colo., 1978), 139; and Thompson, "Congressional Politics of Housing," 87.

39. Thompson, "Congressional Politics," 87. Senator John Stennis, for example, saw in 235 "not a housing measure at all but a major step toward setting up a Federal guaranteed minimum income scheme on a piecemeal basis." *Congressional Record*, 15598.

40. See, for example, U.S. Congress, House, Committee on Banking and Currency Hearing, *Interim Report on HUD Investigation of Low- and Moderate-Income Housing Programs* (Washington, D.C., 1971); Kummerfield, "The Housing Subsidy System," in Daniel Mandelker and Roger Montgomery, eds., *Housing in America* (Indianapolis, 1973), 334–47; Danielson, *Politics of Exclusion*, 87, 100–105; General Accounting Office, Comptroller General of the United States, *Report to the Congress: Need for Fairer Treatment of Homeowners' Claims for Defects in Existing Insured Homes* (Washington, D.C., 1977); Mildred Deyo Roske, *Housing in Transition* (New York, 1983), 258–59.

41. McFarland, *Federal Government and Urban Problems*, 141.

42. U.S. Congress, Senate, Committee on Banking and Currency, Subcommittee on Housing and Urban Affairs, *Progress Report on Federal Housing and Urban Development Programs* (Washington, D.C., 1970), 23.

43. Roske, *Housing in Transition*, 258.

44. U.S. Congress, *Interim Report*, 103.

45. Schussheim, "Toward New Housing Policy," 61.

46. Danielson, *Politics of Exclusion*, 235–36.

47. See Fox, *Metropolitan America*, 198.

48. See Brian Boyer, *Cities Destroyed for Cash* (Chicago, 1973).

49. U.S. Congress, *Interim Report*, 18.

50. Boyer, *Cities Destroyed for Cash*, 6.

51. See, for example, the remarkably strained exchange between Romney and Rep. William Berret (D-Pa.) during a 1971 committee hearing. U.S. Congress, *Interim Report*, 23–24.

52. Robert Schafer and Charles Field, "Section 235 of the National Housing Act," in Jon Pynoos et al., eds., *Housing Urban America*, 2d ed. (Hawthorne, N.Y., 1980, orig. 1969), 492.

53. U.S. Congress, *Interim Report*, 14.

54. Danielson, *Politics of Exclusion*, 100–104.

55. See U.S. Congress, *Interim Report*, 5; Leonard Rubinowitz and Elizabeth Trosman, "Affirmative Action and the American Dream: Implementing Fair Housing Policies in Federal Homeownership Programs," *Northwestern University Law Review* 74:4 (1979): 493–616, esp. 593–95; and Ronald Silverman, "Homeownership for the Poor: Subsidies and Racial Segregation," *New York University Law Review* 48:1 (1973): 72–135.

56. Danielson, *Politics of Exclusion*, 238–39.

57. Ibid., 104.

58. Quoted in General Accounting Office, *Report to the Congress*, 11.

59. U.S. Congress, *Interim Report*, 103.

60. Abbott, *Urban America*, 126. Material in the next paragraph is drawn from Hart-

man, *Housing and Social Policy,* 138; McFarland, *Federal Government and Urban Problems,* 142; U.S. Congress, *Interim Report,* 9, 48, 105; Boyer, *Cities Destroyed for Cash;* and General Accounting Office, *Report to the Congress.*

61. McFarland, *Federal Government and Urban Problems,* 143.

62. John Harrigan, *Political Change in the Metropolis,* 4th ed. (Glenview, Ill., 1989), 362.

63. Hartman, *Housing and Social Policy,* 138. The 5,000 figure was likely a vast underestimate due to HUD's studied number-juggling of its inventory. Boyer calculated at least 8,000 total houses in HUD's Detroit inventory in 1972, including those acquired under other subsidy programs. He forecasted the eventual foreclosure of up to 28,000 homes. Boyer, *Cities Destroyed for Cash,* 9–10.

64. Cushing Dolbeare, "The Low-Income Housing Crisis," in Chester Hartman, ed., *America's Housing Crisis* (Boston, 1983).

65. Danielson, *Politics of Exclusion,* 87–88.

66. See Department of Housing and Urban Development, *1979 Statistical Yearbook* (Washington, D.C., 1980), 186.

67. Ann Markusen and David Wilmoth, "The Political Economy of National Urban Policy in the USA, 1976–81," *Canadian Journal of Regional Science* 5:1 (1982): 125–44.

68. See U.S. Congress, Congressional Budget Office, *Housing Finance: Federal Programs and Issues* (Washington, D.C., 1976).

69. HUD, *1979 Statistical Yearbook,* Table 48.

70. Schussheim, "Toward New Housing Policy," 56.

71. Dolbeare, "The Low-Income Housing Crisis," 51.

72. U.S. Congress, *Housing Finance,* 32–33.

73. Lowi, *The End of Liberalism.*

74. See William Greider, *The Education of David Stockman and Other Americans* (New York, 1982).

75. Kathryn Wylde, "Partnerships for Housing," in Perry Davis, ed., *Public-Private Partnerships* (New York, 1986), 112.

76. Mary Nenno, "H/CD after Reagan," *Journal of Housing* (March–April 1989): 76, 78.

77. Jacobs et al., *Guide to Federal Housing Programs,* 92.

78. "Subsidy recapture" requires homeowners, upon reselling the house, to reimburse the government the lesser of (1) all federal subsidies received; or (2) 50 percent of the home's appreciation in values, minus improvements and sales costs. Jacobs et al., *Guide to Federal Housing Programs,* 106; and HUD communications to the author. While fiscally sound, the provision restrains the upward mobility new home owners might experience under 235.

79. As of September 1990, 179,685 of these early 235 homes still had their federal mortgage insurance in force. All data in these paragraphs are from HUD, *Summary of Mortgage Insurance Operations* (Washington, D.C., 30 September 1990).

80. *Congressional Record,* 14 November 1989, H8604.

81. President's Committee, *A Decent Home,* 1.

82. For dramatic case studies, see Boyer, *Cities Destroyed for Cash.*

83. Kummerfield, "The Housing Subsidy System," 336.

84. See Raymond Struyk, *Should Government Encourage Homeownership?* (Washington, D.C., 1977).

85. Henry Aaron, *Shelter and Subsidies* (Washington, D.C., 1972), 143. On housing means tests, see also Blair Badcock, *Unfairly Structured Cities* (Oxford, 1984), 37.

86. Schafer and Field, "Section 235 of the 1968 Housing Act."

87. Badcock, *Unfairly Structured Cities,* 16.

88. Michael Peter Smith, *City, State, and Market* (New York, 1988), 184.

89. See, for example, Boyer, *Cities Destroyed for Cash,* 4; Davies, "One Third of a

Nation," 45; Hartman, *Housing and Social Policy*, 142; and Struyk, *Should Government Encourage Homeownership?*, 8.

90. Badcock, *Unfairly Structured Cities*, 6, 52. See also, for example, Elkin, "Twentieth-Century Urban Regimes"; Clarence Stone, *Regime Politics: Governing Atlanta, 1946–88* (Lawrence, Kan., 1989); and Smith, *City, State, and Market*.

91. See Charles Lindblom, *Politics and Markets* (New York, 1977).

92. Robert Shapiro and John Young, "Public Opinion and the Welfare State," *Political Science Quarterly* 104:1 (Spring): 82n.

NOEL A. CAZENAVE

Chicago Influences on the War on Poverty

The most controversial component of the War on Poverty in the 1960s was its Community Action Program (CAP). Controversy resulted largely from the CAP because it employed activist professionals, mandated mass-scale resident participation, and encouraged federal-agency-sponsored institutional conflict as a mechanism for social reform. These strategies were tested earlier in the Mobilization for Youth program founded in the late 1950s, and in the early 1960s in the Ford Foundation Gray Areas programs and the President's Committee on Juvenile Delinquency projects. [1] Indeed, the basic models of social expertise and community action employed in those programs were used in Chicago two decades before. [2]

Numerous accounts of the origins of the War on Poverty identify Chicago influences. For example, Daniel Patrick Moynihan mentions the impact of the theories of criminologists Clifford Shaw and David McKay. Both were graduates of what came to be known as the "Chicago School" of sociology, which at that time was the most influential sociology department in the nation. They were also the leaders of the Chicago Area Project, an early community-action-oriented antidelinquency program. In his study of the Mobilization for Youth program, a major laboratory for many of the strategies and techniques of the War on Poverty Community Action Program, Joseph Helfgot identifies three major antecedents. In addition to the Chicago Area Project, he discusses the influences of the settlement-house movement and the Alinsky movement. Alinsky community organization efforts were based in Chicago, and many of the crucial issues and debates facing settlement house workers were acted out in that metropolis. Marris and Rein discuss the influence of key Ford Foundation consultants and juvenile delinquency experts Leonard Cottrell and Lloyd

Ohlin. Both were graduates of the "Chicago School" of sociology. Richard Boone, a former Ford Foundation and later President's Committee staff member, a key planner of the War on Poverty and the Director of the Program Policy and Planning Division of its Community Action Program, was still another graduate of that department.[3]

This article explores two case studies from the period 1939–44 to delineate the dynamics and consequences of the elite competition involved.[4] The first involves social worker Hasseltine Byrd Taylor's report on the social science–dominated Chicago Area Project. The second focuses on the Council of Social Agencies of Chicago study of professional community organizer Saul Alinsky's Back of the Yards Neighborhood Council. These case studies show that those innovations were not simply a result of the gradual evolution of knowledge accumulated through years of research and practice. They occurred through the process of competition between elite groups of social experts.[5] In large part, they were spurred by the conflict between Chicago professional social workers, social scientists, and community organizers over control of programs to meet the needs of low-income urban areas.[6]

In brief, competition between social expert elites played a key role in the evolution of the underlying philosophies and strategies of community change central to the War on Poverty.[7] I hope the following case analyses will further our understanding of how competition between such urban professionals affects urban policy formation, implementation, and consequences.

The Chicago Area Project as Seen by a Social Worker: 1939

While the late 1930s was a time of rapid and innovative change for American society in general, both social workers and social scientists had begun moving away from earlier social-action-oriented approaches to reform.[8] Social work became increasingly preoccupied with more traditional, individualistic, and clinically oriented methods that were seen as being more compatible with their increased emphasis on obtaining and maintaining the status of professionals.[9] Like social workers, American social scientists focused on policy initiatives that were national, rather than local, in scope.[10] With this shift in focus, the sociology department of Columbia University challenged the national dominance of the Department of Sociology of the University of Chicago.[11] Ironically, the national influence of both Chicago social workers and the "Chicago School" of sociology were on the decline at a time when they were key architects of influential strategies of urban reform. The struggle among these experts not only for influence and dominance, but in some incidences, survival, can best be understood in this context.

One of Chicago's most important social-action initiatives at that time was the Chicago Area Project (CAP), which was officially established in 1932 by a group of University of Chicago–trained sociologists. The CAP began as an experimental antidelinquency program that initially operated in three Chicago neighborhoods. Its goal was to go beyond the tendency of psychologists and social workers to treat delinquents as maladjusted individuals in need of therapy, toward approaches designed to change the social environments that sociologists believed resulted in delinquency.[12] The CAP strategy was "community action," which emphasized the involvement of local residents in antidelinquency programs designed to reinstitute the indigenous community-based social controls assumed to be lost as a result of mass-scale urbanization.[13]

The Hasseltine Byrd Taylor Report. In early 1939, Hasseltine Byrd Taylor, self-described social work consultant and former neighborhood house director, initiated a series of written exchanges between herself and the leadership and supporters of the Chicago Area Project.[14] While lasting less than two months, this brief skirmish documents the conflict resulting from an early effort to apply social science expertise to the expansion of local community resident participation in community reform initiatives, which were previously considered by social workers to be their domain. The principals in this conflict thus anticipated many of the issues and debates central to the experimental antidelinquency projects that preceded the Community Action Program of the War on Poverty.

In her letter to Oscar G. Mayer, the president of the Chicago Association of Commerce, Taylor questioned the propriety of hiring Jesse Jacobs, secretary of the Association of Commerce, as CAP associate director.[15] She asked whether this constituted a conflict of interest since Jacobs, through his position with the commerce association, also served as "a trustee to social agencies which participate in the Community Fund of Chicago."[16] Taylor also argued that, even if the CAP did not participate in the fund, there was conflict between its goals and methods and those of other social agencies.

She described the CAP head, Clifford Shaw, as "a research sociologist," who was primarily interested in research and only incidentally concerned about the prevention of juvenile delinquency.[17] Taylor apparently did not view the CAP's use of applied social scientists in delinquency prevention as being indicative of the emergence of a more activist and expanded model of social science expertise.[18]

Taylor did acknowledge the CAP's innovative approach to community organization. But she was especially critical of its emphasis on the use of "natural leaders" to reduce deviance. In contrast, she stressed that traditional social agencies were committed to upgrading the professional education and standards of their workers. It was the responsibility of this trained staff, she argued, to reorient indigenous leadership toward socially acceptable behavior.[19] Social scientists were depicted as being too objective in their acceptance of any naturally existing leadership, regardless of its moral or social direction. As an example of how harmful such an approach could be, Taylor compared this CAP practice to the use of natural leaders in Chicago ward politics and in Hitler's Germany.[20]

Finally, she implied that it was Jacobs's association with the CAP (a rival local social agency) that was a motivating factor in his decision to remove her neighborhood house from the Association of Commerce-approved funding list.[21] In brief, Taylor's letter accused the CAP of operating under a model of social expertise that was largely exploitative, engaging in unfair competition with its rivals, and advocating a model of community action that was not only socially irresponsible but dangerous.

A modified version of that letter was titled "The Chicago Area Project as Seen By a Social Worker." In addition to its title, it differed from Taylor's letter by expunging all references to Jacobs's alleged conflict of interest and her experiences with the CAP staff as a former director of a neighborhood center.[22] CAP sociologist Anthony Sorrentino responded to this version of the Taylor Report.

Sorrentino addressed specifically Taylor's criticisms of: the use of natural leaders, the qualifications of staff members, and the CAP's experimental nature.[23] He justified the use of "responsible local residents" as being central to the CAP program philosophy that "such participation is essential to the reconstruction of the social, moral, and political life of the people residing in deteriorated areas of the city."[24] The composition of the boards overseeing three CAP regional programs was discussed to refute Taylor's claim that it was arbitrary regarding the scruples of the leaders chosen.[25] Sorrentino also discussed the professional background of the seventeen-member CAP staff to counter Taylor's charge that it was "untrained in either social case work or group and recreation work."[26] Finally, in defending the experimental nature of the program, he stressed that the CAP engaged in accepted social work practices, differing from other agencies "in procedure rather than in content." That procedure involved area residents and the coordination of the programs of local institutions.[27]

Another rebuttal charged that Taylor's actions were motivated by personal as well as professional disagreements. That is, Taylor's comments reflected both long-term professional disagreements between sociologists and social workers and her "rather viscious personal opposition to the personnel of the Area Project."[28] The apparent tactic of this memo was to dismiss professional disagreements as being legitimate differences of opinion, while impugning Taylor's motives through the assumption that conflict involving agency turf and personnel was not a permissible topic of discourse.

Taylor's charges did not present a serious challenge to the CAP and its approach to community reform.[29] With its twin resources of social science legitimacy and the advocacy of mass-scale democratic participation, the Chicago Area Project was able to challenge successfully the hegemony of social workers in the area of juvenile delinquency control. In doing so, it anticipated not only key aspects of the basic model of community action used in the War on Poverty, but the major strategy through which social science experts would play a role in its planning and implementation. Before the CAP could enjoy its victory over the hegemony of social work professionals, however, both groups faced a new and significant challenge from the Back of the Yards Neighborhood Council. In that conflict social scientists fought on both sides. However, most allied with the more programmatically conservative social workers.

Saul Alinsky's Back of the Yards Neighborhood Council versus the Council of Social Agencies of Chicago: 1940–1944

In the early 1940s, America's urban landscapes continued to change rapidly in ways that presented both challenges and opportunities to its social work and social science experts. In Chicago a new type of social expert would enter into the fray—the professional troublemaker, as exemplified by Saul Alinsky. The two-month skirmish between Hasseltine Byrd Taylor and the Chicago Area Project provided only a glimpse of a much broader and more enduring conflict.

The Taylor/CAP controversy neither resolved the apprehension of traditional social work professionals about the encroachment of the CAP on their turf nor slowed its movement. Instead, social workers were concerned that with its broad definition of delinquency control the CAP was able to claim most traditional social work activities and programs under its vast and expandable programmatic umbrella.[30]

Traditional social workers were not the only ones to grow wary of the Chicago Area Project. Director Clifford Shaw became skeptical about the

CAP's ability to address problems, the solution to which required more fundamental social and economic changes than local community organization efforts could provide.[31] Saul Alinsky, like Shaw, a University of Chicago–trained sociologist, and a community organizer, was even more disenchanted. Alinsky grew restless as he became convinced that social science and the CAP did not go far enough in addressing the ills of communities plagued by delinquency and other social problems.[32] It was during the late 1930s, ironically, that Alinsky was given the most difficult CAP assignment yet—organizing the slum area upon which Upton Sinclair's novel *The Jungle* was based.

At that time the Congress of Industrial Organizations (CIO) was already engaged in a campaign to unionize the stockyard workers, the chief breadwinners of the "Back of the Yards" neighborhood. Alinsky found himself drawn toward the CIO's efforts just as he became increasingly alienated from the more limited objectives of the CAP. His organization of the entire community exceeded the scope of both the CAP and the CIO plans.[33]

With the organization of the Back of the Yards Neighborhood Council (BYNC), Alinsky also surpassed both Shaw's notoriety and the tolerable bounds of political safety. Fortunately for Alinsky, he was able to parlay that success into a larger neighborhood organization movement by the early 1940s. With this momentum Alinsky built his own organization, the Industrial Areas Foundation (IAF).[34]

Two years later Shaw was still trying to sift out the essence of his CAP from the more controversial elements of Alinsky's BYNC and IAF. In the summer of 1942 he received a letter from the distinguished Harvard University criminologist Sheldon Glueck. Shaw was asked how his program differed from other juvenile delinquency prevention efforts. As an example Glueck mentioned only one program, Saul Alinsky's Industrial Areas Foundation.[35]

Shaw's reply was revealing, both in what was discussed and what was not. There were significant differences in the structure and operations of these two programs. Alinsky's BYNC had a much broader agenda, was overtly political, and was based on a labor union organizational strategy.[36] But Shaw focused exclusively on programmatic outcomes and who got credit for them. He discounted Alinsky's claim of dramatic results in reducing juvenile delinquency in a short period of time, and criticized what he described as the tendency of publicity and credit to be given to "national figures" rather than to local people. This latter criticism indirectly impugned Alinsky's commitment to indigenous leadership.[37]

The Council of Social Agencies Studies the Back of the Yards Neighbor-

hood Council. In Alinsky and the BYNC, Chicago's social work establishment faced foes that, while less prominent than Clifford Shaw's Chicago Area Project, were potentially far more threatening. While the
BYNC lacked the legitimacy of "science," its strength came from the
political salvos it launched in the name of another important American
value, "democracy."[38]

Alinsky assumed a generally more offensive position in his dealings
with settlement house workers than did Shaw's CAP. In her study of the
settlement house movement, Judith Trolander devotes a chapter to what
she refers to as "The Sociological Attack" against settlement houses.[39]
During the four-year period 1940–44, the Council of Social Agencies of
Chicago engaged in a vigorous counterattack. Two years after Alinsky left
the CAP and founded the Industrial Areas Foundation, the Council of
Social Agencies (CSA) mounted a challenge much greater than that
possible by any lone social worker. The CSA launched an investigation of
Alinsky's Back of the Yards Neighborhood Council. Bearing the imprima-
tur of an influential social work network, its inquiry could not simply be
dismissed as a personal attack. In this case it was Alinsky who was forced
to assume a defensive posture.

In January 1942, the CSA authorized a committee "to study the significance of the Back of the Yards Neighborhood Council for agencies in the
field of recreation, informal education and group work."[40] The subdued
and professional tone of its report and correspondence was misleading.[41]
In a letter soliciting Alinsky's cooperation, CSA Division on Education
and Recreation Chairperson William F. Byron frankly acknowledged the
emotional roots of the inquiry. Byron stated that he proposed the study to
bring the "rational element" into play in order to spare CSA members the
type of emotional response they had to the CAP.[42]

In contrast to the Taylor/CAP conflict, in which well-connected "Chicago School" social scientists were aligned against a social worker, the
Council of Social Agencies mobilized social science prestige against
Alinsky, the renegade criminologist. Byron, a Northwestern University
sociology professor, sought unsuccessfully to attract the participation of
renowned University of Chicago sociology professor Louis Wirth.[43] It was
also proposed that the committee's division of labor might include sociologists to review the literature on community organization, providing still
further evidence that the council was prepared to fight sociology with
sociology.

The committee's primary directive was to respond to what in its words
was a BYNC claim to represent "*a new theory of community organization*"
[emphasis in original].[44] To make their case that the BYNC approach was

nothing new, Roosevelt University sociology professor and Committee Chair Arthur Hillman summarized the state of the art of social work community organization.[45] Central to the social worker's approach was the coordination of welfare agencies.[46] In a draft of the committee's report, he explained why the social work approach to community organization stressed councils of social agencies. Since the needs of low-income urban communities were specialized (e.g., housing and recreation), it was essential that community agencies cooperate to address interests that were borderline or overlapping. It was this cooperative activity that social workers referred to as "community organization."[47]

Based on its analysis of written documents, a session with Alinsky, and contacts with other people knowledgeable about the BYNC, the committee concluded that Alinsky's community organization approach was "in line" with existing social work practice and not fundamentally different.[48] The committee did allow that there was evidence supporting the BYNC's "claim to distinction" in its advocacy of a broad base of power and its link between local and large-scale social action.[49] In a response, Alinsky questioned the objectivity of the preliminary report. He was especially disturbed by what he viewed as an attempt to reduce the BYNC to "a conventional community organization, more or less in the category of a social agency."[50]

While the committee expressed great interest in the BYNC's approach to community organization, Alinsky noted that it did not give much attention to its philosophy and methods of community change.[51] The social workers stressed a consensus model as the chief vehicle of change. In contrast, Alinsky used conflict and pressure group tactics.[52] To Alinsky, in comparison with the CSA, the BYNC was "an entirely different animal."[53]

Perhaps a more fundamental issue than the BYNC's uniqueness was the threat Chicago social workers felt it posed to them. The relationship between Alinsky-style organizations and traditional social work agencies was not simply perceived as one of competition over turf, but as a conflict where the presence of indigenous-based neighborhood councils excluded traditional social work agencies headed by professionals. Alinsky did not allay these fears. Indeed, it was reported that in response to a question as to how he knew there was a need for organization in targeted communities. "Mr. Alinsky replied that the secret in the whole business lies in the fact that other organizations collapse shortly after they start."[54]

Again, it appears that the major issue of contention between Alinsky and the social workers was not the BYNC's uniqueness per se, but the role of social work professional expertise in addressing the problems of low-income urban communities. The committee challenged the BYNC's emphasis of indigenous leadership because it saw it as a threat to the social work profession.[55] It argued that while laypersons had a role to play in new BYNC-type initiatives, social work professionals were indispensable. In his critique of social work community organization theory and practice, Hillman concluded that although nonprofessionals may possess community organization skills, professionals were needed for their specialized knowledge of the entire community. It was proposed that professionals would work with local leaders similar to "the role of the expert in government in relation to the political leader who interprets the administrator to the people and the people to the specialist."[56]

The committee was not impressed with Alinsky's arguments that low-income people should represent their own interests. In his response to Alinsky's charge that social work professionals superimposed their wishes on local communities, Hillman suggested that there was a natural link between professionalism and democratic practice. Leadership, he argued, implied followers, and thus, in practice, effective leadership required that the views of those who follow are taken into account. Hillman also argued that there should be concern about the domination by local (nonprofessional) leaders because they were "without the devotion to democratic educational methods which professional people in this field usually espouse."[57]

The committee not only defended the value of social work professionalism but presented it as the standard against which the BYNC's staff should be judged. In this offensive, the Council of Social Agencies employed contradictory tactics in its challenge to the professionalism of the BYNC leadership. The first approach might be termed a rejection tactic since it criticized the BYNC staff for not being more professional. The second was a co-optation tactic, which recognized the BYNC leaders as being professional. In the latter case, however, the committee argued that the BYNC's activities were largely an extension of traditional social work practice and questioned the genuineness of BYNC's indigenous leadership.[58] Through these arguments the chief challenge the BYNC posed to social work professionals was limited to what could be learned from it and incorporated into existing social work practice. No fundamental change was necessary.[59]

Another dispute centered on the issue of objectivity. In response to a social worker's accusation that the BYNC was biased because of its support of area meat-packing workers in a threatened strike, Alinsky admitted that the BYNC was, indeed, partisan. In fact, the BYNC existed specifically to pursue the partisan interests of area residents, he argued.[60] The social worker's claim to objectivity as an occupational value appeared to be more closely aligned with the view of traditional social science experts than Alinsky, whose professional training was as a social scientist and whose community organization theories were heavily influenced by the "Chicago School" of sociology.[61]

The earlier innovations in community organization and professional reform spurred by the Chicago Area Project were due in part to the disenchantment of social science experts with traditional social work practice. However, those initiated by the Back of the Yards Neighborhood Council grew out of the belief that both social science and social work were inadequate in addressing the mass-scale changes occurring in low-income industrialized communities. Just as the CAP's social scientists exploited the American value of "science" to legitimize their work and status, Alinsky's BYNC used "democracy" to legitimize the emergence of a new type of social expert—the professional troublemaker.

The success of the BYNC and its effective rebuttals to many of the CSA's most serious charges was a setback to the professional aspirations of social workers. The result was yet another institutional realignment of Chicago's social experts. The Alinsky/BYNC approach explored different methods and went further than commonly accepted social work practice. The BYNC's broad and comprehensive scope, the inclusion of all major indigenous organizations, and its conflict strategy and tactics suggest that it was indeed significantly different. With the emergence of the BYNC and the national Industrial Areas Foundation, community organization took on a new meaning. It advocated the democratic participation of area residents over CSA professionals. As a result of the conflict between these groups of competing elites, the social workers were forced to adapt as professional reformers were pressured to take a more activist role in the promotion of community change. They could no longer excuse themselves from the heat of battle through claims of professionalism, societal consensus, or objectivity.

Chicago Influences

This article does not argue that specific programs and policies of the War on Poverty were developed as a direct result of conflict between Chicago social workers, social scientists, and community organizers. Its findings do suggest, however, that the emergence of the general context and models of social science expertise and community organization used in the precursors to the War on Poverty were evident in the two Chicago case studies discussed. This does not mean that Chicago was the only location of these skirmishes or that such conflict was limited to the five-year period discussed here. Trolander documents similar battles in other American cities over a twenty-five-year period (1939–65) and shows that they were part of a national conflict between social scientists and social workers over the nature and control of antipoverty program initiatives.

In the conflict between Hasseltine Byrd Taylor and the social science experts of the Chicago Area Project, the social scientists emerged victorious by establishing their legitimacy as scientists, and as professional reformers intent on expanding the base of democratic participation. Science was used to legitimize social science professionals at the expense of traditional social workers. At the same time, the emerging professional-reformer model won social scientists support for their efforts to increase community involvement. In this way, the CAP social scientists placed Taylor in a vise-grip between the professional prestige of science and the popular value of citizen participation.

In the battle of the Council of Social Agencies vs. the Back of the Yards Neighborhood Council there was a shift of professional alignments and the emergence of a new professional group of experts. Unlike the Taylor/CAP controversy, this conflict involved already professionalized experts (social workers *and* social scientists) against a growing movement for indigenous community organization led by professional troublemaker Saul Alinsky. What initially appeared to be a conflict between professionals and nonprofessionals upon closer inspection was a battle between existing social experts and newly emerging professional community organizers as a new model of social expertise. As a result of this conflict, social workers and other professionals were forced to take a more activist role in community matters, one more consistent with a professional reformer model of expertise. Because of the growing value of democratic participation, the conflict inherent in this role of social expert could no longer be dismissed through claims of professionalism and objectivity. The BYNC's emphasis on indigenous leadership opened the way for the use of nonprofessionals in later antipoverty initiatives. Through the challenge of Alinsky's BYNC, social work professionals realized that if they were to survive, their profession must change.

These case studies reveal an increasing commitment to community participation in public-policy formation and implementation processes. The concept of indigenous leadership gained support when Hasseltine Byrd Taylor was unsuccessful in her attempt to portray the Chicago Area Project approach as unprofessional, irresponsible, and dangerous. By surviving the challenge of the Council of Social Agencies, the Back of the

Yards Neighborhood Council further expanded the use of indigenous leadership by the Chicago Area Project. As a result, the BYNC offered a model of community action that stressed a broad and comprehensive scope, the inclusion of all major indigenous organizations, and the use of a conflict strategy of social change. While the CSA raised an important question as to how far down the grassroots leadership of the BYNC actually extended, the BYNC was successful in pushing community organization further in the direction of mass-scale participation.

These findings suggest a link between the models of professionalism and community reform employed during a particular historic period. In the late 1930s and early 1940s that connection was tightened as a result of the shift from a traditional to a professional reformer model of social expertise and the resultant strain it caused. There was a contradiction between experts as professionals (monopolizers of knowledge for career-related pursuits) and as reformers (enhancers of community-wide democratic participation). Such conflict necessitated changes in existing models of professional expertise and community action. The role of social experts was enlarged to include the utilization of professionals in social-action initiatives. The concept of community organization was expanded to permit a broader base of participation and to include the use of disruptive tactics. A model of the professional reformer emerged that was compatible with these changes and was more flexible than earlier models of professionalism and reform, which called for a more rigid division of objectivity and advocacy.

Two decades after the Council of Social Agencies' investigation of Alinsky's Back of the Yards Neighborhood Council, social science experts like Richard Cloward and Lloyd Ohlin, Kenneth B. Clark, and Warren Haggstrom expanded the activist model of social science influenced by Shaw and McKay of the Chicago Area Project into leverage against the social service and political status quo of communities like New York's Lower East Side, Harlem, and low-income areas of Syracuse, New York. Their prestige as social scientists legitimized their plans for community change, which sometimes were implemented through militant social-action strategies and tactics reminiscent of those of America's most renowned community agitator, Saul Alinsky.

This study of Chicago influences on the War of Poverty suggests two issues that merit further exploration in future historical research on the evolution of U.S. urban policy. First, historical analysis cannot only help us better understand the commonly stressed ways in which national urban policies affect cities, but how the political characteristics and professional conflicts of influential cities affect the development of federal urban policies. Finally, historical research of the role of elites in municipal conflicts can increase our understanding of precisely how urban policies and pro-grams emerge. The preceding analysis suggests that the development of urban reform initiatives is not simply the product of the rational accumula-tion of knowledge and techniques. Urban policy is affected by competi-tion among elites and the efforts of professionals to resolve conflicts within their own changing work requisites and roles.

University of Connecticut

Acknowledgments

This research was made possible by a grant-in-aid from Temple University and grant RLL-8807980 from the National Science Foundation. The author wishes to thank Leo C. Rigsby, Department of Sociology, Temple University; Judith Trolander, Department of History, University of Min-nesota, Duluth Campus; Donald C. Reitzes, Department of Sociology, Georgia State University; Mary Jo Deegan, Department of Sociology, University of Nebraska; and Gaye Tuchman, Department of Sociology, University of Connecticut, for their helpful comments and suggestions. I would also like to thank my research assistant, Dena R. Wallerson, for proofreading this article.

Notes

1. Joseph H. Helfgot, *Professional Reforming: Mobilization for Youth and the Failure of Social Science* (Lexington, Mass., 1981), 29–31; Daniel Knapp and Kenneth Polk, *Scouting the War on Poverty: Social Reform Politics in the Kennedy Administration* (Lexington, Mass., 1971), 4–5; Peter Marris and Martin Rein, *Dilemmas of Social Reform: Poverty and Commu-nity Action in the United States,* 2d ed. (Chicago, 1982), 14–25; John H. Laub, *Criminology in the Making: An Oral History* (Boston, 1983), 212.

2. Helfgot, *Professional Reforming,* 16–18; Judith Ann Trolander, *Professionalism and Social Change: From the Settlement House Movement to Neighborhood Centers, 1886 to the Present* (New York, 1987), 167.

3. Daniel P. Moynihan, *Maximum Feasible Misunderstanding: Community Action in the War on Poverty* (New York, 1969). Helfgot, *Professional Reforming;* Marris and Rein, *Dilemmas of Social Reform;* Sanford D. Horwitt, *Let Them Call Me Rebel: Saul Alinsky—His Life and Legacy* (New York, 1989). Conference Proceedings, "Poverty and Public Policy. The 1973 Group Discussion of the Kennedy Administration Urban Poverty Program and Policies," vol. 1, John F. Kennedy Library. Ohlin, 61–61a.

Lloyd Ohlin, the first head of the Office of Juvenile Delinquency of the President's Committee recalled that he and James McCarthy, the action director of Mobilization for Youth, met with Alinsky in Chicago for an eight-hour conversation.

4. This article provides the early historical background of a larger study of the use of social science experts and community participation in precursors to the War on Poverty. The goal of that project is to explore the potential and limitations of the use of social science experts in the promotion of resident participation in community reform initiatives.

5. For an example of historical research using his approach, see Trolander, *Professionalism and Social Change*, chap. 7, "Settlement Houses Lose Influence: The Sociological Attack," 139–57. It is also important to note how, despite their periodic conflicts in Chicago, these different categories of social experts shared common roots in the "Chicago School" of sociology.

6. Trolander, *Professionalism and Social Change*. Trolander treats the conflict between social science experts and settlement house workers as central to the evolution of antipoverty strategies and to the use of professionals in their planning and execution. This approach is consistent with what Robert R. Alford and Roger Friedland, in *Powers of Theory: Capitalism, the State, and Democracy* (Cambridge, 1985), refer to as "the managerial perspective." In contrast to the pluralist view of the power structure, the managerial or competing-elite perspective stresses the importance of power and conflict in public-policy formation and implementation. It does not assume this process to be either objective or rational. Instead, it is seen as being dominated by various competing groups of elites and the important organizations they control.

7. Conference Proceedings, "Poverty and Public Policy," vol. 2, John F. Kennedy Library, 407. The term "social experts" is used by Francis Fox Piven to refer to social scientists. Here it refers to social scientists, social service providers, professional community organizers, and others who specialize in social issues.

8. Geoffrey Perrett, *Days of Sadness, Years of Triumph: The American People, 1939–1945* (New York, 1973).

9. John H. Ehrenreich, *The Altruistic Imagination: A History of Social Work and Social Policy in the United States* (Ithaca, N.Y., 1985), 122.

10. Martin Bulmer, *The Chicago School of Sociology: Institutionalization, Diversity, and the Rise of Sociology Research* (Chicago, 1984); Trolander, *Professionalism and Social Change*.

11. Bulmer, *The Chicago School of Sociology*. In addition, the largely male University of Chicago sociologists and the mostly female social workers were still experiencing the "chill" associated with the polarization of these professions into separate departments and schools. Robert E. L. Faris, *Chicago Sociology: 1920–1932* (San Francisco, 1967), 13. See also Rosalind Rosenberg's *Beyond Separate Spheres: Intellectual Roots of Modern Feminism* (New Haven, 1982), 50.

12. Jon Snodgrass, "The American Criminological Tradition: Portraits of the Men and Ideology in a Discipline" (Ph.D. diss., University of Pennsylvania, 1972).

13. Anthony Sorrentino, "The Chicago Area Project After 25 Years," *Federal Probation* (June 1959): 40–45.

14. Taylor to Oscar G. Mayer, 11 February 1939, Box 27, Folder 5, Clifford R. Shaw Papers, Chicago Area Project Records, Chicago Historical Society (hereafter Clifford Shaw Papers).

15. Ibid., 1, 5.

16. Ibid., 1.

17. Ibid.

18. Scholars of the War on Poverty and its forerunners have suggested that the emergence of the professionalization of reform, which eventually entailed a shift from a traditional scientific to a more activist applied model of social science expertise, was a key factor in making these initiatives possible. Knapp and Polk, *Scouting the War on Poverty*, trace the beginning of the professional reform movement back to the New Deal. They explain the movement from the greater emphasis on scientific expertise in the 1930s to that of democratic participation characteristic of the 1960s as the result of an intentional "constituency shift" of the federal government toward the urban poor. As compared to the more tradi-

tional model of scientific expertise, the professional-reformer approach was more likely to advocate activist social science as a way of promoting greater indigenous resident participation in community programs (5).

19. Taylor to Mayer, 11 February 1934, Clifford Shaw Papers, 1.

20. Ibid., 3.

21. Ibid., 6–7.

22. Hasseltine Byrd Taylor, "The Chicago Area Project As Seen By a Social Worker," Box 27, Folder 4, Clifford Shaw Papers. As a result, the letter provided less information as to the specific incidents that sparked the controversy. In its sanitized version, the new document appeared to be a reasonably objective social work critique of a new social reform initiative.

23. Hasseltine Report, Anthony Sorrentino, Box 27, Folder 4, Clifford Shaw Papers, 1.

24. Ibid., 1.

25. Ibid., 1–2.

26. Ibid., 2–3.

27. Ibid., 4. For Sorrentino's account of this controversy, see Anthony Sorrentino, *Organizing Against Crime* (New York, 1977), 89–90. Sorrentino discusses meetings where he says Taylor attempted to organize other social workers against the CAP.

28. Malcolm McCallum to A. G. Montgomery, 16 March 1939, Box 27, Folder 5, Clifford Shaw Papers, 5.

29. Jesse A. Jacobs to Carroll H. Sudler, Jr., 3 April 1939, Box 27, Folder 5, Clifford Shaw Papers. In his summation of the impact of her attack, Jesse Jacobs wrote an apparent supporter that it "seems to have done the Area Project a great deal of good. In fact, it turned out to be the best sort of publicity."

30. Horwitt, *Let Them Call Me Rebel*, 53–54.

31. Jon Snodgrass, "Clifford R. Shaw and Henry D. McKay: Chicago Criminologists," *The British Journal of Criminology* 16 (January 1976): 16. According to Snodgrass, as early as 1935 Shaw concluded that the CAP did not adequately address the problems of the poor. Snodgrass states that because of its close ties to industry (e.g., its board composition and funding sources), "the CAP was cosmetic rather than surgical; the approach was almost trivial in the face of the realities of Chicago politics and economics." (For responses to Snodgrass's assertion, see the Sorrentino and Puntil interviews in the appendix to Laub's *Criminology in the Making*.) While the CAP was able to go further in its focus on the immediate environment than the approach of traditional social work, neither was able to address the serious social and economic dislocations cities faced as a result of rapid industrialization.

32. See David P. Finks, *The Radical Vision of Saul Alinsky* (New York, 1984), 20.

33. Horwitt, *Let Them Call Me Rebel*, 68.

34. Ibid., 102, and Finks, *The Radical Vision of Saul Alinsky*, 23.

35. Sheldon Glueck to Clifford Shaw, 23 July 1943, Box 15, Folder 14, Clifford Shaw Papers.

36. Horwitt, *Let Them Call Me Rebel*, 68.

37. Shaw to Glueck, 6 August 1942, Box 15, Folder 14, Clifford Shaw Papers.

38. In *Professionalism and Social Change*, Trolander (29) states that settlement house workers were attacked for being paternalistic and nondemocratic outsiders whose primary function was social control.

39. Ibid., 139–57.

40. William F. Byron to Louis Wirth, 18 February 1942, Box 241, Folder 7, Welfare Council of Metropolitan Chicago Records, Chicago Historical Society (hereafter Welfare Council Records).

41. In *Let Them Call Me Rebel*, Horwitt (135) also notes that the source of social workers' concern was the same as that of the earlier Taylor attack on the CAP—a feeling

that social work professionals were being shut out of solutions to the problems of lower-class communities in the nation's industrialized cities.

42. Byron to Alinsky, 25 January 1942, Box 251, Folder 7, Welfare Council Records.

43. Byron to Wirth, 18 February 1942, Box 251, Folder 7, Welfare Council Records. "Proposal for the Study of the Significance of the Back of the Yards Neighborhood Council," Box 251, Folder 7, Welfare Council Records.

44. "Proposal for the Study of the Significance of the Back of the Yards Neighborhood Council," Box 251, Folder 7, Welfare Council Records.

45. Arthur Hillman Vita, Arthur Hillman Papers, Box 1, Vita, Articles, The University of Minnesota Social Welfare History Archives. Hillman completed his doctoral work in sociology and social service administration at the University of Chicago in 1940.

46. Arthur Hillman, "Principles of Community Organization" (tentative statement for consideration by a committee of the Council of Social Agencies of Chicago), Box 251, Folder 7, Welfare Council Records.

47. "Preliminary Report for Discussion by Executive Committee. General Principles of Community Organization and a Statement on the Back of the Yards Neighborhood Council. By a Committee of the Division on Education—Recreation. Council of Social Agencies of Chicago," Box 251, Folder 7, Welfare Council Records.

Hillman noted, however, that community organization could go beyond traditional social work practice, as was the case in the field of social action, where the social worker emphasized his or her role as citizen. In the final version of this document, the specific reference to the cooperative activity of councils of social agencies and Community Chests was deleted.

48. Ibid., 7.

49. "Preliminary Report for Discussion by Executive Committee," Box 251, Folder 7, Welfare Council Records, 7. Donald C. Reitzes and Dietrich C. Reitzes argue in *The Alinsky Legacy: Alive and Kicking* (Greenwich, Conn., 1987) that Alinsky was heavily influenced in his thinking about community organizing by University of Chicago sociologist Robert Park's observation that communities are not self-sufficient and autonomous entities that can be understood independent of broader societal changes occurring outside their borders.

50. Alinsky to Byron, 12 April 1943, Box 251, Folder 7, Welfare Council Records, 4.

51. Ibid., 3.

52. Trolander, *Professionalism and Social Change.*

53. Alinsky to Byron, 12 April 1943, Box 251, Folder 7, Welfare Council Records, 2. The committee saw BYNC's claim to uniqueness as being based on an indigenous neighborhood movement, as well as on its comprehensiveness and its recognition of the role of external national forces. In contrast, traditional social agencies focused on a single problem and treated their target areas as isolated and self-contained communities. Minutes of Meeting of the Committee on the Back of the Yards Neighborhood Council, 6 April 1942, Box 251, Folder 7, Welfare Council Records. Alinsky also identified the BYNC's inclusion of all organizations within a community, its emphasis on the rights of community residents, its partisan nature, and its use of conflict tactics as characteristics that distinguished it from the traditional social work approach to community organization. Minutes of Meeting of the Committee to Study the Significance of the Back of the Yards Neighborhood Council, 29 April 1942, Box 251, Folder 7, Welfare Council Records. See also Saul Alinsky's "Community Analysis and Organization," *American Journal of Sociology* 46 (1941): 41–47.

54. Minutes of Meeting of the Committee to Study the Significance of the Back of the Yards Neighborhood Council, 29 April 1942, Box 251, Folder 7, Welfare Council Records, 4.

55. "Preliminary Report for Discussion by Executive Committee," Box 251, Folder 7, Welfare Council Records.

56. Hillman, "Principles of Community Organization," Box 251, Folder 7, Welfare Council Records.

57. Ibid., 2.

58. On the one hand, the committee questioned whether Alinsky's role in the BYNC was, to use rhetoric he used while employed in the CAP, "superimposed" as merely an extension of traditional social work practice. On the other hand, the committee charged that Alinsky and the BYNC executive director, Joseph B. Meegan, were not indigenous leaders; Alinsky because he was not a "Back of the Yards" resident and Meegan because of the resources available to him as head of an area recreation center. "Preliminary Report for Discussion by Executive Committee," Box 251, Folder 7, Welfare Council Records, 7–8.

59. "Proposal for the Study of the Significance of the Back of the Yards Neighborhood Council," Box 251, Folder 7, Welfare Council Records.

60. Alinsky to Byron, 12 April 1943, Box 251, Folder 7, Welfare Council Records.

61. See Wayne McMillen, "The Content of Professional Courses in Community Organizations," The Social Service Review 9 (1935): 68–82.

SY ADLER

The Evolution of Federal Transit Policy

The first major piece of national transit legislation was enacted in 1964. By 1969 the Urban Mass Transportation Administration was the subject of a highly critical analysis by staff investigators for a Congressional Appropriations Committee, and in the early 1970s industry analysts sharply critiqued the rationality of urban transit policy in general. In 1981 the Comptroller General of the U.S. reported to Congress that the demand for transit subsidies was approaching crisis proportions.[1] The U.S. government has come to play a greater role in the transit industry than do most European counterparts, provides more passenger subsidy per ride than any other country, and, though transit is everywhere subsidized, the U.S. federal government subsidizes a greater share of industry costs than most other national governments.[2] This article examines the circumstances under which this particular industry-government relationship developed. As part of this industrial policy discussion, the article also looks at the culture of discourse that was present during the early intervention period and that has been characteristic of the transit policy community since that time.[3]

David Jones argues that the federal program failed to address the underlying causes of the widespread financial distress of the urban transit industry during the post–World War II period, a reflection of the fact that "virtually no attention was given to the economics of transit operations." He critiques federal government intervention on the grounds that "policy was being built for and around the racehorses, not the workhorses, of the transit industry," by which he means that policy focused on the suburb-to-central city journey rather than on the intra-urban travel that was the bread and butter of city transit properties. Moreover, he claims that the federal bureaucracy charged with administering the transit program consistently deferred to local priorities and judgments.[4]

This article argues that transit policy was indeed captured—at the outset—by central business district activists in cities across the country seeking to enhance the locational advantages of their place in the face of increasingly intense competition from suburban business centers. The mayor of Atlanta, testifying to a congressional committee in 1961 on behalf of the American Municipal Association and the U.S. Conference of Mayors, precisely articulated the theme that Jones pinpoints as leading to policy failure: "The greatest dilemma is this. Mass transportation has failed to keep pace with the explosive growth of our suburban areas. . . . Our mass transportation facilities must be stretched out into these new suburban areas. . . . Most of the strangling congestion on our central city streets results from the fact that private operators find it unprofitable to expand their services into the less densely populated suburban areas. It is a vital public necessity that such service be provided. . . . If they are vital public necessities, yet unprofitable to operate privately, they must be subsidized."[5]

The central city focus of the federal program reflected a strategic shift by transit advocates in congressional policy-making tactics, away from the commuter railroad problems of a few big metropolitan areas—and the jurisdiction of the congressional commerce committees that dealt with railroad transportation matters—toward a broader concern with urban transportation and related land-use issues. The constituency for intervention was broadened, and the issues were addressed by the more interventionist and city-oriented banking and currency committees. However, shortly after the legislative breakthrough in 1964, the transit program and its implementing bureaucracy were moved to the newly established Department of Transportation, rather than being permanently lodged with the Department of Housing and Urban Development. Although it was not especially controversial at the time, the shift institutionalized a set of conflicts between Transportation's continuing efforts to rationalize the supply of transit facilities and deeply rooted congressional efforts to subsidize the competitive exertions of central city constituents.

These conflicts, whether expressed on the terrain of land use or of transport supply, were present in the original debates regarding the nature and purposes of transit policy, and reflected a growing executive branch concern with rationalizing the national government's myriad interventions in these spheres.[6] This rationalizing concern, which characterized both Republican and Democratic administrations and grew in intensity as congresionally driven program subsidies escalated, is one of the key dimensions of transit industrial policy analyzed below. However, before turning to a discussion of the dynamics of intervention, the article first grounds the evolution of federal policy in the context of local responses to the decline of the mostly privately owned transit industry during the 1940s and 1950s.

Responding to Industry Decline

As the financial and service problems of urban transit worsened in the post–World War II period, industry leaders advocated several steps to restore profitable operations and to prevent government takeovers of private properties. However, as the limits of these responses became increasingly evident to central city business and to political and technical activists, and as competition between central business districts and growing outlying business centers intensified, downtown interests sought to create regionwide governmental transit agencies that would invest in the types of services and facilities that would enhance the accessibility and reception capacity of the core. Representatives of outlying business centers resisted these initiatives, which produced governmental transit agencies with limited capabilities. These local political constraints, combined with state legislative reluctance to subsidize urban projects, reinforced a turn by downtown activists to the federal government.

In order to reverse the declining fortunes of their industry, leaders exhorted transit firms to pursue several different strategies. These ideas were widely discussed in the industry press and successes were loudly trumpeted to encourage others to adopt the innovations. First and foremost, transit properties were advised to establish and maintain close working alliances with downtown merchants and property owners, major newspapers, and city political officials. The key to these alliances, according to their industry leadership, was an awareness of shared fate. The financial future of all the alliance partners was intimately related to the health of the downtown economy, and transit operators had to convince these others that a thriving central business district required a viable transit system.[7]

Solid working relationships would, in turn, facilitate the adoption of various street and parking management tactics that would expedite the flow of surface transit vehicles, thereby improving the efficiency of operations. These included the elimination of on-street parking in the downtown area during the day or at least during peak periods, the provision of fringe parking/shuttle bus service, controls on turning movements, and the radical notion of reserving traffic lanes on the main downtown routes exclusively for transit vehicles during rush hours. New Orleans and Chicago set up fringe lots in the late 1940s. Philadelphia banned on-street parking downtown during the 1952 Christmas shopping season, and later generalized the practice, following a suggestion made by the major transit company there, and in early 1956 Nashville set up the first traffic lane reserved exclusively for buses.[8] Nashville's mayor Ben West, who was also a leading activist in the American Municipal Association during the 1950s, was hailed as a hero by the industry. The editors of *Mass Transportation* wrote in their report on the 1956 American Transit Association convention that "the best speech . . . was given by Mayor Ben West of Nashville, Tennessee. But we had the feeling that there was not complete realization by transit men that here, in the person of this energetic mayor and in the things that have been accomplished in Nashville, was *everything* transit seeks in the way of city operation."[9]

Transit industry leaders also hoped that an alliance with downtown interests would lead to support for a set of long-sought changes in the regulatory environment within which privately owned firms operated, and in fare practices. These were aimed at reducing costs, boosting productivity, and enhancing revenues. The industry sought emancipation from what were perceived to be oppressive franchise taxes and gross revenue levies; rigid rate structures, which made it impossible to raise and lower fares in a timely manner; and severe constraints on operators' capacity to drop service on unprofitable lines. Houston, for example, lowered gross receipts taxes in 1952, and the press kept a scoreboard of reductions in various taxes and forms of regulatory relief granted by states and cities around the country.[10]

On the revenue side, industry leaders called for the introduction of distance-based or zonal fare structures and peak period pricing. Industry analysts noted that while off-peak riding was precipitously declining, peak-priced ridership was holding its own. Moreover, the postwar round of fare increases was driving away the short-haul passenger. In early 1956 Toledo instituted a downtown free fare zone as part of a zone fare system, and the St. Louis transit company reduced off-peak fares for downtown trips during shopping hours and also worked out a deal with downtown merchants to subsidize shopper travel.[11]

While the transit industry promoted these institutional, fare, and traffic management changes, their alliance partners representing downtown sought a variety of service innovations in return for their support. These had mostly to do, as the Atlanta mayor told the Congress in 1961, with extending service to rapidly developing suburban areas, and providing peak-period express service between these outlying areas and the central business district. These were the sorts of services that investors rooted in downtown sought to deploy in order to counter the competitive threat posed by suburban business centers and their acres of free parking. These were, however, the most costly services for the transit industry—already reeling from the financially devastating effects of the peaking problem—to supply.[12]

The St. Louis Public Service Company, the major transit supplier in that city, was widely regarded as "The Showpiece of the Transit Industry," largely because of the property's heroic efforts to respond, on behalf of downtown, to the suburban challenge. The company instituted a number of peak-period express bus routes between outlying areas and the core and ran shopper expresses as well. It utilized park-and-ride lots in suburban areas and fielded the nation's largest fleet of air-conditioned buses. The company president lobbied incessantly for exclusive bus lanes on the downtown streets, as had been introduced in Nashville. Nashville Transit initiated De Luxe commuter service using a subscription bus approach in early 1955, as did the Cincinnati operation, and the Washington, D.C., transit firm proposed to offer subscription-type club express service. These were aimed at attracting the long-distance traveler.[13]

While there was some movement in the direction of these sorts of peak period, long-distance express services, privately owned firms generally resisted downtown pleas to increase significantly their offerings in this area. Pacific Electric Railway in Los Angeles, which had resumed a limited number of express runs in 1946 that had been suspended during the war explained that "express service during the peak hours of travel has stimulated such peak hour travel without any appreciable effect on the mid-day or off-peak travel. It is a well known fact that all peak-hour travel, while undoubtedly of material benefit to the community served and to the passengers using it, has had a detrimental effect upon the earnings of the Company."[14] While deteriorating financial circumstances sharply constrained the capacity of private firms to provide these sorts of services, the few city-owned transit systems in the country were checked by municipal boundaries. The San Francisco Municipal Railway, for example, inaugurated express services from outlying parts of the city and put buses on freeways as quickly as segments opened to traffic, but Muni could not penetrate the rapidly growing sections of the peninsula south of the city or extend into the eastern or northern parts of the bay region.[15]

As a result of the financial exhaustion of the private companies and the limits of city-based public alternatives, downtown activists initiated movements to create regionwide governmental transit agencies with the politi-

cal and financial power to provide the kinds of facilities and services that
were seen as crucial to the survival of the central business district. These
same activists were also in the forefront of the drive to launch a massive
freeway building program that would include urban extensions of the
interstate system. Nashville mayor Ben West, hero of the transit industry,
was also the chair of the American Municipal Association's Highways
Committee. Testifying before the U.S. Senate Public Works Committee
in 1955 about the national highway program, he articulated the cities'
interest in metropolitan freeways and explained that a large-scale federal
program was necessary because of rural domination of state legislatures.
"We are going to be lost balls in the high weeds," he said, "because we
cannot get enough money [from the states] to take care of that tremendous load of cost of acquisition of rights-of-way."[16]

Downtown activists sought transport facilities that would radiate from
the core into outlying areas. Combining freeway and transit facilities
within the same right-of-way—a set of downtown/radial corridors—was
their ideal configuration. Such transport facilities would enable people to
make increasingly lengthy, metropolitan-scale trips quickly, and, together
with parking lots, would supply the central business district with virtually
unlimited reception capacity. The idea surfaced in Detroit in a 1920s
report by a group of five prominent businessmen calling for the construction of a network of "superhighways" that would incorporate transit in the
median strip. Rail transit in freeway medians was the objective of a Los
Angeles Chamber of Commerce–led movement in that region in the late
1940s, and the first such facility in the U.S., a rail line in the median strip
of the Congress Street Expressway in Chicago, opened in 1958.[17] However, creating the governmental capacities that were necessary to finance
such multimodal corridor projects, as well as separate transit facilities, was
quite difficult politically.

California central business districts experienced the full force of suburban competition more intensely than elsewhere during the early postwar
period. Efforts to create regional transit agencies in three California urban
areas during the 1940s and 1950s reveal the political conflicts that at-
tended these downtown responses. These conflicts would shortly characterize other metropolitan areas as well. When the Los Angeles Chamber
of Commerce launched its drive to create a rapid transit district that
would place rail lines in several downtown/radial freeways—which the
Chamber had played a leading role in winning—opposition surfaced in
the large number of outlying business centers, within as well as without
the city, to the new governmental entity. The basis of resistance was
straightforward, reflecting the fundamental way in which the intense

competition between business centers in the region to maintain and attract mobile capital investment structured the dynamics of transport politics: outlying business center representatives opposed subsidizing transport
projects that would primarily benefit the Los Angeles central business
district.[18]

The intense political conflict surrounding the downtown-oriented transit initiative produced, in 1951, the Los Angeles Metropolitan Transit
Authority, which so clearly reflected the stalemate that prevailed in the
region that it was thoroughly paralyzed for several years. In 1957 this
regional government agency was finally enabled to buy out the private
firms, but was too financially and politically constrained to implement
much of the key elements of the downtown program.[19]

A downtown San Francisco–led rapid transit movement emerged shortly
after its Los Angeles counterpart, which eventually succeeded in building
the Bay Area Rapid Transit (BART) system. However, the same conflicts
that characterized the Los Angeles experience surfaced in the Bay region,
nearly derailing the project there as well. In the end, a much smaller system
than transit activists originally conceived was built. During the early years
of the transit movement in the Bay Area, the main line of conflict sepa-
rated downtown activists in San Francisco and Oakland, with the Oakland
leadership perceiving the San Francisco proposal as yet another attempt by
its larger competitor to defend the historic pattern of regional domination
and prevent downtown Oakland from playing the hegemonic office-
commercial role in the rapidly growing East Bay portion of the region. The
Bay Area Rapid Transit Commission was created in 1951, during the same
legislative session as its Los Angeles analogue, and was equally as constrained. During the next few years, however, San Francisco and Oakland
activists reached an accommodation—built around an underwater trans-
bay tube—that promised to permit both downtowns jointly to penetrate
rapidly growing suburban areas.

The Bay Area Rapid Transit District, created in 1957, reflected the San
Francisco–Oakland settlement; however, the growth of several business
centers on the peninsula south of San Francisco during the 1950s led to
another rupture. Santa Clara County, which contains San Jose, refused to
join the District, and San Mateo County, immediately south of the city,
withdrew from the District a few years later. Financing for a much trun-
cated three-county system, rather than the six-county network sought by
San Francisco activists, was approved by the district electorate in 1962,
and limits on the district's bonding capacity further constrained system
design and construction.[20]

Their efforts earned BART district activists a hero's welcome at congressional hearings, though. Senator Harrison Williams of New Jersey, the leading transit advocate in Congress, praised district representatives for doing "what in many areas has seemed almost impossible, to get the whole region, or most of the region, into a governing unit . . . each jealous, of course, of its own sovereignty, and have done an even harder job of giving them the power to raise the money." Following successful passage of the BART bond issue, Williams described it as "a governmental miracle that your people . . . voted to tax themselves for this magnificent proposed rapid transit line."[21]

While the downtown Oakland leadership struggled with San Francisco over a regional rapid transit system, they faced their own local crisis. Oakland and several other smaller cities in the East Bay were served by Key System Transit Lines, one of the handful of big-city transit properties—St. Louis Public Service was another—controlled by National City Lines (NCL). NCL sought to maintain the profitability of its transit empire in large part through an effort to hold down wages, a strategy that produced a great deal of bitterness on the part of the unionized workers who toiled on its properties, particularly in the many smaller cities where NCL's wage discipline was especially strict. The Amalgamated Association of Street, Electric Railway, and Motor Coach Employees of America, which represented most NCL workers, also deeply resented the company's policy of refusing to submit contract disputes to arbitration. As NCL sought to hold the line on wages during the protracted period of industry decline, strikes on NCL properties increased in frequency, and the company was quite willing to take lengthy strikes in order to enforce its bargaining position.

The downtown Oakland leadership had to stand idly by while a Key System refusal to arbitrate provoked a seventeen-day strike in 1947 and a strike lasting two and a half months in 1953, severely affecting downtown business and retail sales. The latter strike was widely interpreted as an NCL effort to force a government buy-out of the property; the arch-conservative Oakland leadership reluctantly moved to comply. Blessed by Joseph Knowland, publisher of the Oakland *Tribune* and a leading activist in the right wing of the state and national Republican party, a coalition of downtown business, political and technical people sponsored the creation of the Alameda–Contra Costa Transit District, to take over Key System and provide transit service that would strengthen downtown Oakland's position in the East Bay. Key System had always staunchly resisted extending lines into growing areas and providing express services to the core. Knowland explained to his associates: "I am not an advocate of public ownership, as such. But we are here confronted with a condition, not a theory."

The Oakland-centered regional transit government that Knowland and colleagues created was endowed with the broadest range of political and financial power of any such entity created before federal governmental intervention. The district was the only one in the country with an elected board of directors and unlimited power to tax property within its jurisdiction, and it was granted a larger proportional bonding capacity than was its larger Bay Area counterpart. However, even the powerful downtown Oakland coalition was constrained in its drive to encompass the entire East Bay region within its district's domain. Substantial portions of both Alameda and Contra Costa counties successfully resisted incorporation into the transit district, seeking instead to foster the growth aspirations of their own business centers. [22]

Similar competition-driven dynamics were in evidence elsewhere in the country as well. The Manhattan-centered plan of the New York–New Jersey Metropolitan Rapid Transit Commission drew the same kind of fire as in the Los Angeles and San Francisco–Oakland metropolitan areas. Business and political leaders in the larger New Jersey cities attacked the understanding that informed the commission's rail transit plan—that the metropolitan area constituted a single, integrated social and economic unit focused on the Manhattan central business district—and resisted the creation of a region-wide government agency that would impose the commission's plan on them. [23] Efforts to create a Baltimore-centered metropolitan transit authority were similarly stymied for several years during the 1950s, and the Chicago Transit Authority repeatedly failed to secure the capacity to implement major extension programs. [24] In Washington, D.C., the House District of Columbia Committee decided that approval should be sought for only that portion of a proposed rail rapid transit system for the national capital region that was mainly within the District of Columbia due to serious suburban uncertainties regarding the location of the proposed rail lines. [25]

In mid-1961, just as the drive for federal intervention in transit was gathering steam, the trade journal *Metropolitan Transportation* surveyed the thirteen major regional transport agencies then functioning, including the New York City Transit Authority. All of these were constrained in various jurisdictional and/or financial ways from fully implementing the downtown corridor program, and in many other areas local conflicts had prevented the emergence of regional agencies at all. [26] The transit districts and authorities, such as the Los Angeles Metropolitan Transit Authority, instituted as much long-distance, peak-period express service as they could. However, a combination of political conflict at the metropolitan level and state-level unwillingness to subsidize urban transport projects limited the capacities of the new agencies to act. City support for federal intervention, for both downtown/radial freeways and transit, increased in relation to these political obstacles.

The Dynamics of Federal Intervention

Downtown activists were supported in their natural legislative effort by some commuter railroads, the Railway Progress Institute representing rail equipment manufacturers, and the Institute for Rapid Transit, which included rail transit operators, equipment manufacturers, and transport planning and engineering consulting firms. They were championed by a growing number of congressional representatives who sought to advance the interests of their constituents. However, this alliance confronted a tentative executive branch. Tentativeness was a product of two contradictory sets of pressures bearing on top officials of both political parties and their executive appointees. On the one hand, national leaders of both parties sought to use metropolitan programs, including transit, to solidify relationships between national and local party organizations and to enhance the party's electoral appeal among target groups at the local level. The Democrats used urban programs aimed at traditional big-city strongholds in the Northeast, Midwest, and West during the Kennedy-Johnson years, and the Republicans adopted their own version aimed at suburban voters and the newer cities of the South, Southwest and Western areas during the Nixon period.

Executive branch officials, however, were also concerned about rationalizing the national government's growing involvement with metropolitan area problems. They worried about the budgetary impacts of the increasing amounts of subsidy, the extent to which the many programs were effectively coordinated, and the efficiency with which program objectives were addressed. Party-building and electoral concerns, along with congressional advocacy, have produced periodic transit program expansion. Rationalization efforts have sought continually to rein in subsidy commitments and discipline the allocation process according to efficiency objectives. Both tendencies are responses to the competition between places to maintain and attract mobile capital investment at the local level. Spatial competition engenders a continuing demand for transport projects that will create and maintain location advantages; executives continually search for ways to contain the fiscal crisis tendencies inherent in the growing number of project proposals.

The kinds of transit initiatives that downtown activists sought from the federal government to overcome their political and financial obstacles fell into three main categories: (1) institutional and financial access to interstate highway rights-of-way in order to realize fully the promise of the downtown/radial transport corridor; (2) grants to construct radial rapid-transit facilities—for rail and bus rapid transit, both inside freeways and separately—that would penetrate rapidly growing suburban areas; and (3) subsidies for equipment and labor to operate the new peak-period services. It took varying lengths of time to achieve these objectives. Institutional commitments at the national level were fairly easily secured. Subsidies for equipment preceded major support for construction and right-of-way acquisition, and operating subsidies were the most difficult to accomplish. By the mid-1970s, though, all the elements were in place.

City officials, local transit activists, and congressional advocates began calling for access to freeways during debates on the national highway program in the mid-1950s. The American Municipal Association resolved at its annual convention in 1957 that the federal Bureau of Public Roads should authorize plans and specifications for the inclusion of transit facilities as an eligible federal cost in the planning of the urban segments of the new interstates. The idea was also boosted by Harland Bartholomew, one of the nation's leading urban planners and the chairman of the National Capital Planning Commission. He said in 1957 that he would ask District of Columbia highway officials to reserve the median strips of two proposed highways for mass transit, and the proposed transportation plan released by the Bartholomew Commission in 1959 called for extensive bus and rail use of freeway rights-of-way and lanes as well.[27]

As part of the Kennedy administration's response to the downtown coalition's transit initiative, the president called for a report on the nation's mass-transit problems and needs to be jointly prepared by the Housing and Home Finance Agency and the Department of Commerce. This 1962 report concluded that "the Bureau of Public Roads will in the future (a) permit the reservation of highway lanes for the exclusive use of specific types of motor vehicles when comprehensive transportation plans indicate this to be desirable, and (b) encourage the development of rail transit and highway facilities in the same right-of-way whenever more effective transportation will result."[28] In his transportation message to the Congress, presented shortly after receipt of the report, President Kennedy said that he had endorsed the recommendations, and during congressional testimony the federal highway administrator said that the Bureau of Public Roads was implementing what the President had approved, referring specifically to the charge given designers of the congressionally authorized Shirley Highway in the Washington, D.C., area to consider the inclusion of special bus lanes. The administrator also, however, called attention to the fact that funds to implement the transit portion of any joint use plan were not yet generally available.[29]

Walter McCarter, a former Chicago transit official and now president of the Institute for Rapid Transit recalled at congressional hearings in 1963 that he had worked closely with former Bureau of Public Roads chief Tom McDonald in the late 1940s on planning the jointly used Congress Street Expressway, and that McDonald had told him at the time that "If he had had the power . . . he would not have allowed an expressway to be built in any metropolitan area without a median strip wide enough for a private right-of-way [for mass] transportation. He did not have the power at that time."[30] The mayor of Seattle, representing the American Municipal Association, also called on Congress to provide funds for advance right-of-way acquisition so that space might be reserved for transit.[31]

The first major piece of transit legislation, in 1964, made available federal grants for land acquisition, new equipment purchase, and facility construction. Money for land would enable local transit agencies to begin implementing their share of corridor development. Funds for equipment would permit locals to modernize and upgrade their vehicles and facilities. This element also amounted to a protectionist industrial adjustment policy aimed at stabilizing the rail equipment manufacturers who were prominent members of the transit coalition, and who stressed to Congress the dispersed character of their industry—plants in 468 cities in all but three continental states—and the likelihood of hiring back many of their workers who had been laid off in 1961.[32] Construction grants would help to underwrite radial projects aimed at penetrating rapidly growing suburban areas. However, the amounts of money involved were modest. This reflected the still rather narrow basis of support for a program of transit intervention, which was concentrated among those urban areas where downtown already confronted suburban competition, and where existing private and public transit firms were clearly unable to help the central business district compete.

The next major expansion of the transit program was in 1970, as national Republicans deployed a metropolitan strategy aimed at newer cities in the South, Southwest, and West whose core areas were now beginning to feel the same sorts of competitive pressures as earlier had the older urban centers, and whose transit firms were now similarly financially exhausted. A lobbyist for the transit coalition noted that "now we have new horizon cities—younger and more expansive metropolitan areas in all sections of the country—wanting to build rapid rail systems to their suburbs. . . . In the next 20 years, all the new systems now on the drawing boards will be aimed at that 10 per cent of the SMSA . . . populations made up of commuter riders."[33] Republicans and southerners were attracted to a program aimed at suburban constituencies. The amounts available for facility expansion and equipment were increased, and highway fund monies were made available for exclusive or preferential bus lanes and related uses. The 1973 highway act liberalized the use of funds for bus-transit-related purposes.[34]

Subsidizing the operation of expanded peak-period services was the one remaining item on the downtown coalition agenda. When he presented the Kennedy administration's transit proposal to Congress in 1963, Housing and Home Finance Administrator Robert Weaver was asked, "Do we envision, after making a Federal investment at the capital end of the structure . . . making future Federal contributions in the form of subsidies for the operation of these facilities?" Weaver responded, "We have never advocated such subsidies, and we have no intention of doing so."[35] Following passage of the 1964 legislation, though, Senator Harrison Williams, the leading congressional champion of transit, introduced a bill calling for operating subsidies, which failed. Once again, following the successful passage of the 1970 transit bill, the coalition sought operating subsidies. After a protracted campaign, in 1974 the Nixon administration decided to adopt, as part of a rationalization strategy discussed below, a revenue-sharing approach within which local agencies could choose to allocate resources to capital or to operations and maintenance expenditures.[36] The final piece of the downtown coalition program was now in place.

Rationalizing Federal Government Intervention

A key objective for national government executives has been to reduce the threat to the treasury of long-term subsidization.[37] Several different ways of achieving this object have been tried. They have included national mandates that metropolitan areas created region-wide government agencies with the power to plan and to manage transport facilities. Research and development aimed at boosting productivity was sponsored as well. When mandates to plan proved inattentive to efficiency concerns, attention to these concerns was mandated. They waged ideological campaigns against expensive projects. Executive branch officials continually sought ways to minimize the role of legislative politics in decision-making, in the face of constant efforts by congressional advocates to champion the projects of their constituents. As the subsidy costs of the transit program grew, executives sought to restructure the industry through privatization and other marketlike strategies primarily aimed at strengthening management's capacity to reorganize the labor process and to reduce the wage bill. The focus of rationalization efforts shifted over time from increasing the efficiency and effectiveness of intervention in the urban development process to reining in the fiscal-crisis machine that had evolved.

Addressing downtown coalition transit proposals, Eisenhower administration executives called for comprehensive metropolitan land-use and transportation planning that would determine the nature and level of transit requirements and integrate transit and highway expenditures. These suggestions echoed concerns voiced by leading urban planners around the country following passage of the interstate highway program in 1956. In his 1960 congressional testimony on an early transit bill, Eisenhower's commissioner of urban renewal also stressed the absence of metropolitan governmental organizations that could finance and manage coordinated transport systems. These concerns, about governmental planning and management capacity at the metropolitan level, and about the nature and extent of subsidization, were present in the Kennedy administration as well.[38]

In 1961 the Kennedy administration supported increasing federal support for planning. Housing and Home Finance Administrator Robert Weaver wrote to President Kennedy, and testified to Congress shortly thereafter, that "unless cities prepare and adopt comprehensive community plans, including mass transportation plans as an integral part thereof, they may waste both their own and Federal funds and may aggravate rather than correct problems of urban congestion, haphazard development, and deterioration." Plans were intended to protect the value of investments that local and federal governments were about to undertake.[39] Kennedy wrote to Congress that his proposed legislation would "stimulate urban areas to establish areawide agencies empowered to plan, develop, and operate transportation systems."[40] This was reinforced by the stipulation, contained in the joint report of the Secretary of Commerce and the Housing and Home Finance Administrator, that, after 1 July 1965, only those highway projects that were consistent with areawide plans for a balanced transportation system would be approved. Kennedy also said that an approved comprehensive plan and "the existence of a suitable organization representing all, or substantially all, of the local governmental units in the metropolitan area" were absolute requisites to federal subsidy.[41] Weaver highlighted the central importance of this last point to the national executive: "It [subsidy] has to go to some place where there is a central approach to the problem, or else we are going to dissipate our funds entirely and make chaos, rather than an improvement."[42]

The emphasis on planning, governmental organization, and need assessment in the early 1960s reflected the Democratic interest in party building and electoral support in central cities as well as a more general national executive interest in rationalizing the government's intervention in the urban development process. The institutional innovations were aimed at helping downtown activists achieve what they were unable to put in place at the metropolitan level due to spatial competition-induced political conflict and state legislative opposition. At the same time, executives placed the transit program in the context of increasing the efficiency of other federal programs aimed at central city support, including freeway building, urban and community renewal, and housing.

In his 1962 transportation message Kennedy discussed the essential need "to conserve and enhance values in existing urban areas," and the importance of promoting "economic efficiency and livability in areas of future development." He also noted that there was a need to intervene "to assure more effective use of Federal funds available for other urban development and renewal programs."[43] Lyle Fitch, president of the Institute of Public Administration, which did the research for the joint HHFA-Commerce study mentioned above, articulated this point clearly in his 1962 testimony to Congress: "In downtown areas the Federal Government is making very large investments for redevelopment and housing and so from the point of view of preserving the Federal investment already made and in prospect, it is highly important that we assist mass transportation."[44] Building local capacity to plan and evaluate was critical because, as Weaver told Congress, "This is a complex country, it is a heterogeneous country, and it is very difficult for us to get any staff in Washington that is going to be able to make this evaluation in every community. It is our feeling very strongly that this has to be a matter of local responsibility. . . . And once you depart from this . . . you are going to have a situation where the Federal Government is going to be dipping into a series of local situations, which is disastrous."[45]

Echoing a comment made by Eisenhower's urban renewal chief, Weaver also told Congress that the government lacked both theory and data to discipline the nature and extent of federal subsidy: "I think . . . the biggest unexplored area—and one would assume there was a great deal of knowledge, but there really isn't—is the effect of more prompt, more satisfactory, more comfortable, more expeditious mass transit upon the rider. . . . [I]f you increase the service and if you make it . . . a little more reasonable, is the ridership going to increase? Because if this is true, then you have a whole set of economic possibilities. If it isn't true, then you are in an entirely different situation."[46] Weaver was here articulating an "economist" approach to policy analysis and intervention—a concern with the elasticity of demand for transit—to go along with the traditional government preference that in the case of infrastructure projects the user-pay principle be applied to the greatest practical extent. Economist forms of reasoning would become increasingly important in the executive branch, especially after the institutional focus of the transit program shifted from its origins in land use and urban development to transport supply.

Interestingly, a little later in 1962 Senator Frank Lausche of Ohio, who was sponsoring a competing piece of transit legislation that did not include federal grants, showcased the only available example of precisely the sort of research that Weaver had described. Professor Leon Moses, research director at Northwestern University's Transportation Center, told a congressional committee about analyses that he was doing using Chicago travel data. The research question Moses discussed with Congress was: "What price structure would serve to divert automobile users to public transportation[?]" He noted that "no one else I know of has such figures or has been interested in doing such a study, and yet this is the essential criteria necessary for a bill to subsidize mass transit, if you are going to subsidize it, and have some notion of what the costs are going to be." He warned that "the experience in Chicago . . . proves it would be extremely difficult to carry out diversion, and extremely expensive. . . . [T]he cost of the program could exceed the cost of many other subsidy programs we are now involved in."[47]

Congressional transit champion Harrison Williams mocked the caution counseled by the economist approach. Specifically attacking Moses, Williams told Lausche's committee, "There was one witness in particular who seemed agitated about the fact that we don't know with any scientific exactitude how much it would cost to divert X number of riders from their automobiles to their next best choice of public transportation. I just wonder where this country would be today if we had to await answers to similar questions about other problems facing the Nation. We would certainly have a lot of busy and well-paid researchers tucked away in our universities. . . . For the sad thing is that the question this witness thought was in urgent need of answering is completely irrelevant to the problem at hand." Williams cited evidence from the Boston area, and from Philadelphia, where improvements in service had been associated with increases in transit patronage to counter the claim that not enough was known about the dynamics of ridership. He also argued that the comprehensive planning requirements in his proposed legislation "which would determine the need, the value, the economic feasibility, and the utility of any particular transit service—is the key to the wise and prudent use of Federal funds." Williams agreed with Weaver that a metropolitan-level planning capacity was essential because a national bureaucracy had no business telling local people how to solve their problems.[48]

The lack of interest in creating a substantial expert capacity at the national level, or in getting a handle on likely future levels of subsidy demand, reflected the congressional concern to advance the downtown agenda as far and as quickly as possible. Comprehensive planning was an arena within which to defend the interests of central business districts within metropolitan areas, and both Congress and the executive branch supported such an effort. However, suburban opposition to the re-centralizing aims of such plans was increasing in intensity; it was a very weak hook upon which to hang a strategy aimed at rationalizing the urban development process.

The failure of authoritative metropolitan land-use planning agencies to emerge increased the significance attached by downtown activists to transport facilities. In the absence of plans that would maintain historic patterns of land use, they looked to the new metropolitan-scale projects to shape the dynamics of growth, so as to maintain the hegemony of the central business district in the face of suburban business center competition. Ironically, just as the federal government was committing its resources to using transport investments to shape the pattern of future metropolitan development, transportation planners engaged in plan preparation at the metropolitan level were concluding that it was essentially too late to accomplish this. There was already so much transport capacity in place that even the addition of a planned network of freeways and transit lines would at best marginally influence the pattern of metropolitan land use.[49]

The politics of transport planning in Washington, D.C., provided early evidence of the obstacles confronting the planning strategy. A survey of mass-transportation needs was mandated by Congress. The steering committee overseeing the preparation of this survey decided not to publish a 1959 report prepared by the Institute of Public Administration—the only one of the support studies done for the mandated survey that was not published—because they disagreed with the institute's proposal to create a transportation organization embracing all modes of transport that would be closely related to an effective regional planning agency. The institute's report to the Secretary of Commerce and the Housing and Home Finance

Administrator a few years later recommended that transit legislation contain a requirement for a regional planning process backed up by a regional
decision-making authority. These requirements were left vague in the
bills submitted to Congress.[50]

Congressional responsiveness to downtown concerns was the key element in the policy-making process. This prevented the establishment of a
framework conducive to an economically rational policy of transit industry adjustment. The executive branch was able to resist one particular
effort at obtaining subsidy, though: that of the Los Angeles Metropolitan
Transit Authority to secure a federal guarantee of revenue bonds the
Authority wished to sell to finance construction of a downtown/radial rail
transit system. President Kennedy had referred in his transportation message to very specialized situations in which such a guarantee might be
appropriate. Senator Clair Engle of California told his colleagues that he
believed that "the language contained in the President's message—I
worked very closely with the staff people who wrote that message—was
placed in there because of the Los Angeles situation," and he sponsored a
bill that would create the possibility of such a federal guarantee. However,
largely based on Treasury Department opposition to a financing technique
that might interfere with its debt-management and long-term bond-
financing requirements, Engle's measure failed to pass.[51]

Following the 1964 legislation, Congress added funds for research and
training, as well as money for planning, engineering, and designing transport projects. Whether operating increasingly decimated private firms or
continuing to operate the new governmentally owned transit systems, decades of retrenchment had produced a generation of transit managers who
were inexperienced in image-building, marketing, technological innovation, and other forms of entrepreneurial activity. Moreover, the industry's
poor financial prospects had held few attractions for a younger generation
of managerial activists. Congress also added funds for technologically-
oriented development. In the early 1970s, though, following several years
of increasing demand for downtown/radial rail rapid transit systems, the
executive faced, for the first time, applications for funds that would exceed
available monies.[52] The issue of prioritization posed a crucial test of the
executive's capacity to conduct a rational industrial policy as well as to
rationalize its own intervention.

Congress had closely questioned Robert Weaver about how the executive would establish priorities before the 1964 act. Weaver answered that
top priority would be given to those projects that were an integral part of
authoritative comprehensive plans. In addition, the government would
support local efforts to deal with an emergency situation in which an area

was threatened with the imminent loss of transit service.[53] However, serious questions regarding intervention choices did not arise during the first few years following program start-up.

The question of allocation policy was complicated by the shift of the transit subsidy program to the Department of Transportation in 1968. The culture of Transportation disposed transit executives to the strict economist approach to financing infrastructure that characterized the department. Allocation policy was a highly controversial issue when Transportation was created in 1966. The most controversy was generated by a section in the original proposal for the department that would have authorized the Secretary of Transportation to develop uniform standards and criteria for evaluating all federal investments in proposed transport projects. This clearly represented an effort to rationalize the transport investment process; all projects would be subjected to a total systems-oriented cost-benefit analysis. Representatives of the many modal interests were extremely concerned about this proposed section, and, with highway activists in the forefront, they persuaded Congress to restrict dramatically the scope of authority granted to the executive branch. While Congress determined to reserve for itself the lead role in project decision-making, however, the department continued to stress greater economic rationality in its varied interventions.[54] Grant Davis noted that "the bills which have been submitted [to Congress] by the [Department of Transportation] reflect its philosophical orientation which favors utilization of the market mechanism and the elimination of excessive subsidy. Congress has not acted favorably to any of the recommendations by the department to increase user charges and thereby insure that transportation users pay their 'fair share.' Furthermore, when appearing before congressional committees, the organization is not held in high esteem."[55]

The departmental concern with rationalization was reinforced by top-level appointments made by Nixon's Urban Mass Transportation Administrator in 1969. Most of these went to people with considerable managerial experience in the defense and aerospace industries rather than, as had been the case with the original federal transit program staff, to those with backgrounds in land transportation, urban planning, and transportation economics. A hardware orientation persisted within the agency, which was closely linked to efforts to enhance productivity within the transit industry.[56] In an industry where wage costs account for the great bulk of operating expense, substituting capital for labor as a method of increasing productivity had a great deal of surface economic appeal. Moreover, given the extreme physical deterioration of the industry during its protracted period of decline, new technology had marketing appeal as well. The savings theoretically available from the substitution of multicar trains operated by one person for a multitude of buses each operated by a driver was a major justification for the rail transit demands that were surfacing.

The large number of downtown alliances seeking subsidy for expensive capital projects generated a great deal of budgetary anxiety. The White House had fears about the capacity of national transit executives to develop and implement a method for rationalizing access to subsidies when demand exceeded available grant funds. They were concerned that Congress would be irritated—and would intervene—when particular projects failed to secure funding commitments. In September 1973 the Office of Management and Budget instituted a moratorium on new projects involving railways and deleted all UMTA-requested money for rail projects in fiscal year 1975. An ideological campaign against rail projects was waged by the Department of Transportation and the UMTA administrator. UMTA also instituted an elaborate set of project planning requirements, including demands for cost-effectiveness analyses and the explicit inclusion of low-capital-cost approaches among the alternatives analyzed at the metropolitan level.[57]

Altshuler and Curry sympathized with the procedural demands elaborated by federal bureaucrats in their efforts to "avoid becoming caught in the middle of local controversies, to limit demand for the scarce resources at their disposal, and to require both statutory compliance with comprehensive planning requirements and the highest standards of professional practice without appearing to impose their own values upon urban regions." Along with other transit industry activists and analysts, however, they felt that form was now driving substance out of transportation planning; the quality of governmental decision-making was suffering as a result of the emphasis on procedure.[58]

While UMTA struggled to sort out the mushrooming number of rail project proposals, the Nixon administration saw financial problems intensifying when the downtown coalition's demand for operating subsidies gathered strength in the early 1970s. Academic analysts and national transit executives forecast dire consequences if operations were subsidized. They predicted that subsidies would be used inefficiently to expand services, and that the fares charged for additional services would be far below the cost of their provision. In addition, they argued that transit workers would win substantial pay increases because the subsidies would undermine managerial resolve to impose wage discipline on organized labor.[59] However, in the face of these plausible, articulate warnings, the administration was still forced to respond to the downtown demand to increase the most costly sort of service to provide—long-distance, peak-period routes connecting downtown with low-density suburban areas.

The executives chose to do so by embedding a local choice to use subsidy funds for either capital or operating expenses in a revenue-sharing format. The White House wanted to reduce the discretion available to executive branch officials because discretionary authority stimulated congressional efforts to influence its exercise. An approach that used formulas to allocate funds, combined with local choice about spending, was intended to minimize congressional intervention in the subsidy allocation process. If the executive could not rationalize its own allocation process, then setting an overall limit and shrinking the executive's decision-making sphere appeared to the administration as an attractive strategy to rationalize its own intervention. In the latter 1970s, though, Congress continued to increase the amount of subsidy available, as well as intervene in the rail project approval process over which federal executives still exercised discretion. [60]

The evolution of local and federal programs of financial support, adapted to the pressures of spatial competition at the metropolitan level, exacerbated the financial troubles of the transit industry. The critics of operating subsidies were right. The new services often carried relatively light loads. At the same time, transit labor was able to secure wage gains enabling them to keep pace with workers in other local government sectors during a very inflationary period. Moreover, transit worker resistance limited management's ability to reintroduce work practices that would soften the consequences of the continuing concentration of patronage in the peak hours, such as part-time labor and more split-shifts. Transit units also bitterly resisted efforts to contract out work to nonunion firms. The result of these dynamics was a dramatic decline in industry productivity. [61]

The crisis was political as well as financial. Outlying business center coalitions increasingly saw needs for locally-responsive transport going unmet while downtown coalition projects absorbed ever more subsidy. Many central business districts did so well strengthening their competitive position—with freeways as well as transit—that few financial resources remained to subsidize the transport-related growth aspirations of outlying areas beginning to experience suburban gridlock. Public-sector transit crisis has, in turn, generated a new round of efforts to restructure the industry and rationalize federal intervention, although the current situation is more complicated because of the presence of suburban business center activists in local, state, and federal political arenas. As a result of international competition, subsidy possibilities are now more constrained than during the 1960s and 1970s as well.

The Culture of Policy Discourse in Urban Transit

One of the more controversial reports prepared during the early legislative debates was *Technology and Urban Transportation,* by John R. Meyer, John F. Kain, and Martin Wohl. It was commissioned by the Panel on Civilian Technology, which was set up under the joint sponsorship of the President's Special Assistant for Science and Technology, the Chairman of the Council of Economic Advisers, and the Secretary of Commerce. The report was presented in June 1962 and released—though neither published nor endorsed—in October.[62] Their charge was to identify areas for useful research in urban transportation. The authors construed their mandate broadly, discoursing on the present and likely future course of metropolitan development and the resulting significance for transport requirements. They also did cost comparisons between different modes of urban transit, reflected on the deep importance of social relations for a full understanding of transport supply and demand, and addressed the equity aspects of policy. The report exemplified the economist approach, stressing the need to evaluate the full costs of a proposed intervention through a comprehensive, systemwide analysis, to find ways of using existing resources more efficiently, rather than simply to expand capacity whenever bottlenecks appear, and to deploy a system of user charges to induce efficient behavior. The authors challenged many of the arguments being advanced on behalf of rail rapid transit projects. Within the industry, which was familiar with its contents, the report and the critical commentary it sparked generated a "bus versus rail" controversy, but the issues it raised went far beyond modal conflict.

Meyer, Kain, and Wohl called attention to the "underlying forces for decentralization [which] would be operative independent of any public policy influences since they are attributable to fundamental changes in technology, income levels and consumer tastes. . . . [T]he availability and use of transit does not seem to be a sufficient or a necessary condition for creating density or downtown growth and, conversely, provides no major retardant or preventive to the development of new employment opportunities in the urban ring."[63] Following an analysis of the comparative bus and rail transit costs of supplying a hypothetical downtown commuter trip, they argued that if the capacity of urban highways was efficiently utilized during peak hours, as a result of the use of priority access for transit vehicles and a set of charges for congested failures, foreseeable levels of travel demand could be accommodated.

In addition to their concern with efficient capacity utilization, Meyer, Kain, and Wohl also addressed the social and equity aspects of transit policy. They hypothesized that declines in off-peak shopping transit trips were related to the recent desegregation of buses in the South, and to a desire for racial segregation elsewhere as well. They forecasted a bimodal distribution of transit ridership; high-income executives, technicians and their secretaries, on the one hand, and unskilled labor used in service industries, on the other, mainly recruited from minority groups. They noted "the tendency of people with high incomes to substitute long distance commuting for direct solutions to the problems created by restrictions placed upon minority housing opportunities," suggesting that "it might be better to attack the housing segregation problem itself rather than attempting to perpetuate it by subsidizing additional transportation facilities for those whose travel demands are created by a search for segregation." In the absence of restrictions on minority housing choices, a major resettlement of higher-income people closer to the central business district—where many such people worked and would increasingly work in the future—might occur, which, they believed, would greatly reduce, or even eliminate, the commuting problem.[64]

Technology and Urban Transportation was bitterly attacked by the Institute for Rapid Transit as "replete with fallacious theories and assumptions, erroneous mathematical analyses, and prejudiced and undocumented conclusions." The institute, which was composed primarily of activist engineers working in transit operations, system design, and equipment manufacturing, was especially concerned about what it considered to be a distorted and biased cost comparison between bus and rail transits. However, the institute, which had positioned itself as a leading member of the downtown coalition seeking federal transit subsidy, also questioned Meyer, Kain, and Wohl's claim about the irreversible nature of the decentralizing forces: "The authors appear to be entirely blind to . . . downtown building booms [in New York and Chicago] and the national movement for strengthening and expanding central business districts. Surely the private interests, as well as local and federal governments in many instances, which are investing large sums of money in the downtown areas of the nation's great cities, do not accept the author's contention that the downtown area with its high concentration of population and activity is a thing of the past."[65]

Senator Harrison Williams also voiced his concern about *Technology and Urban Transportation*. He worried that the authors were making a sweeping claim about what mode of transit was best for all metropolitan areas, when it was certainly "not the job of the federal government or others to tell a metropolitan area what modes of transportation it should have." Williams also thought that "it might be better to await the results from San Francisco before transit is consigned to the junk heap." The senator doubted that the authors, "who were asked to identify useful technological research areas, were fully qualified as observers of the social and economic urban scene" to comment on racial segregation. He questioned whether their suggestion to attack the housing problem rather than subsidizing transit "would also apply to future highway as well as transit expenditures, and whether the authors would go so far as to say that the problem of traffic congestion should be attacked by a program to get people to live within walking distance of their place of work," the implications being that they would be unwilling to extend the logic of their analysis in this manner, and in any case the latter notion was beyond the pale.[66]

Meyer, Kain, and Wohl's claim about the immutability of the forces producing decentralization—and that transit institutions and investments should efficiently serve these underlying forces—was the most serious challenge to planners, most of whom wanted to subordinate transport projects to land-use plans aimed at strengthening central business districts. In contrast to the economist discourse embodied in *Technology and Urban Transportation*, planners' discourse stressed a set of policy choices premised on the malleability of the future pattern of urban development. In a book based on the analytical work done for the joint Commerce-HHFA study discussed earlier, Lyle Fitch and his Institute of Public Administration associates noted that "certain factors point to increased decentralization if past trends continue. But should they continue? Do we want density or dispersion? Do we prefer urban areas with a single center or with many functional nuclei? Should suburbs be integrated into the urban region or be largely self-contained? How should they be related to each other and to the central city? Do we want even development or urban land or clusters leaving sections of open space? These are questions which are unanswered in most developing urban areas and which vitally concern transportation planning as well as urban design."[67]

Fitch and associates set out both sides of the debate between those who argued the "indispensability of the central city to our culture and economy" and the decentralists, who emphasized "the inevitability or desirability of dispersion of enterprises and population . . . throughout an urban region." They linked these positions on urban form to positions on transport supply, characterizing Meyer, Kain, and Wohl as highway proponents who questioned "whether grade-separated mass transportation has an important role in the future urban complex," and who held that "planning should focus on the widely decentralized type of city, which is made possible and best served by the automobile."[68] At the national level, planning discourse focused on the subordination of transport projects to comprehensive land-use plans, leaving the resolution of the urban form debate to metropolitan planning processes. Fitch and associates justified intervention to subsidize transit on the basis that automotive transport in urban areas was subsidized, thereby distorting supply-and-demand choices, concluding that "if for historical reasons (good or bad), one mode of transportation is being subsidized by a certain amount per passenger trip, competing modes should be subsidized by at least roughly corresponding amounts per trip." Metropolitan planning aimed at reaching consensus on urban form goals would then take place without the distorting effects of unequal subsidy.[69]

Economist Leon Moses clearly expressed the focus of planning discourse at the local level as it contrasted with the economist emphasis on efficient capacity utilization. When he discussed with Congress the economist advice to increase the price of commuting by automobile as a way of inducing efficient capacity utilization, he cautioned that "city planners . . . whose real concern is not traffic congestion and the inefficient use of highway capacity—viewed as a resource—but the economic future of our mature, central cities, should pause before accepting it," because instead of commuters shifting to transit in response to the price increase, "there is a strong possibility that the core area's traffic problem will be solved by reducing the number of people who work there."[70] Working within the context of spatial competition, local planners and political leaders evaluated transport strategies from the perspective of their impacts on particular places; the place competition dynamic was absent from Meyer, Kain, and Wohl's analysis of policy conflict. Spatial competition would also prevent the emergence of consensus about metropolitan form goals that Fitch hoped planning would produce.

As was the case with Leon Moses's testimony regarding the elasticity of demand for transit, *Technology and Urban Transportation* played a minor role in legislative debates. The report was referred to by a few others, usually to support a critique of proposed legislation. The Investment Bankers Association of America cited the report to support their claim that "population growth in metropolitan areas has not been accompanied by a corresponding increased need for urban mass transit facilities," and that any transit subsidies should come from local governments rather than the national treasury.[71] The American Road Builders' Association cited the paper to support its view that while a great deal was uncertain regarding commuter transportation problems, there was no question regarding the need for expressways; transit considerations, therefore, should not in any way compromise the integrity of the highway program.[72] The Amalgamated Association of Street, Electric Railway, and Motor Coach Employees of America pointed to the report to illustrate its concern that the federal government would be subsidizing automation. Meyer, Kain, and Wohl had discussed the possibilities of automated buses operating in special guidance lanes as a way of reducing labor costs, and automating fare collection and vehicle loading and unloading. These sorts of technological changes, which, the union argued, would threaten the jobs and the living standards of transit workers, required provisions that would protect workers who were adversely affected. Analysts of the 1964 transit act have all noted the critically important role played by organized labor in the legislative success of the bill. Reflecting the weight of organized labor in Democratic party politics at the national and local levels, transit unions were able to secure institutional guarantees aimed at ensuring that their members would not bear a disproportionate share of the burdens of industrial adjustment. Labor was thus positioned to seriously challenge management efforts to restructure the work process.[73]

Regarding the lessons to be learned from San Francisco, however, Meyer, Kain, and Wohl's critique of the BART plan anticipated later work critical of that system and of other rail transit ventures.[74] They pointed out that a fixation on achieving very high average speeds on the line-haul portions of the Bay Area system had led to poor station spacing and location choices that would reduce access to potential patrons and lengthen door-to-door travel times, thereby depressing patronage. Their hypothesis of a link between racial segregation and rail transit investment would be supported as well. The transit lobby's coordinator during the 1970 legislative campaign said, "The Southerners in Congress are quite open about its being a white commuter program; Atlanta, for example, is downright blunt about it. . . . [T]here is no question the realization by politicians of who is going to benefit from the program—the middle and the upper middle class—isn't an enormous tactical aid for us in working with Congress, especially Republicans and Southerners."[75] The attributes of an economically viable transit system that they set out—differentiated services adapted to diverse consumer demands—became the objective of Reagan administration executives in the 1980s.

Planner desires to use transport investments to shape the pattern of metropolitan development and to strengthen the position of central business districts would continue to clash with economic admonitions that such efforts were both utopian and elitist, and that services instead should efficiently serve expressed patterns of demand.[76] The planner's reliance on the growth-shaping potential of transport, though, reflected an effort to substitute transport projects for land-use plans. In the absence of plans that would constrain the use of projects to create location advantages for competing places, a great deal of growth-inducing transport capacity was put in place. The planning ideal, articulated by one of the charter members of the Urban Mass Transportation Administration, was to "plan our cities so that the demand for transportation is not allowed to expand without limit in the first place."[77] Instead, competition to retain and attract mobile capital rendered the planning ideal infeasible and overwhelmed economist efforts to rationalize the transit industry.

Senator Williams said to Institute for Rapid Transit president Walter McCarter, "You and I and others of like mind are going to have to preserve downtown commerce for the chamber of commerce." He phrased it this way because the U.S. Chamber of Commerce opposed federal intervention. "Of course," he continued, "in doing it, we will make transportation available to the suburbanite who needs the city, wants the city."[78] During the 1960s and early 1970s the concerns of large urban areas occupied a place near the top of the national agenda; downtown coalitions were able to overcome resistance to intervention. The way these coalitions shaped the transit industry adjustment policies that resulted generated fiscal and political crises. A rationalizing transit policy would have led to a concentration of shrinking industry energies on those services that could be most efficiently provided and the creation of new industrial means to serve those markets that required different approaches. This would have included breaking apart large, difficult-to-manage transit organizations and dramatically altering labor policies. The outcome, however, was very different. During the latter 1970s national executives attempted to discipline the subsidy allocation process through planning mandates. The Reagan administration, which had little interest in the big cities and in governmental intervention in domestic matters, tried more direct approaches to rationalize intervention. These included continuing efforts to eliminate, or at least to reduce, operating subsidies, the use of performance standards to allocate resources, and support for privatizing the very services that had been the heart of the downtown coalition program. These strategies at the national level accompanied suburban business center demands in many metropolitan areas to reorient the services provided by regional transit agencies to facilitate their own growth aspirations and to change institutional structures and finance mechanisms if necessary to do so.[79] This much more complex, competitive metropolitan environment is the current context for efforts to once again restructure the transit industry; the dynamics that characterized the first phase, though, continue to influence policies of industrial adjustment.

Portland State University

Notes

1. Michael Danielson, *Federal-Metropolitan Politics and the Commuter Crisis* (New York, 1965); George Smerk, *Urban Transportation: The Federal Role* (Bloomington, 1965); Lewis Schneider, "Urban Mass Transportation: A Survey of the Decision-Making Process," in Raymond Bauer and Kenneth Gergen, eds., *The Study of Policy Formation* (Glencoe, Ill., 1968); Royce Hanson, "Congress Copes with Mass Transit," in Frederick Cleaveland, ed., *Congress and Urban Problems* (Washington, D.C., 1969); John Burby, "Mass Transit Agency Faces Planning, Staffing Problems in Shift from Rags to Riches," *National Journal*, 3 October 1970, 2152; David Miller, ed., *Urban Transit Policy: New Perspectives* (Lexington, Mass., 1972); Comptroller General of the United States, *Soaring Transit Subsidies Must be Controlled* (Washington, D.C., 1981).

2. John Pucher, "Urban Public Transport Subsidies in Western Europe and North America," *Transportation Quarterly* 42 (July 1988).

3. David Vogel, "Government-Industry Relations in the United States: An Overview," in Stephen Wilks and Maurice Wright, eds., *Comparative Government—Industry Relations* (Oxford, 1987); R. Kent Weaver, *The Politics of Industrial Change* (Washington, D.C., 1985); Wyn Grant, *Government and Industry: A Comparative Analysis of the U.S. Canada and the U.K.* (Aldershot, England, 1989).

4. David Jones, *Urban Transit Policy: An Economic and Political History* (Englewood Cliffs, N.J., 1985), 120, 121.

5. William Hartsfield, in *Urban Mass Transportation—1961*, Committee on Banking and Currency, U.S. House of Representatives, 87th Cong., 1st sess., June 1961, 72.

6. Lawrence Brown, *New Policies, New Politics: Government's Response to Government's Growth* (Washington, D.C., 1983).

7. "Dear Mr. City Official," *Mass Transportation* 48 (August 1952); "A Bold Plan to Get People to Ride More," 51 (September 1955); *Passenger Transport*, 26 January 1953.

8. David Markstein and Myles Jarrow, "Fringe Parking—Shuttle Bus Plan Proves Successful in New Orleans and in Chicago," *Mass Transportation* 45 (March 1949); *Passenger Transport*, 5 December 1952 and 12 December 1952; Robert Mitchell, "A Diet for Vehicular Traffic or Starvation for Transit," *Mass Transportation* 48 (June 1952); Henry Barnes, "Traffic Engineering and Mass Transportation," *Mass Transportation* 48 (August 1952); "Nashville Reserves a Separate Lane for Buses," *Mass Transportation* 52 (February 1956).

9. "The ATA Convention in St. Louis," *Mass Transportation* 52 (October 1956): 25–26.

10. "A Plea for Emancipation," *Mass Transportation* 46 (May 1950); *Passenger Transport*, 14 November 1952, 13 February 1959.

11. Peter Kocan, "Why Not Charge the Rush Hour Rider?" and David Canning, "Let Your Schedule Maker Set Your Rates," *Mass Transportation* 45 (December 1949); Peter Kocan, "Four Years of Fare Increases," *Mass Transportation* 46 (January 1950); "Bold Experiment in Toledo," *Mass Transportation* 52 (January 1956); W. C. Gilman and Company, *St. Louis Metropolitan Area Transportation Study 1957–'70–'80* (New York, 1959).

12. Jones, *Urban Transit Policy*.

13. "The Showpiece of the Transit Industry," *Mass Transportation* 52 (September 1956); "Nashville Transit Initiates De Luxe Commuter Service," and "Capital Transit Proposes Club Express Service," and John Jones, "Cincinnati Inaugurates Club Flyer Service," *Mass Transportation* 51 (February 1955).

14. Pacific Electric Railway Company, *Rebuttal Testimony and Exhibits in Case 4843* (Sacramento, 1947), 20.

15. Seymour Adler, *The Political Economy of Transit in the San Francisco Bay Area, 1945–1963* (Washington, D.C., 1980).

16. Ben West, in *National Highway Program*, Committee on Public Works, U.S. Senate, 84th Cong., 1st sess., 1955, 196–99.

17. Donald Davis, *Conspicuous Production: Automobiles and Elites in Detroit, 1899–1933* (Philadelphia, 1988); Los Angeles Chamber of Commerce, Rapid Transit Action Group, *Rail Rapid Transit—Now!* (Los Angeles, 1948); Darrel Ward, "Chicago Denounces New Concept in Rapid Transit," *Mass Transportation* 58 (March 1962).

18. California Assembly, *Preliminary Report of the Assembly Investigating Committee on Traffic Control*, Assembly Journal, 23 March 1948, 448; *Santa Monica Evening Outlook*, 18 April 1949; *Southwest Wave*, 11 March 1948; Sy Adler, "The Transformation of the Pacific Electric Railway: Bradford Snell, Roger Rabbit, and the Politics of Transportation in Los Angeles," *Urban Affairs Quarterly* 27 (September 1991).

19. Sy Adler, "Why BART but no LART? The Political Economy of Rail Rapid Transit Planning in the Los Angeles and San Francisco Metropolitan Areas, 1945–1957," *Planning Perspectives* 2:2 (1987).

20. Adler, *The Political Economy of Transit in the San Fransico Bay Area, 1945–1963*.

21. Harrison Williams in *Urban Mass Transportation—1962*, Committee on Banking and Currency, U.S. Senate, 87th Cong., 2d sess., April 1962, 156; *Urban Mass Transportation—1963*, Committee on Banking and Currency, U.S. Senate, 88th Cong., 1st sess., 1963, 86.

22. "That St. Louis Arbitration," *The Motorman, Conductor and Motor Coach Operator* 55 (August 1947); D. McClurg, "30th Convention Notes," 57 (November 1949); "Proceedings of the Thirty-Third Convention," 63 (November 1955); *Oakland Tribune*, 12 September 1956; Adler, *The Political Economy of Transit in the San Francisco Bay Area, 1945–1963*.

23. Jameson Doig, *Metropolitan Transportation Politics and the New York Region* (New York, 1966).

24. "Baltimore Group to Offer Ownership Plan," *Passenger Transport*, 25 November 1955; "Baltimore Transit Bills Die in State Legislature," *Passenger Transport*, 5 April 1957; "City Presents Plan for Baltimore Area Transit Authority," *Passenger Transport*, 13 February 1959; "Study Commission Drafts New Bill to Create Transit Authority for Metro Baltimore Area," *Passenger Transport*, 8 January 1960; H. Polland, "What's Ahead in '64—Chicago," *Metropolitan Transportation and Planning*, January 1964, 29.

25. William Murin, *Mass Transit Policy Planning: An Incremental Approach* (Lexington, Mass., 1971).

26. "Is a Super Agency the Answer?" *Metropolitan Transportation* 57 (August 1961).

27. "AMA adopts 1957 Policy Statement on Mass Transit," *Passenger Transport*, 11 January 1957; "Editorial," *Mass Transportation* 53 (December 1957); "Provision for Mass Transit Should Be Considered in Planning New Highways," *Passenger Transport*, 31 January 1958; "Urge Transit Strips in D.C. Highways," *Passenger Transport*, 15 November 1957; "Express Bus, Rapid Transit Network Proposed at D.C." *Passenger Transport*, 17 July 1959.

28. "Joint Report to the President by the Secretary of Commerce and the Housing and Home Finance Administration," in *Urban Mass Transportation—1962*, Committee on Banking and Currency, U.S. Senate, 87th Cong., 2d sess., 72.

29. "A Message from the President of the United States, 1962" in George Smerk, ed., *Readings in Urban Transportation* (Bloomington, 1968), 309; Rex Whitton in *Urban Mass Transportation—1962*, Committee on Banking and Currency, U.S. Senate, 129.

30. Walter McCarter in *Urban Mass Transportation—1963*, Committee on Banking and Currency, U.S. Senate, 151.

31. Gordon Clinton in *Urban Mass Transportation—1963*, 190–91.

32. Holcombe Parkes in *Urban Mass Transportation Act of 1962*, Committee on Banking and Currency, U.S. House of Representatives, 87th Cong., 2d sess., 439–40.

33. William Lilley III, "Urban Interests Win Transit Bill With 'Letter-Perfect' Lobbying," *National Journal*, 19 September 1970.

34. George Smerk, *The Federal Role in Urban Mass Transportation* (Bloomington, 1991), 115–19.

35. Robert Weaver in *Urban Mass Transportation Act of 1963*, Committee on Banking and Currency, U.S. House of Representatives, 88th Cong., 1st sess., 42.

36. Smerk, *The Federal Role in Urban Mass Transportation*, 123–29.

37. Dennis Quinn, Jr., *Restructuring the Automobile Industry* (New York, 1988).

38. E. Williams, Jr., and D. Bluestone, *Rationale of Federal Transportation Policy* (Washington, D.C., 1960), 52–54; David Walker in *Metropolitan Mass Transportation*, Committee on Banking and Currency, U.S. House of Representatives, 86th Cong., 2d sess., 1960, 7.

39. Robert Weaver in *Urban Mass Transportation—1961*, 4–5.

40. John F. Kennedy in *Urban Mass Transportation—1961*, 4.

41. Ibid., 4; "Joint Report to the President by the Secretary of Commerce and the Housing and Home Finance Administration," in *Urban Mass Transportation—1962*, Committee on Banking and Currency, U.S. Senate, 74.

42. Robert Weaver in *Urban Mass Transportation—1961*, 25.

43. "A Message from the President of the United States, 1962," 302–6.

44. Lyle Fitch in *Urban Mass Transportation Act of 1962*, 475.

45. Robert Weaver in *Urban Mass Transportation Act of 1962*, 90–91.

46. Robert Weaver in *Urban Mass Transportation—1962*, Committee on Banking and Currency, U.S. Senate, 116.

47. Leon Moses in *Urban Mass Transportation—1962*, Committee on Commerce, U.S. Senate, 37–50.

48. Harrison Williams in *Urban Mass Transportation—1962*, Committee on Commerce, U.S. Senate, 135.

49. Melvin Webber, "Transportation Planning Models," *Traffic Quarterly* 15 (July 1961).

50. Murin, *Mass Transit Policy Planning*, 50.

51. Clair Engle in *Urban Mass Transportation—1962*, Committee on Banking and Currency, U.S. Senate, 123; Alan K. Browne, "Financing California Rapid Transit," *Traffic Quarterly* 17 (January 1963).

52. Smerk, *The Federal Role in Urban Mass Transportation*, 97–103, 131.

53. Robert Weaver, *Urban Mass Transportation Act of 1963*, 60.

54. Richard Barsness, "The Department of Transportation: Concept and Structure," *Western Political Quarterly* 23 (September 1970); Herman Mertins, Jr., *National Transportation Policy in Transition* (Lexington, Mass., 1972).

55. Grant Miller Davis, *The Department of Transportation* (Lexington, Mass., 1970), 190.

56. Edmond Kanwit, "The Urban Mass Transportation Administration: Its Problems and Promise," in David Miller, ed., *Urban Transportation Policy: New Perspectives* (Lexington, Mass., 1972).

57. Smerk, *The Federal Role in Urban Mass Transportation*, 131–32.

58. Alan Altshuler and Robert Curry, "The Changing Environment of Urban Development Policy—Shared Power or Impotence?" *Urban Law Annual* 10:3 (1975).

59. William Lilley III, "Transit Lobby Sights Victory in Fight for Massive Subsidy Program," *National Journal*, 4 March 1972.

60. Smerk, *The Federal Role in Urban Mass Transportation*, 132; U.S. Urban Mass Transportation Administration, *Feasibility of Federal Assistance for Urban Mass Transportation Operating Costs* (Washington, D.C., 1971); "Mass Transit: The Expensive Dream," *Business Week*, 27 August 1984.

61. Don Pickrell, "Federal Operating Assistance for Urban Mass Transit: Assessing a Decade of Experience," in Transit Pricing and Performance, *Transportation Research Record 1078* (Washington, D.C., 1986).

62. John R. Meyer, John F. Kain, and Martin Wohl, *Technology and Urban Transportation* (Washington, D.C., 1962); Joseph Ingraham, "Car-Bus Transit for Cities Urged," *New York Times*, 30 October 1962.

63. Meyer, Kain, and Wohl, *Technology and Urban Transportation*, 21.

64. Ibid., 42–43, 46–49, 58, 91, 94, 97–98, 112–14.

65. "An Evaluation of a Report Entitled 'Technology and Urban Transportation,'" *Institute for Rapid Transit Newsletter* 4 (August 1963): 5–9.

66. Harrison Williams, Jr., "Who's Right in Rail-Bus Row?" *Metropolitan Transportation* 59 (January 1963): 25.

67. Lyle Fitch and Associates, *Urban Transportation and Public Policy* (San Francisco, 1964), 20.

68. Ibid., 20–21.

69. Ibid., 156.

70. Leon Moses in *Urban Mass Transportation—1962*, Committee on Commerce, U.S. Senate, 48, 50.

71. Investment Bankers Association of America in *Urban Mass Transportation—1963*, 398–403.

72. American Road Builders' Association in *Urban Mass Transportation Act of 1963*, 555–57.

73. Bernard Cushman in *Urban Mass Transportation—1963*, 328–29; See the sources cited in note 1.

74. Meyer, Kain, and Wohl, *Technology and Urban Transportation*, 106; Melvin Webber, *The BART Experiment: What Have We Learned?* (Berkeley, 1976).

75. William Lilley III, "Urban Interests Win Transit Bill With 'Letter-Perfect' Lobbying," *National Journal*, 19 September 1970, 2026.

76. Peter Hall and Carmen Hass-Klau, *Can Rail Save the City?* (London, 1985); Martin Wachs, "U.S. Transit Subsidy Policy: In Need of Reform," *Science*, 30 June 1989; *New Urban Rail Transit: How Can Its Development and Growth-Shaping Potential Be Realized?* Committee on Banking, Finance, and Urban Affairs, U.S. House of Representatives, 96th Cong., 1st sess., 1980; Andrew Hamer, *Selling Rail Rapid Transit* (Lexington, Mass., 1976).

77. Kanwit, "The Urban Mass Transportation Administration," 86–87.

78. Harrison Williams in *Urban Mass Transportation—1963*, 150.

79. Sy Adler, *Understanding the Dynamics of Innovation in Urban Transit* (Washington, D.C., 1986).

MARTIN V. MELOSI

Down in the Dumps: Is There a Garbage Crisis in America?

The pariah garbage barge on a two-month odyssey with 3,100 tons of unwanted trash drew throngs of sightseers and reporters Sunday as it anchored just outside New York Harbor while city officials decide its fate.
—*Houston Chronicle,* 18 May 1987

The trek of the *Mobro* is well known. On 22 March 1987 the fully loaded garbage barge left Islip, New York, looking for a landfill that would take its unwanted cargo. Five states—North Carolina, Louisiana, Alabama, Mississippi, and Florida—as well as three countries, Mexico, Belize, and the Bahamas, had banned the barge from unloading. Reluctantly, the captain turned the *Mobro* toward home, where it received an unceremonious, and dispirited, welcome.

The garbage barge story was a journalist's delight. It highlighted New York's chronic problems of service delivery. Metaphorically, it exposed the insensitivity of the Sunbelt toward the plight of the Snowbelt. And it graphically demonstrated the dilemma of the modern "garbage crisis" in America.

Talk of a garbage crisis goes back at least to the early 1970s—a period of heightened environmental awareness—and stressed the same issues swirling through the media almost two decades later. In 1973 the National League of Cities and the U.S. Conference of Mayors issued a report in which they identified as culprits the "skyrocketing" volume of solid waste and the "sharp decline" in available urban land for disposal sites:

> The disposal of wastes and the conservation of resources are two of the greatest problems to be understood and solved by this nation in

the latter third of this century. With almost half of our cities running out of current disposal capacity in from one to five years, America's urban areas face an immediate disposal crisis.[1]

The acknowledgment of a crisis in waste volume and a crisis in landfill space persisted into the 1990s. "Many cities are rapidly approaching a garbage and trash crisis: no place to put it," noted a 1987 study.[2] Other studies, placing the center of the crisis in the East, also affirmed its national scope: "The magnitude of New York's dilemma may be exceptional, but the general problem itself is not: though reliable nationwide numbers are hard to come by, cities everywhere seem to be running out of places to put their garbage."[3] Sylvia Lowrance, director of EPA's Office of Solid Waste, echoed this general sentiment: "In some sections of the country [the crisis is] very acute today. They literally do not have any more landfill space. In other sections of the country, it's a crisis that's going to overwhelm them soon, if localities and citizens don't take steps today to plan for tomorrow."[4]

Some observers view the crisis in different terms. A special report in *World Waste* stated that beyond the unavailability of disposal sites loomed a "liability insurance crisis" for operators. "The cost of insurance, when available, has mushroomed almost overnight for very limited coverage." This problem has arisen because insurance companies purportedly were reducing coverage for businesses with high liability risk and because courts were awarding large sums to litigants claiming damages in solid waste cases.[5]

In a widely discussed article in the *Atlantic Monthly*, archaeologist-turned-garbologist William Rathje questioned the standard perception of the crisis:

> The press in recent years has paid much attention to the filling up (and therefore the closing down) of landfills, to the potential dangers of incinerators, and to the apparent inadequacy of our recycling efforts. The use of the word "crisis" in these contexts has become routine. For all the publicity, however, the precise state of affairs is not known. It may be that the lack of reliable information and the persistence of misinformation constitute the real garbage crisis.[6]

Rathje has rightly questioned the almost universal acceptance of a "garbage crisis." And, through extensive research, he has attempted to offer correctives to long-held beliefs about issues such as America's waste habits, the biodegradability of discards, and the viability of recycling.[7] Yet the notion of crisis still needs to be confronted in more detail. To what extent has there been and does there continue to be a crisis? If there is a crisis, what is its nature? Is it national in scope?

The "garbage crisis," as it has been characterized, is a call for action but also a comforting label for a complex set of problems. It is comforting because the notion of "crisis" confers upon the problem relatively tangible, concrete properties, which may be resolved through equally tangible, concrete solutions—new technology, effective management, or popular will. Yet "crisis" denies the complexity of the problem and ignores its persistence over time, failing to determine whether it is chronic, recurrent, or temporary.

By separating the collection and disposal system into its component parts, the nature and extent of the garbage crisis may come into focus. This article will examine five significant elements of that system—quantity and composition of the wastes, collection, disposal, management, and regulation. Through a comparison of past and current experiences and practices, it should become clear that the garbage crisis largely represents a set of chronic problems with deep historical roots.

Quantities and Composition of Wastes

There is little doubt that the vast amount of waste produced in the United States contributes significantly to the problem of collection and disposal. The sheer magnitude goes back at least to the nineteenth century, long before the post–World War II "throwaway society." Between 1900 and 1920 each citizen of Manhattan, Brooklyn, and the Bronx produced 160 pounds of garbage, 1,231 pounds of ashes, and 97 pounds of rubbish annually. A researcher at MIT calculated in 1911 that if New York City's refuse were gathered in one place, "the resulting volume [would be] over three times that of the great pyramid of Ghizeh, and would accommodate one hundred and forty Washington monuments with ease."[8]

In recent years the volume of municipal solid waste (MSW) has increased to staggering proportions. Between 1920 and 1965 refuse production rose from 2.8 to 4.5 pounds per capita. From 1968 to 1988 it increased almost 30 percent—from 140 million tons per year to 180 million tons. While the amounts per capita have leveled off at about four pounds per capita annually, population increases will result in a steady rise in aggregate discards.[9]

While the quantity of waste is a contributing factor to the garbage problem, it is not the only problem. Composition of materials in the current waste stream may contribute more to a crisis than sheer quantities. The composition of waste presents "front-end" as well as "back-end" dilemmas. For example, the generation of waste calls into question the rationale for consuming scarce resources and at the same time leads to demands for the quick and efficient disposal of society's discards. The current waste stream includes a complex mix of hard-to-replace as well as recyclable materials and a vast array of toxic substances. How best to collect these materials, yet alone how to dispose of them, challenges traditional solid waste practices.

Collection and disposal systems in the nineteenth century were initially designed to deal with large amounts of organic material, such as food waste and horse manure, as well as wood and coal ash and an assortment of rubbish. For many years, little was known about the long-term environmental consequences of disposing of waste—beyond a growing suspicion about the potential health hazards of putrefying organic materials. Consequently, collection and disposal systems were chosen to conform with the popular notion of "out of sight, out of mind."[10]

As more was learned about the changing nature of the waste stream over time, older collection and disposal methods came into question. Sometimes these methods were modified, but rarely were they abandoned. No consensus has been reached on how best to adjust to the changing composition of wastes. In recent years, as Table 1 shows, paper has represented the largest percentage of municipal waste, and it continues to increase. Yard and food wastes, the major organic discards, have steadily declined. Plastics, a new element in the waste stream since World War II, represent a relatively small but rapidly increasing portion of the total. Inorganic materials are scant in terms of percentage but include many household chemicals with potentially serious environmental implications.

The nature of the waste stream, at least since 1960, suggests important "front-end" problems. Of all the discarded items, paper, plastics, and aluminum have grown steadily as a percentage of the total MSW.[11] The use of these materials reflects a substantial increase in packaging waste and a wide variety of additional uses for paper.

Few would disagree that rampant consumerism, especially since World War II, has been a major contributing factor to the solid waste problem. The conclusion that excessive packaging is the whole problem misstates the case, however. Between 1958 and 1976 packaging consumption rose by 63 percent. But rapid growth in aggregate packaging waste has not continued into the 1980s and 1990s. For example, between 1970 and 1986 packaging as a component of MSW increased only 9 percent, while durable items increased 35 percent; clothing/footwear, 88 percent; nondu-

Table 1. Gross Discards in Municipal Solid Waste (in percentages)

Discards	1960	1970	1986	2000
Paper	34.0	36.5	41.0	44.9
Glass	7.4	10.5	8.2	7.0
Metals	12.0	11.4	8.7	8.3
Plastics	0.5	2.5	6.5	8.2
Rubber, leather, textiles, wood	7.8	7.8	8.0	7.0
Food waste	13.9	10.6	7.9	6.4
Yard waste	22.9	19.3	17.9	16.6
Misc. inorganic	1.5	1.6	1.7	1.7

Source: U.S. EPA, "The Solid Waste Dilemma: An Agenda for Action: Background Document" (Washington, D.C., September 1988), 1–9.

rables, 300 percent; office and commercial paper, 69 percent; and newspapers/magazines/books, 40 percent.[12]

A more critical issue with packaging, both in terms of "front-end" and "back-end" problems, involves the changes in package composition. Paperboard cartons, plastic jugs, and plastic jars have replaced glass milk bottles and other glass containers; aluminum beverage cans have replaced steel cans; and plastic grocery bags are replacing paper bags. In 1985, 47 billion pounds of plastics were produced in the United States. Of the 39 billion pounds consumed domestically, 33 percent was used for packaging. More than half of the discarded plastics is from packaging. The dependence on plastics requires extensive use of petrochemical and other feedstocks and results in discards of substantial bulk—if not weight—in landfills. Plastics pose a health hazard when burned in incinerators and demand more complex recycling methods than glass or paper. Additional problems arise if packages are composed of several materials.[13]

In the case of paper, not only has the amount of discards increased, but the use has changed. While some forms of packaging are no longer made of paper products, other uses for paper have been growing. Office paper and commercial printing papers have mounted, while newsprint as a percentage of total MSW has remained constant. The rise in the use of computer printouts, direct-mail advertising brochures, and the output from high-speed copiers is particularly significant. The potential for recycling paper is great, although paper and paperboard of various types are often mixed in landfills and thus must be recycled at the source. Even with source separation, effective techniques for converting all but newsprint and clean, white paper into new products are not yet viable in the market.

The problem with paper is compounded by another disposal issue: it adds significantly to the volume of waste in a greater proportion than weight. In 1986 approximately 50 million tons of paper products were dumped in landfills or were incinerated, representing 35.6 percent of MSW by weight disposed that year. The volume, however, was much greater. Since most projections about aggregate discards are calculated by weight, paper's contribution to the disposal problem is often underestimated, even after compaction. [14]

There is little doubt that variety and complexity of discards compounds the problem of volume. Questions of excessive waste generation and the squandering of resources, issues generally ignored in the past, become more crucial when the composition of solid waste is given parity with waste volume. It is particularly important to remember that the composition of materials in the waste stream is dependent on several external factors, including patterns of consumption and production, the availability and use of new materials and new technologies, and the obsolescence of older materials and older technologies. Without the industry's paying careful attention the kind of materials entering the waste stream, and without recognizing that composition is generally in flux, collection and disposal practices can prove ineffective and, in some cases, obsolete.

Collection

Collection of solid waste has long been regarded as a cumbersome, labor-intensive, and expensive venture, but not as a major factor in the garbage crisis. Surveys of refuse collection going back to the 1890s came to the important, if not startling, conclusion that there was no single "best" method of collection. Some cities chose to collect unseparated discards; others experimented with source separation. Regardless of the method, collection was difficult because it was costly and rarely equitable. Historically, collections were most frequent in the business districts and less frequent in outlying areas or poorer neighborhoods. As more affluent suburbs grew, some cities diverted collection teams from inner-city routes to upper- and middle-class neighborhoods. [15]

Considering the problems associated with it, collection should be given more attention in the dialogue about the garbage crisis. Surveys estimate that from 70 percent to 90 percent of the cost of collection and disposal in the United States goes for collection alone. Conservative estimates placed the annual cost of solid waste management in 1974 at $5 billion, with collection and delivery of wastes to disposal sites accounting for nearly $4 billion.[16] In addition, recent studies indicate that the disparity between the budgeted amount for collection and the actual cost may be great.[17]

Refuse collection can be characterized more by economies of density than by economies of scale. For example, a doubling of the tonnage collected per mile may reduce the average cost by as much as 50 percent. Longer hauls to disposal sites or transfer stations, on the contrary, significantly increase cost. This suggests that population diffusion or deconcentration, as in the case of the modern metropolis, is the enemy of efficient and economical collection.[18]

After World War II, the introduction of compaction vehicles, which compress wastes to about 30 percent of the curbside volume, yielded a significant technology to take advantage of economies of density. The use of transfer stations—points at which collection trucks can unload into larger vehicles or temporary storage facilities—also helped to ease the problem of distant collections. Mechanization, however, was not a simple technical fix for collection. While some solid waste managers hoped that mechanization would reduce reliance on hand labor (and thus cut down on accident claims and forestall messy labor disputes), collection remains labor-intensive. Labor problems continue to plague collection services in many cities, especially in cases where race is intermingled with an assortment of worker grievances.[19]

Reliance on a mechanized fleet to collect refuse also has environmental repercussions. As one study noted: "The emissions from the massive fleet of garbage trucks, the traffic congestion aggravated by the trucks, the littering caused by trash blown off the trucks, and the disposal processes themselves all contribute to environmental disturbances which would not have occurred if there were no wastes."[20]

In recent years, collection has resurrected some old issues. As will be discussed later, the debate over privatization of service delivery rages in some cities. From the consumer's perspective, frequency of service remains a key concern. Rising interest in recycling is reopening the question of source separation versus mixed-refuse collection—a point of contention going back to the late nineteenth century—and likely will affect collection strategies for both public and private service providers in the near future.

Do these collection problems contribute to a garbage crisis? Perhaps. Knotty issues surrounding collection are simply inherent in the process itself. What the collection problems expose—like the changing waste composition—is the significance of external factors that influence quality of service. Modification in the structure and size of cities, changes in population distribution, and increasing environmental awareness all have powerful effects on collection.

Disposal

Sanitary Landfills

If there is a garbage crisis, it has been most closely linked with the problem of disposal, especially the shrinking of landfill sites. In 1988 Karen Tumulty of the *Los Angeles Times* wrote that "Fresh Kills, New York's only remaining big landfill, also symbolizes a crisis that faces communities throughout the Northeast. When it runs out of space around the turn of the century, 7.1 million people will have to find something else to do with three quarters of their trash."[21] One solution is exporting wastes, as in the case of the *Mobro,* but this action smacks of desperation by those who have given up on a purely local solution. Three northeastern states— New Jersey, Pennsylvania, and New York—already export eight million tons of garbage a year, with much of it deposited in the Midwest.[22]

There is no value in minimizing the disposal crisis. It is real, and it is serious. But it is at once a less universal problem in some respects and a more complex problem than often portrayed. The crisis is less universal because regional differences in available sites for landfills are so great; it is more complex because the landfill problem exposes an array of perplexing issues, from exporting waste to environmental degradation.

The most striking aspect of the sanitary landfill is how widely acclaimed it became as a universally accepted panacea. No other American disposal option has been lauded in this manner. Modern sanitary landfills originated in Great Britain in the 1920s under the term "controlled tipping." American versions were first attempted in the 1930s in New York City and in Fresno, California. During World War II, the Army Corps of Engineers experimented with landfills; after the war several cities adopted the technique. In the 1950s the Sanitary Engineering Division of the American Society of Civil Engineers prepared a manual on sanitary landfilling that became a standard guide.[23] During the 1950s and 1960s the prevailing wisdom among those involved in solid waste management was that sanitary landfilling was the most economical form of disposal, and at the same time it offered a method that produced reclaimed land.[24]

By the 1970s solid waste professionals and others began to doubt the adequacy of the sanitary landfill to serve the future needs of cities. The major point of discussion was the problem in acquiring adequate space.

Ironically, what made sanitary landfills attractive as a disposal option—availability of cheap and abundant land—was the very argument used in the 1970s to discredit it. Siting new landfills became problematic in some parts of the country. Many communities simply did not set aside land specifically designated for waste disposal facilities. Part of the reason was that physically or environmentally marginal land, or land perceived to be environmentally marginal, was no longer available. In competition with other land uses, landfills quickly dropped down the list of priorities. The strong consensus favoring sanitary fills also meant that other disposal options received much less attention, and in many cases languished.[25]

Availability of land was only the most obvious point of contention. Landfill siting is treacherous business because of citizen resistance and increasingly rigid environmental standards. A great deal has been made of the NIMBY syndrome—Not in My Back Yard—which reveals growing skepticism with the environmental soundness of landfills. Equally important, NIMBY has received wider press coverage because of attempts to site landfills beyond the inner-city along the urban fringe, where the population is not characteristically poor. In Contra Costa County, California, all the proposed sites for new landfill spaces were to be located on the predominantly blue-collar east side of the county. The organizer of an east county coalition, WHEW (We Have Enough Waste), stated: "Whenever there are undesirable things to be located, if there is a dump or a jail, where do you look? East county! Is it fair that east county citizens be the recipients of all the garbage for the rest of the county?"[26] Even the once passive or politically neutered neighborhoods are fighting back, unwilling to provide dumping space for the whole city or county.

Growing concern that sanitary landfills are not as sanitary as their name implies has given citizen groups and others weapons to resist new sitings. Birds, insects, rodents, and other animals that frequent landfills can carry pathogens back to people. Even in the most pristine facility, this problem cannot be wholly eliminated. In addition, if not properly lined, landfills pose a threat to ground and surface water, especially through leachate. There is also concern about contamination from hazardous materials and incinerator ash that find their way into the landfills from home and factory.[27] As Rathje noted, "The potentially toxic legacy of landfills that may long ago have been covered over by hospitals and golf courses illustrates one of the terrible ironies of enlightened garbage management: an idea that seems sensible and right is often overtaken by changes in society and in the contents of its garbage."[28]

By current estimates, 75 percent to 85 percent of the waste generated in the United States ends up in landfills, while the total number of sites are declining. Aggregate statistics paint a gloomy national picture of the phasing out of the sanitary landfill as the single disposal option in American cities. According to the EPA, half of the nation's approximately six thousand landfills will be closed by 1995. Since 1978, fourteen thousand facilities—or 70 percent of all landfills—were closed. And most significant, newer ones are not coming on line to replace the older ones. In 1988 only 9.5 percent of the landfills were less than five years old, whereas 46 percent were more than fifteen years old and 30 percent more than twenty years old. In the early 1970s, 330 to 400 municipal landfills were built each year. In the 1980s the annual figure dropped to between 50 and 200.[29]

What is a crisis for some communities is only a distant danger for others. Regional differences in availability of landfill space have made it difficult to alert cities to what some believe to be a national plight. Landfills are most highly concentrated in a few locations, namely, the New England states, New York, Wisconsin, Texas, and California. Maine, New York, Wisconsin, Texas, and California account for 40 percent of all municipal landfills in the country. Wisconsin, with only 2 percent of the population in the United States, has 15 percent of the landfills.[30]

It is likewise difficult to generalize about landfill capacity. Between 1980 and 1984, for example, the Delaware Solid Waste Authority established three new landfills and expanded the state's available capacity to an estimated twenty-five to thirty years. In the Southwest, Arizona and New Mexico appear to have no capacity crisis. Low population density and greater land availability undermine problems faced in other areas. Also, since groundwater aquifers in the Southwest tend to be much farther below the surface than elsewhere, the fear of contamination from leachate is minimal. Even within states great variation exists. Rural areas generally do not experience disposal problems to the same degree as urban centers. In some states the reverse is true.[31]

It is not sufficient to make a case for a national crisis in disposal based simply on the shrinking of landfill space. The cumulative result of the cost of disposal, environmental risk factors, management problems, compliance with regulations, and the squandering of resources combines to exacerbate the problem for those communities faced with the need for immediate action, and serves as a warning for those yet to face such a dilemma. The assumption of a crisis or pending crisis also has increased in intensity because of the prevailing belief that no single alternative method of disposal offers a better solution than landfilling.

What, then, is the crisis of the landfill? Lack of sites? Encroachment on residential neighborhoods? Threats to groundwater? All of these? In one sense, disposal in general constitutes a problem that has never been solved in the past and is unlikely to be solved in the future. The adage that we cannot solve the garbage problem, only manage it, has validity. If sanitary landfills deserve crisis status, it is because American cities have depended on a one-dimensional disposal system for at least forty years and have not adequately prepared the way for viable alternatives.

Incineration

Of the available alternatives to sanitary landfills, incineration has had the strongest following. Since the first "cremator" was built in the United States in 1885, incineration seems to have offered a simple yet effective solution to reducing the volume of waste. Fire appeared to be the perfect disinfectant, leaving only an ash residue. But incineration never achieved the status of the sanitary landfill. It was embraced by one generation of engineers and policymakers, only to be rejected by the next. Experiments at the turn of the century led American cities to attempt to utilize original English-designed "destructors," but they had a difficult time adapting them to American conditions. Throughout the early twentieth century incinerators met with uneven success in American cities. In the 1930s they had a brief resurgence—600 to 700 cities and towns employed the technology, and incineration became responsible for the disposal of 5 percent to 10 percent of the solid waste. By 1966, however, the total had declined to 265, and by the end of 1974 one expert estimated that only 160 plants were in operation. In 1988 only 3 percent of MSW was incinerated.[32]

These figures do not speak well for the second most popular disposal technology. But incineration continues to reappear in the disposal debate because it drastically reduces waste volume and takes up relatively limited space in comparison to a landfill. At the same time, the shortcomings of incineration—high capital costs and air pollution—never allowed it to compete effectively.

Two types of waste combustion facilities, both with roots in the late nineteenth and early twentieth centuries, continue in use. The first is a facility that burns waste only to reduce the volume to be landfilled. For the most part, this type of plant was built before 1975 and is relatively small (with a capacity of fewer than 1,000 tons per day). It is typically a mass-burn unit; that is, it combusts waste with none or very little preprocessing. The second type is the waste-to-energy facility, which burns the waste but utilizes the resulting hot flue gases to produce steam for the production of electricity or for sale directly to users of thermal energy. This unit became popular during the energy crisis in the 1970s as an alternative to the use of fossil fuels. The waste-to-energy plant can employ mass-burn techniques or can be a refuse-derived-fuel (RDF) facility. The RDF plant preprocesses waste, employing shredders, screens, and separators to isolate the combustible material. The resulting residue can be turned into pellets, then stored or transported to be used at a later time. The pellets burn hot and evenly and can be combusted in specially designed boilers. At present, however, very few plants densify RDF and burn it.[33]

Despite the sophistication of modern incinerators, by 1988 only 134 waste-reduction-only (38) and waste-to-energy (96) facilities were in operation. Of that number only 18 were new waste-to-energy plants starting up in 1988. The highest concentration of these facilities is east of the Mississippi River. However, EPA projections suggest an almost 50 percent increase in incinerator capacity by 1992. No fewer than 126 communities are in various stages of project planning. If only some of the plants are completed, about 25 percent of the total solid waste in the United States will be burned by 1994.[34]

The reversal of the disposal trend suggests the pressure felt by some communities to develop disposal alternatives, especially communities where landfills have become a liability or a less viable option. Like landfilling, incineration has encountered public resistance. Incinerators are much easier to site in an urban setting, but fear of air pollution makes them as unwelcome as any landfill.

The debate over incineration is a classic confrontation between those with faith in technology to overcome social and economic problems versus those who are suspicious of the "technical fix." In theory, waste-to-energy offers two major advantages: an efficient means to reduce the volume of wastes, and the production of a valuable by-product. Proponents do not deny the potential environmental hazards associated with burning waste, but they are inclined to believe that while older facilities usually failed to meet new emissions standards, newer waste-to-energy facilities can withstand the performance test.[35]

Critics of incineration question the efficiency of the plants and bemoan the squandering of resources that provide the feedstock, fearing the environmental impact of their use. They are not willing to give the facilities the same latitude as proponents. Allen Hershkowitz put the case succinctly: "Garbage burning generates a range of pollutants, including gases that contain heavy metals and dioxins and that contribute to acid rain. Moreover, incinerators require a new breed of secure landfills that accept only the toxic ash they generate."[36] Less subtle in his criticism, environ-

mentalist Barry Commoner has referred to the new generation of incinerators as "dioxin-producing factories," and through his leadership citizens
groups in New York City have managed to delay the development of an
elaborate resource-recovery program there.[37]

The Washington-based Institute for Local Self-Reliance has strongly
criticized incineration; it also rejects sanitary landfilling as a viable disposal option for urban centers. This appraisal has focused on cost factors
and environmental implications. In fact, the institute has linked the two
by arguing that "because of unresolved, environmental regulatory requirements, the ultimate cost of mass burn facilities [and presumably sanitary
landfills] is not fully known." The institute has taken a strong stand in
favor of resource recovery, but in the form of recycling and waste minimization rather than waste-to-energy facilities. One report stated that the
use of the term "resource recovery" by advocates of incineration is misleading: "While it is true that such technologies recover heat . . . and the
heat can be used with varying efficiencies to produce steam or electricity,
they recover no other resources. From an environmental standpoint, they
concentrate toxicities and distribute contaminants into air, soil and
groundwater."[38]

Recycling

The long-standing debate over landfilling versus incineration has taken a
new turn in recent years. Recycling has emerged as an alternative disposal
strategy. Once regarded as a grassroots method of source reduction and a
relatively innocuous protest against overconsumption in the 1960s, recycling emerged in the 1980s as an alternative to—or at least a complement
to—more traditional disposal methods. Recycling has become a disposal
option in the same sense that energy experts consider conservation as an
energy source—a kind of negative sum that stretches existing resources
and generates less waste that would otherwise be dumped or burned. An
Oregon engineer told the American Institute of Chemical Engineers,
"Once ridiculed as an ineffective hobby of environmentalists, [recycling]
is now regarded as an essential component of solid-waste management and
a cost-effective way to reduce dependence on landfills."[39]

In the late nineteenth century, "scow-trimmers" sorted through New
York's rubbish as it was loaded onto barges headed out to sea. The recovered material was sold to junk dealers. Sorting plants were set up in some
cities to remove materials with resale value from collected refuse. During
both world wars, resource recovery was regarded as a patriotic duty and a
means to acquire salvageable materials to aid in the prosecution of the

war. Industrial expansion in wartime increased the demand for rubber, aluminum, tin, and paper. Conservation of food and fuel were encouraged on the domestic front to increase supplies for the war effort. In the 1970s interest in resource recovery emerged again, this time in the wake of the burgeoning ecology movement and the energy crisis.[40]

Recycling in the United States is, as Neil Seldman stated, "at the takeoff stage." Many problems need to be resolved. What kind of incentives should be used to get the compliance of households, businesses, haulers, and manufacturers? What about mandatory recycling laws? Should there be a clear policy of government procurement of recycled products? How much attention should be paid to recycling literacy? And the biggest question of all: Can markets be found and developed to take the increasing volume of recyclables?[41]

As solid-waste managers, private industry, and citizens groups struggle with these questions, pressure to find practical answers is coming in the form of recycling programs springing up all across the country. Before 1980 fewer than 140 communities in the United States had door-to-door recycling collection service. Estimates for the 1990s put the total at more than 1,000. In 1989 more than 10,000 recycling drop-off and buy-back centers were in operation, as well as more than 7,000 scrap processors.[42]

A major goal for most communities and the nation in general is to increase the recycling rate, which stood at 10 percent in the late 1980s. An EPA draft report in 1988, "The Solid Waste Dilemma: An Agenda for Action," called for a national recycling goal of 25 percent by 1992. Some communities are claiming achievements beyond that national standard. Portland, Oregon, claims 26 percent; Montclair, New Jersey, 30 percent; and Islip, New York, the home of the *Mobro*, 35 percent. Several states have begun aggressive recycling programs, including Connecticut, New Jersey, New York, Pennsylvania, and Rhode Island in the East, Florida in the South, and Oregon in the West.[43]

Recycling, moreover, has developed strong political and social appeal. While not inexpensive to implement, recycling puts policymakers on the side of conservation of resources as well as giving concerned citizens a way to participate in confronting the solid waste dilemma. But skeptics of the new faith in recycling persist, and cautionary notes append many enthusiastic reports. Still, the perception of recycling as an answer to the nation's disposal problem has given it strong momentum in the 1980s. Its linkage to waste reduction and waste minimization as a means to conserve resources and reduce pollution has attracted new followers. A powerful argument is that the environment can be protected from many pollutants by reducing the amount of waste produced, thus reducing the need to find ways to treat the unwanted residues. But just as the sanitary landfill came to be viewed as a disposal panacea, only to be discredited later, the euphoria over recycling will need to be tempered with a strong record of tangible results.[44]

Management

"There is nothing as crucial to an alderman as garbage." So spoke Alderman Roman Pucinski of Chicago in 1984.[45] Many people would agree. And many would argue that interest-group politics alone explains the garbage crisis in America. In a 1988 issue of *Forbes*, James Cook observed:

> Pitted against one another are environmental groups, consultants, manufacturers, government agencies, politicians, homeowners. The waste-to-energy companies fear the move to recycling will shut them out of the market. Scrap dealers worry that the recyclers will walk away with their business. The battery, container and plastics producers suspect that regulation will limit their growth. And extreme environmentalists don't like the idea that somebody else might have a partial claim on the truth.
>
> You have local communities pitted against resource recovery projects, environmentalists against the EPA, the EPA against everybody. Only the landfill operators are left smiling cheerfully at the rapid rise in tipping fees.[46]

It is difficult to deny the confusion and complexities that the surfeit of interest groups brings to the garbage problem—and the harrowing task of political leaders to sort out the relevant issues. But political circumstance alone does not explain priority-setting for individual cities, nor does it address the means to confront the so-called garbage crisis. The way in which solid waste is managed within local government may play a crucial role in the means to a solution, or, indeed, it may be part of the problem itself.

Beginning in the late nineteenth century, a major concern of city government was to determine who was responsible for delivering needed services such as refuse collection and disposal. The concentration of people in the teaming industrial cities made private action impractical. The real choice was between contracting or establishing a municipal service. The contract approach was initially more popular because it required little or no capital outlay while still allowing some municipal supervision. Besides, cities at the turn of the century were constrained from expanding their authority by hostile rural-dominated state legislatures that did not want cities to increase power at their expense. The popularity of the contract system was short-lived, however, especially when the garbage problem ceased to be recognized simply as a nuisance and was considered a major health hazard. Since most cities assumed responsibility for public health, municipal collection and disposal of refuse appeared to be the best means of assuring proper sanitation. In 1880 only 24 percent of cities surveyed in the census had municipally operated garbage-collection systems; by 1924 the figure had risen to 63 percent.[47]

As municipal service expanded in the larger cities at least, private firms lost residential accounts and concentrated on commercial and industrial waste collection and other specialized collection functions. The trend toward municipal collection began to reverse itself in the 1950s and 1960s. As cities annexed greater numbers of suburban communities, they often contracted with the existing private firms rather than expand the municipal service. In addition, the shift to a more competitive system was accelerated by the change from separate to mixed refuse collection and demands for greater efficiency. With the ban on backyard burning of trash in many cities during the 1970s, trash collecting became mandatory along with garbage collecting. The increased volume of collectible wastes led several cities to contract part of the service while maintaining a portion of their original routes. Dissatisfaction with municipal service led several private collectors, because of their expanded role in residential collection, to claim that they could compete favorably with their public counterparts.[48]

During the 1960s a few large hauling firms bought up smaller companies in a number of cities. These "agglomerates" soon acquired both residential and industrial customers and offered an array of services—including disposal. By 1974 these large firms held contracts in more than three hundred communities. Between 1964 and 1973, 65 percent of cities surveyed operated some sort of collection service, but the proportion of cities with exclusively municipal collection declined from 45 percent to 39 percent.[49]

Debate over "privatization" of collection services became the battleground for confronting a wide array of issues surrounding the problem of solid waste. The major issue was not simply a question of who was more efficient or who was cheaper—although these were key points of argument—but who had control and who made decisions about the disposition of the wastes.

In many ways the shift to private services happened more easily than anticipated. A 1981 study of ten cities (ranging in size from 35,000 to 593,000) noted that the switch to private collection was widely supported without significant opposition within the city bureaucracies or among municipal unions.[50] Significant reductions in the cost of service were achieved in the first year of the contract, no doubt reflecting the goal that supporters hoped to achieve. Key factors contributing to support for the private contracts included: (1) shifts in federal or state regulations that compelled cities to reexamine their collection systems; (2) a reduction in city resources through rising costs, inflation, a declining tax base, and/or a local tax revolt; and (3) the efforts of private firms, especially with national bases, to provide information about private services and to promote privatization. These factors, rather than any clear geographic patterns, appear to have influenced the decisions—although city size was important. Large cities, with entrenched, centralized, and professional public-works systems, tended to resist contracting more vigorously than smaller cities.[51]

The trend toward more privatized collection appears to be continuing into the 1990s. In 1988 the National Solid Waste Management Association stated that more than 80 percent of the nation's garbage was collected by private companies, either under government contract or working directly for local residents. Between 1973 and 1982 the number of communities with private collection increased from 339 to 486. Private control of disposal facilities, however, is much less dramatic. From 1973 to 1983 the number of communities contracting for refuse disposal increased from 143 to 342. While this growth was significant, it is not comparable to growth in private collection. In 1987 only 22 percent of municipal governments had contracted with private landfills or combustion facilities, although 32 percent had made plans to hire a contractor in 1989. In 1988 only 15 percent of the country's landfills (but about half of the resource-recovery plants) were private.[52]

The privatization trend, especially in collection, suggests a dramatic swing of the pendulum in the operation phase of solid waste management. But with respect to the question of ultimate responsibility for collection and disposal services, privatization is simply a complicating factor, one that makes the debate over a garbage crisis murkier. A recent study noted that competition, rather than the type of ownership per se, appears to be the most important factor in efficiency of service. The trend toward consolidation in the waste disposal industry could strongly affect the nature of competition, and thus the relationship with municipal governments in setting policy. The three firms that dominate the industry—Browning-Ferris Industries, Waste Management, and Laidlaw of Canada—have substantially more leverage than the myriad small companies they have replaced or have absorbed.[53]

Competition also exists among various governmental entities in the form of jurisdictional rivalries. One report noted that "solid waste disposal is rapidly becoming an intrastate, as well as interstate, matter."[54] A variety of new arrangements have emerged out of the realization that the garbage problem is infrequently contained within the city limits or within a particular jurisdiction. Some areas have tried interlocal agreements, countywide systems, multicounty corporations, or intrastate planning bodies. Often born of necessity, these arrangements speak to the complex problems of collection and disposal, but like the emergence of privatization, they require substantial attention to determine lines of authority in the decision-making process.

The question "Who is in charge?" is particularly significant because of the recent commitment of both public and private entities to "integrated waste management" systems. The EPA recommends:

> . . . using "integrated waste management" systems to solve municipal solid waste generation and management problems at the local, regional, and national levels. In this holistic approach, systems are designed so that some or all of the four waste management options (source reduction, recycling, combustion and landfills) are used as a complement to one another to safely and efficiently manage municipal solid waste.[55]

In setting such a worthy but ambitious goal, the EPA and others are treating "integrated waste management" as a solution to the garbage crisis. However, proponents of the idea may not have given sufficient attention to the fact that attempts to implement "integrated waste management" come with the risk of sharpening the traditional rivalry between public and private forces seeking to control collection and disposal systems.

Regulation

The EPA's promotion of the concept of "integrated waste management" suggests a significant role for the federal government not only in setting a national agenda for solid waste but in setting an expanded regulatory role. Especially since the 1960s, the federal government has broadened the scope of the waste problem, stressing its significance as an environmental issue with national repercussions.

Until the mid-1960s, collection and disposal were considered functions of local government. Understood to be a fundamentally urban problem, their management was linked to concerns over population growth and city expansion. As late as 1963, the Advisory Commission on Intergovernmental Relations concluded that collection and disposal of solid wastes, according to one observer, "had no significant economic, social, or other spillover effects, and could therefore be safely left to local management."[56]

The recognition in the 1960s that solid waste was part of a more general national environmental problem quickly led to the assumption that control limited to the local level would be inadequate to deal with a problem that extended beyond the city limits of every community. In time, solid waste was elevated to the stature of "third pollution," alongside air and water pollution.[57] The significance of the change in perspective about solid waste as an environmental danger was at least as pivotal as the transformation of refuse in the nineteenth century from a "nuisance" to a "health hazard."

In a special message on conservation and restoration of national beauty, President Lyndon Johnson called for "better solutions to the disposal of solid waste" and recommended federal legislation to assist state governments in developing comprehensive disposal programs and to provide research and development funds. Soon after Johnson's speech, Congress passed the Solid Waste Disposal Act as Title 2 of the 1965 amendments to the Clean Air Act.

The Solid Waste Disposal Act recognized the mounting quantities and changing character of refuse. It also noted the inability of current methods to deal with the problem and the failure of resource-recovery programs to convert waste economically into usable by-products. The primary thrust of the act was to "initiate and accelerate" a national research and development program and to provide technical and financial assistance to state and local governments and interstate agencies in the "planning, development, and conduct" of disposal programs. The Department of Health, Education, and Welfare was given advisory powers over local solid waste regulation.

The act represented the first significant recognition of solid waste as a national problem, but it was incomplete in its assessment. Primary focus was on disposal of waste, not collection. Furthermore, the act failed to mandate a regulatory authority to deal with broader issues related to refuse.[58]

After the Solid Waste Disposal Act was passed, President Johnson, with the advice of his Scientific Advisory Committee, called for a special study of the solid waste problem. Members of the White House staff, with representatives from the Public Health Service, the Departments of Agriculture, Defense, and the Interior, and other groups, produced the 1968

National Survey of Community Solid Waste Practices. Although the samples chosen were incomplete and the execution imperfect, the survey helped to fill the "data gap" and led to other statistical compilations.[59]

To refine the 1965 act, Congress passed the Resource Recovery Act in 1970. This legislation shifted emphasis of federal involvement from disposal to recycling, resource recovery, and conversion of waste to energy. It created the National Commission on Materials Policy to develop a national policy on materials requirements, supply, use, recovery, and disposal. Another feature of the 1970 legislation was the stipulation that a national system be implemented for storing and disposing of hazardous wastes.[60]

Both the 1965 and 1970 acts led the states to become more deeply involved in what until that time had been a local issue. Responding to federal legislation, pressure; or incentives, states began to enact solid waste management statutes and to designate one of its agencies a solid waste management office. They were usually of two types: public health or environmental protection agencies. The state programs, however, showed little uniformity. Some were staffed by as many as sixty-two people or as few as one. They operated with budgets ranging from $1.2 million to no budget at all. The typical program could be found near the lower end of the range. The most significant immediate result was the development of solid waste management plans—a prerequisite for receiving federal funds. Often built on the plans of counties and/or municipalities, these programs stressed issues of disposal more than collection.[61]

The Resource Conservation and Recovery Act (RCRA) passed in 1976, and reauthorized as the Hazardous and Solid Waste Amendments of 1984, was the first comprehensive framework for hazardous waste management in the United States. Of particular significance for municipal solid waste was Subtitle D, which provided for development of environmentally sound disposal methods and the protection of groundwater with new landfill standards. To achieve sound methods of waste disposal and to encourage the conservation of resources, RCRA outlined plans for federal financial and technical assistance to state and local jurisdictions for the development of solid waste management plans that would lead to cooperation among federal, state, and local governments and private industry. The 1984 amendments substantially tightened standards with respect to landfills. According to one analyst: "Simply put, the premise of RCRA is that the solid waste problem is a result of our industrial society. As such, the true costs of disposal should be borne by those benefitting from the products that generate the waste. Therefore, once the subsidy of the cheap landfill is removed, other more advanced technologies will develop."[62]

The federal legislation originating in the 1960s and extending into the 1990s has not simply set new guidelines for action but has changed the workings of waste-disposal regulation as well. Especially under RCRA, the EPA has acquired extensive regulatory authority over municipal solid waste, especially in the design and operation of landfills and incinerators.[63]

The increase in federal authority was not immediate, nor is it absolute in the 1990s. Initially the enforcement of the 1965 act fell to the Public Health Service, an agency of HEW, and to the Bureau of Mines in the Department of Interior. The Public Health Service was given responsibility for municipal wastes, while the Bureau of Mines supervised mining and fossil-fuel waste from power plants and industrial steam plants. With the creation of the Environmental Protection Agency in 1970, responsibility for most refuse activities was transferred to it. In the 1970s the Office of Solid Waste (OSW) acquired the authority to conduct special studies of problems related to solid waste, to award grants, and to publish guidelines.

The establishment of OSW provided a degree of stability—if not permanence—for federal solid-waste programs, but not without controversy. Since a primary function of the EPA was to aid in the control and elimination of pollution, several officials preferred to concentrate on the problem of hazardous wastes and de-emphasized solid waste management issues as envisioned in the 1965 and 1970 acts. In the mid-1970s the EPA proposed a drastic cutback in the federal solid-waste program and recommended that federal activities be limited to regulating hazardous wastes. When Congress and state and local groups balked at this stance, the EPA backed away from this extreme position and announced its willingness to continue to develop and promote resource-recovery systems and technology. But when the immediate threat of the energy crisis had passed and belt-tightening provisions began to cut into the EPA's budget in the early 1980s, the agency all but turned away from the municipal solid waste issue.[64]

With public attention alerted to a pending "garbage crisis" and with the strengthening of RCRA provisions affecting MSW in the mid-1980s, the EPA was back in the middle of the municipal solid waste debate—along with such other federal agencies as the Office of Technology Assessment. The issuance of "The Solid Waste Dilemma" was a clear statement of the EPA's desire to set the tone for attacking the crisis. Speaking about the EPA's new role, especially in light of the establishment of the Office of Pollution Prevention, director William Reilly stated, "That is going to be the hallmark of this place—pollution prevention and reduction at the source."[65]

But the return of the EPA has engendered several responses. While some have applauded the resolve of the federal government to join the garbage crisis battle, others argue that the increase in regulatory authority has not been matched with action. William Kovacs, chief counsel of the House Subcommittee on Transportation and Commerce (with primary jurisdiction over solid and hazardous waste) during the enactment of RCRA, observed that the EPA's "implementation of RCRA can only be described as tardy, fragmented, at times nonexistent, and consistently inconsistent."[66] For those living under the new standards, especially local and state governments, various waste-disposal authorities, and private businesses, such animism at the national level often produces confusion over the type and extent of compliance with new rules, and sometimes fosters suspicion and cynicism over federal intrusion into local affairs.

For optimists, the expanded role of the federal government in the solid-waste debate may mobilize Americans to action. For pessimists, it may simply add one more discordant voice to a tone-deaf choir. At the least, federal involvement may produce a more middle-of-the-road effect, as law professor Peter S. Menell observed: "Despite the lethargy of the federal government in promulgating regulations, the solid waste crisis has renewed interest in solid waste regulatory policy both at EPA and in Congress."[67]

The solid-waste problem in the United States is too complex simply to regard it as a crisis. Implied in this usage of "crisis" is the assumption that society has reached a point beyond which we can expect nothing less than a dangerous outcome. But being perched on the edge of disaster suggests one of two extreme results—either we must resign ourselves to an unpalatable outcome or we must take immediate action to forestall the worst case. Either way, the call to a crisis oversimplifies the solid-waste problem. Much of what has come to be considered the "garbage crisis" is not the product of immediate past practices or present inaction, but a series of chronic problems, interrelated in such a way as to defy a simple solution. The difficult task is trying to determine what needs careful, steadfast action and what needs immediate action.

Those things that fall into the category of chronic problems include: the unwieldy volume of waste, inherent problems associated with collection, the impulse to depend on a single disposal option rather than developing a clear disposal strategy, emphasis on "back-end" solutions to what may be "front-end" problems, the debate over public-versus-private operation and management, and jurisdictional disputes over regulation.

Those problems especially in need of immediate attention, some of which may be at the crisis state, include: increasing amounts of toxic materials in the municipal waste stream, the squandering of limited resources, lack of viable landfill space, and increased levels of air and water pollution. Some of these problems exhibit regional variations in intensity, such as landfill siting (although most communities will need to confront this issue at some point). Others are more universal, as in the case of consumption of scarce or otherwise valuable resources.

In some respects, dealing with the chronic problems may prove more difficult than confronting those deemed to be at a crisis point. By no means is this distinction between chronic problems and crisis state purely semantic. Nor is it meant to diminish the significance of the solid-waste problem. Clearly, the broad acceptance of a "garbage crisis" derives much of its power from the fact that, since the 1970s at least, the problem of waste was given greater credit for environmental degradation than before. What had been a nuisance in the nineteenth century became a major environmental blight in the twentieth century. With a keener understanding of its complexities and nuances, the search for remedies to the garbage crisis may produce more long-lasting results.

University of Houston

Acknowledgment

I would like to acknowledge the financial support of the National Endowment for the Humanities and the University of Houston Energy Laboratory for completion of this article.

Notes

1. National League of Cities and United States Conference of Mayors, *Cities and the Nation's Disposal Crisis* (Washington, D.C., March 1973), 1. See also Michael R. Greenberg et al., *Solid Waste Planning in Metropolitan Regions* (New Brunswick, N.J., 1976), 11–22; Brian J. L. Berry and Frank E. Horton, *Urban Environmental Management* (Englewood Cliffs, N.J., 1974), 376–77.

2. Homer A. Neal and J. R. Schubel, *Solid Waste Management and the Environment: The Mounting Garbage and Trash Crisis* (Englewood Cliffs, N.J., 1987), 5.

3. Robert Emmet Long, ed., *The Problem of Waste Disposal* (New York, 1989), 9. See also Newsday, *Rush to Burn: Solving America's Garbage Crisis?* (Washington, D.C., 1989).

4. "An Interview with Sylvia Lowrance," *EPA Journal* 15 (March–April, 1989): 10.

5. "Leaders Waste No Time in Facing Tough Issues," *World Wastes* 29 (January 1986): 13–14.

6. William L. Rathje, "Rubbish!" *Atlantic Monthly*, December 1989, 99.

7. See ibid., 99–106, 108–9; William Rathje and Barry Thompson, *The Milwaukee Garbage Project* (Washington, D.C., 1981).

8. Quoted in Martin V. Melosi, *Garbage in the Cities* (College Station, Tex., 1981), 23–24.

9. Projections of eight pounds per capita for the 1980s was a miscalculation. Rathje argues that even four pounds per capita may be too high, estimating instead about three pounds. See Alfred J. Van Tassel, ed., *Our Environment: The Outlook of 1980* (Lexington, Mass., 1973), 460; Melosi, *Garbage in the Cities*, 191; U.S. Environmental Protection Agency, "Characterization of Municipal Solid Waste in the United States: 1990 Update; Executive Summary" (Washington, D.C., 13 June 1990), 3; Rathje, "Rubbish!" 101.

10. See Melosi, *Garbage in the Cities*, 22ff.

11. EPA, "Solid Waste Dilemma: Background Documents," 1–18 and 1–19.

12. Lewis Erwin and L. Hall Healy, Jr., *Packaging and Solid Waste* (Washington, D.C., 1990), 19; Melosi, *Garbage in the Cities*, 210.

13. EPA, "The Solid Waste Dilemma: An Agenda for Action: Appendices A-B-C" (Washington, D.C., 1988), A.C-1 to A.C-15; EPA, "Solid Waste Dilemma: Background Document, 1–19 and 1–20.

14. EPA, "Solid Waste Dilemma: Appendices A-B-C," A.A-1 to A.A-48.

15. Melosi, *Garbage in the Cities*, 156–58. For an alternative perspective on the widely held view that collection service generally has been inadequate in neighborhoods heavily populated with minorities and/or the poor, see Bryan D. Jones, *Service Delivery in the City* (New York, 1980), 118–35.

16. American Public Works Association, *Solid Waste Collection Practice* (Chicago, 1975), 1. See also Arthur J. Warner, Charles H. Parker, and Barnard Baum, *Solid Waste Management of Plastics* (Washington, D.C., December, 1970), 4–5.

17. E. S. Savas, "How Much Do Government Services Really Cost?" *Urban Affairs Quarterly* 15 (September 1979): 23–42.

18. Peter Kemper and John M Quigley, *The Economics of Refuse Collection* (Cambridge, Mass., 1976), 109–11.

19. APWA, *History of Public Works in the United States*, 442, 444–46. See also Martin V. Melosi, "Waste Management: The Cleaning of America," *Environment* 23 (October 1981): 10; Van Tassel, ed., *Our Environment*, 467. For some insight into the life of garbage workers, see Stewart E. Perry, *San Francisco Scavengers* (Berkeley, 1978).

20. Neal and Schubel, *Solid Waste Management and the Environment*, 29.

21. Karen Tumulty, "No Dumping (There's No More Dump)," *Los Angeles Times*, 2 September 1988, 1.

22. Casey Bukro, "Eastern Trash Being Dumped in America's Heartland," *Houston Chronicle*, 24 November 1989, 1F. See also Lori Gilmore, "The Export of Nonhazardous Waste," *Environmental Law* 19 (Summer 1989): 879–907; Jim Schwab, "Garbage In, Garbage Out," *Planning* 52 (October 1986): 5–6.

23. The guide defines sanitary landfilling as "a method of disposing of refuse on land without creating nuisances or hazards to public health or safety, by utilizing the principles of engineering to confine the refuse to the smallest practical area, to reduce it to the smallest practical volume, and to cover it with a layer of earth at the conclusion of each day's operation, or at such more frequent intervals as may be necessary." See C. L. Mantell, *Solid Wastes* (New York, 1975), 71–72; APWA, *History of Public Works in the United States*, 450.

24. Melosi, *Garbage in the Cities*, 219.

25. See J. J. Dunn, Jr., and Penelope Hong, "Landfill Siting—An Old Skill in a New Setting," *APWA Reporter* 46 (June 1979): 12.

26. See Peter Steinhart, "Down in the Dumps," *Audubon*, 19 May 1986, 106.

27. Neal and Schubel, *Solid Waste Management and the Environment*, 116; Sue Darcey,

"Landfill Crisis Prompts Action," *World Wastes* 32 (May 1989): 28; Joanna D. Underwood, Allen Hershkowitz, and Maarten de Kadt, *Garbage* (New York, 1988), 8–12.

28. Rathje, "Rubbish!" 103.

29. Figures vary widely on what constitutes a landfill for purposes of evaluation. One report set the number of MSW landfills in 1986 at 9,284, with a sharp drop by 1988. Another stated that in 1980 the United States had 93,384 landfills—77,087 industrial sites and 15,577 municipal facilities. The EPA figure of 6,000 seems to reflect accurately the total MSW fills, taking into account the heavy attrition in sites during the 1980s. See "Municipal Solid Waste Management: An Integrated Approach," *State Factor* 15 (June 1989): 2; National Solid Waste Management Association, "Landfill Capacity in the Year 2000" (Washington, D.C., 1989), 1–3; Edward W. Repa, "Landfill Capacity: How Much Really Remains," *Waste Alternatives* 1 (December 1988): 32; Ishwar P. Murarka, *Solid Waste Disposal and Reuse in the United States*, vol. 1 (Boca Raton, Fla., 1987), 5; "Land Disposal Survey," *Waste Age* 12 (January 1981): 65.

30. EPA, "Solid Waste Dilemma: Background Documents," 2.E-1.

31. U.S. Congress, Office of Technology Assessment, *Facing America's Trash: What Next for Municipal Solid Waste?* (Washington, D.C., 1989), 273–74. See also Long, *The Problem of Waste Disposal*, 9–10.

32. Melosi, "Waste Management," 12; Melosi, *Garbage in the Cities*, 47–49; Greenberg et al., *Solid Waste Planning in Metropolitan Regions*, 8; O. P. Kharbanda and E. A. Stallworthy, *Waste Management* (New York, 1990), 67.

33. According to Harvey Alter, manager of the U.S. Chamber of Commerce's Resources Policy Department, there may be as few as two plants in the country that densify. Letter, Harvey Alter to Martin Melosi, 19 April 1991.

34. EPA, "Solid Waste Dilemma: Background Document," 2.D-1–2.D-3, 2.D-5. See also Harvey Alter, "The History of Refuse-Derived Fuels," *Resources and Conservation* 15 (1987): 251–75; Alter, "Energy Conservation and Fuel Production by Processing Solid Wastes," *Environmental Conservation* 4 (Spring 1977): 11–19; Van Tassel, ed., *Our Environment*, 464–65; David A. Tillman, Amadeo J. Rossi, and Katherine M. Vick, *Incineration of Municipal and Hazardous Solid Wastes* (New York, 1989), 1, 59–61, 113–17; Long, *The Problem of Waste Disposal*, 11, 15–16, 18, 20–21; Robert Zralek, "Energy from Waste," *APWA Reporter* 48 (August 1981): 15–16; K. A. Godfrey, Jr., "Municipal Refuse: Is Burning Best?" *Civil Engineering* 55 (April 1985): 53–56; David Sokol, "Contracting for Energy," *American City and County/Resource Recovery* (1988): RR22, RR24.

35. Schwab, "Garbage In, Garbage Out," 7.

36. Allen Hershkowitz, "Burning Trash: How It Could Work," *Technology Review* (July 1987): 27. When the article was written, Hershkowitz was director of solid waste for INFORM, a New York environmental research group. He is now employed by the NRDC.

37. Dioxin is a generic term for approximately 75 chemical compounds with the technical name polychlorinated dibenzo-p-dioxins (PCDDs). PCDFs, or furans, are a related group of 135 chemicals often found in association with PCDDs. Both can be released into the air as a residue of burning. While the potential effects of dioxins and furans on humans are serious, there has been substantial debate on the conclusiveness of testing because measurement of exposure is imprecise, separating the effects of dioxins from other toxic substances is difficult, and the latency period for potential effects may be as long as twenty years or more. See James E. McCarthy, "Incinerating Trash: A Hot Issue, Getting Hotter," *Congressional Research Service Review* 7 (April 1986): 19–20. See also Tillman, Rossi, and Vick, *Incineration of Municipal and Hazardous Wastes*, x; Citizens Clearinghouse for Hazardous Wastes, Inc., "Incineration: The Burning Issue of the 80's" (July 1985), 11–13, 26–41; Janet Marinelli and Gail Robinson, "Garbage: No Room at the Bin," *The Progressive* (December 1981): 24–25; Institute for Local Self-Reliance, "An Environmental Review of Incineration Technologies" (October 1986): 1–43.

38. Institute for Local Self-Reliance, "An Environmental Review of Incineration Tech-

nologies," 8. See also Neil Seldman, "Waste Management: Mass Burn Is Dying," *Environment* 31 (September 1989): 42–44.

39. Quoted in Long, *The Problem of Waste Disposal*, 17. See also Tillman, Rossi, and Vick, *Incineration of Municipal and Hazardous Wastes*, ix; Marinelli and Robinson, "No Room at the Bin," 26.

40. Melosi, *Garbage in the Cities*, 222; Melosi, *Coping with Abundance* (New York, 1985), 91–97, 185–89; Suellen M. Hoy and Michael C. Robinson, *Recovering the Past: A Handbook of Community Recycling Programs, 1890–1945* (Chicago, 1979), 4, 8–10, 15–19, 22.

41. Seldman, "Waste Management," 43–44. See also Schwab, "Garbage In, Garbage Out," 9; T. Randall Curlee, "Plastics Recycling: Economic and Institutional Issues," *Conservation and Recycling* 9 (1986): 335–50; EPA, *Recycling Works!* (Washington, D.C., January 1989); Nicholas Basta, "A Renaissance in Recycling," *High Technology* 5 (October 1985): 32–39; Barbara Goldoftas, "Recycling: Coming of Age," *Technology Review* (November–December 1987): 30–35, 71; Anne Magnuson, "Recycling Gains Ground," *American City & County/Resource Recovery* (1988), RR10. Recycling is already a major component of waste programs in Europe and Japan. In fact, the Japanese are the world's leader in the field. See Hershkowitz, "Burning Trash," 28.

42. "Municipal Solid Waste Management," 6.

43. See NSWMA, "Solid Waste Disposal Overview" (1988), 2; Cynthia Pollock, "There's Gold in Garbage," *Across the Board* (March 1987), 37; "Municipal Solid Waste Management," 7; "Newark Claims East Coasts' Largest Recycling Program," *World Wastes* 31 (December 1988): 47–49.

44. *Waste minimization* is a broader term than *waste reduction*. It appears in the 1984 amendments to the Resource Conservation and Recovery Act of 1976 and includes waste reduction, recycling, and the treatment of wastes after they are generated. According to Kirsten U. Oldenburg and Joel S. Hirschhorn, "Waste minimization combines the concepts of both prevention and control and its goal is generally understood to be the avoidance of land disposal of hazardous wastes regulated under RCRA." See Oldenburg and Hirschhorn, "Waste Reduction: A New Strategy to Avoid Pollution," *Environment* 29 (March 1987): 17–20, 39–45.

Unlike the various disposal options, waste reduction and waste minimization are moving into relatively uncharted waters. In a society conditioned to deal with its waste problems from the "back end," "front-end" solutions go beyond technical fixes and management efficiencies toward lifestyle and behavioral changes. See Craig Colten, "Historical Development of Waste Minimization," *Environmental Professional* 11 (1989): 94–99; Masood Ghassemi, "Waste Reduction: An Overview," *Environmental Professional* 11 (1989): 100–116; EPA, "Waste Minimization: Environmental Quality with Economic Benefits" (Washington, D.C., October 1987).

45. "Garbage at the Crossroads," *Chicago Tribune*, 1 February 1984, 1.

46. James Cook, "Not in Anybody's Backyard," *Forbes*, 28 November 1988, 172.

47. The notion that refuse was a health hazard grew out of English studies in the mid-nineteenth century that linked communicable disease to filthy environmental conditions. This revelation led to the use of "environmental sanitation" to combat disease. After 1880 "contagionists" made great strides in convincing sanitarians and public health officials that many diseases had a bacteriological cause, and environmental sanitation, while still in practice, was subordinated to more modern epidemic-combatting practices. See Melosi, *Garbage in the Cities*, 12, 26–33, 80–84, 113–14, 153–55, 197–207.

48. E. S. Savas, "Intracity Competition Between Public and Private Service Delivery," *Public Administration Review* 41 (January–February 1981): 47–48.

49. APWA, *History of Public Works in the United States*, 446–47. See also Dennis Young, *How Shall We Collect the Garbage?* (Washington, D.C., 1972), 8; APWA *Solid Waste Collection Practice* (Chicago, 1975), 236–37; E. S. Savas, *The Organization and Efficiency of Solid Waste Collection* (Lexington, Mass., 1977), 43.

50. The cities in the study were: Camden, New Jersey; Middletown and Akron, Ohio; Pekin and Berwyn, Illinois; Kansas City, Missouri; Covington, Kentucky; Gainesville, Florida; and New Orleans and Oklahoma City.

51. Eileen Brettler Berenyi, "Contracting Out Refuse Collection: The Nature and Impact of Change," *Urban Interest* 3 (1981): 30–42. Municipal collection tended to predominate in the South during the 1970s, while franchise collection was much more common in the West. See Savas, "Solid Waste Collection in Metropolitan Areas," in Elinor Ostrom, ed., *The Delivery of Urban Services* (Beverly Hills, 1976), 211–13, 219–21, 228. The question of efficiency of private service has been tested in various studies. Several claimed that private collection is cheaper, although economies of scale play an important role. Small-scale systems of fewer than 1,000 pickup units have shown a diseconomy. See John N. Collins and Bryant T. Downes, "The Effect of Size on the Provision of Public Services: The Case of Solid Waste Collection in Smaller Cities," *Urban Affairs Quarterly* 12 (March 1977): 345. See also James T. Bennett and Manuel H. Johnson, "Public Versus Private Provision of Collective Goods and Services: Garbage Collection Revisited," *Public Choice* 34 (1979): 55–63; Franklin R. Edwards and Barbara J. Stevens, "The Provision of Municipal Sanitation Services by Private Firms," *Journal of Industrial Economics* 27 (December 1978): 144; Julia Marlow, "Private Versus Public Provision of Refuse Removal Service: Measures of Citizen Satisfaction," *Urban Affairs Quarterly* 20 (March 1985): 355–63; Michael R. Fitzgerald, "The Promise and Performance of Privatization: The Knoxville Experience," *Policy Studies Review* 5 (February 1986): 606–12.

52. NSWMA, "Privatizing Municipal Waste Services: Saving Dollars and Making Sense" (1988), 1–5. See also "Landfill Capacity in the U.S.: How Much Do We Really Have?" (18 October 1988), 5; Joseph Hagerty, Joseph Pavoni, and John Heer, Jr., *Solid Waste Management* (New York, 1973), 17.

53. John Vickers and George Yarrow, *Privatization: An Economic Analysis* (Cambridge, Mass., 1988), 41. See also Charles G. Burck, "There's Big Business in All That Garbage," *Fortune*, 7 April 1980, 106–12; "An Overwhelming Problem Offers Business Opportunities," *Chemical Week*, 27 July 1988, 22–26; Nancy Shute, "The Selling of Waste Management," *Amicus Journal* 7 (Summer 1985): 8–17; Janet Novack, "A New Top Broom," *Forbes*, 28 November 1988, 200, 202; Harold Gershowitz, "Managing Solid Waste in Future Societies," *American City and County* 104 (September 1989): 44, 46.

54. Bill Wolpin and Lourdes Dumke, "Former EPA Administrator: Regs Will Move Industry," *World Wastes* 32 (May 1989): 36.

55. EPA, "The Solid Waste Dilemma: An Agenda for Action" (February 1989), 2. See also EPA, "Decision-Makers Guide to Solid Waste Management" (November 1989); NSWMA, "Landfill Capacity in the Year 2000," 2–3.

56. Frank P. Grad, "The Role of the Federal and State Governments," in Savas, *Organization and Efficiency of Solid Waste Collection*, 169.

57. See William E. Small, *Third Pollution: The National Problem of Solid Waste Disposal* (New York, 1970).

58. Melosi, "Waste Management," 7. See also Grad, "The Role of the Federal and State Governments," 169–70; APWA, *History of Public Works in the United States*, 453; Peter S. Menell, "Beyond the Throwaway Society: An Incentive Approach to Regulating Municipal Solid Waste," *Ecology Law Quarterly* 17 (1990): 671. The act authorized more than $60 million for the program during a four-year period for the Department of Health, Education, and Welfare, and more than $32 million for the Bureau of Mines. The amounts actually appropriated were somewhat less. See Stanley E. Degler, *Federal Pollution Control Programs* (Washington, D.C., 1971), 37.

59. Melosi, "Waste Management," 7. See also APWA, *Municipal Refuse Disposal*, 346–47.

60. Melosi, "Waste Management," 7; Degler, *Federal Pollution Control Programs*, 37–38.

61. Grad, "The Role of the Federal and State Governments," 169–83; William L.

Kovacs, "Legislation and Involved Agencies," in William D. Robinson, ed., *The Solid Waste Handbook* (New York, 1986), 9; Berry and Horton, *Urban Environmental Management*, 361–62. States have a variety of functions relative to solid waste that may not be handled effectively on the federal level, such as permitting of landfills, monitoring of incinerators, and dealing with various resource-recovery issues. For example, see Jeffrey B. Wagenbach, "The Bottle Bill: Progress and Prospects," *Syracuse Law Review* 36 (1985): 759–97.

62. Kovacs, "Legislation and Involved Agencies," 10, 12–18. See also Erwin and Healy, *Packaging and Solid Waste*, 80; EPA, "Report to Congress: Solid Waste Disposal in the United States, Executive Summary" (October 1988). It should be noted that, as of the mid-1980s, air pollution from nonhazardous waste incineration is regulated only if the waste originates from municipal sources. Nonhazardous waste incinerated by industry is not regulated by the federal government except for provisions of the National Ambient Air Quality Standards. See Calvin R. Brunner, *Incineration Systems* (New York, 1984), 16.

63. See Menell, "Beyond the Throwaway Society," 671–72.

64. Melosi, "Waste Management," 7–8; Office of Technology Assessment, *Facing America's Trash*, 299; *The Environment Index, 1973*, 8.

65. Dombrowski, "Reilly Predicts More Regs and Higher Disposal Costs," 39. See also EPA, "Solid Waste Dilemma: An Agenda for Action," 8–11.

66. Kovacs, "Legislation and Involved Agencies," 19.

67. Menell, "Beyond the Throwaway Society," 674.

HAROLD L. PLATT

World War I and the Birth of American Regionalism

Soon after American entry into World War I, Colonel Charles Keller of the Army Corps of Engineers confronted an emergency on the home front that threatened to stymie victory abroad. For several years, the West Point career officer had been in charge of overseeing the development of hydroelectric power at Niagara Falls, New York. Now Keller began receiving urgent messages from manufacturers in nearby Buffalo complaining that shortages of electricity were preventing them from producing vital materials such as high-grade steel for shell casings, aluminum for airplanes, chlorine for poison gas, and other electrochemicals.

The assistant to the Chief Engineer applied his considerable expertise to meeting this critical demand for more energy, but the situation only grew worse. Icy conditions during the unusually harsh winter of 1917–18 cut the flow of power to only twenty percent of normal, while a severe coal famine thwarted plans to use alternative steam generators in the local area. Keller faced similar frustrations in adding new supplies of electricity. Generator equipment took years to build, and high interest rates precluded even stopgap measures to construct transmission lines to Buffalo's factories from other utility companies with greater reserve capacity. Army Corps engineers faced similar defeats throughout the industrial heartland in meeting the power needs of a nation at war. Electric shortages reduced production levels from New England to Ohio and all the way to Alabama. In his final report, the engineer had to admit that "notwithstanding the organization and work of the power section the country was still, practically a year and a half after the declaration of war, unable to proceed to the execution of a comprehensive program for taking care of our ascertained power needs of the near future."[1]

Across town from Keller's office, another group of war managers was fighting the battle of the home front with much greater success. The government needed to build ships at an unprecedented rate. But planners soon learned that it was difficult to keep workers on the job when they could not find decent housing. Unlike the career officers of the Army Corps, the volunteers involved in building these accommodations represented a diverse mix of housing reformers, architects, city planners, and developers. For them, the war suddenly offered a unique opportunity to put untested theories into practice. Almost overnight, blueprints were lifted off drawing tables to become living communities complete with up to two thousand inhabitants. "For the first time," according to a recent assessment of this extraordinary experience, "professionals and large building firms were enabled to try out the principles of industrialized construction, scientific planning, and centralized management with mass housing." Before the armistice of November 1918 brought the program to an abrupt end, the Emergency Fleet Corporation and the U.S. Housing Corporation had completed fifty-five projects with accommodations for nearly one hundred thousand people.[2]

The unparalleled strains and opportunities presented by World War I affected not only government administrators in Washington but the entire population of the nation's industrial cities. In a land of plenty, critical shortages suddenly appeared that threatened the very survival of urban America, especially during the fearsome winter of 1917–18. For the first time, city dwellers confronted terrifying famines of food and fuel, exacerbated by a virtual gridlock of the nation's transportation system. By January 1918 the breakdown of the war machine became so severe that President Woodrow Wilson had to order a complete shutdown of all business and trade east of the Mississippi River in a desperate effort to clear clogged railroad tracks.[3] For city officials, municipal engineers, factory owners, shop-floor supervisors, business managers, and other decision-makers, there was no escape from the battle of the home front. Although Wilson's emergency measure was temporary, the impact of the war at home continued to upset the normal routines of urban America. Besides suffering periodic shortages of coal and food for the next two years, the cities were hammered by a series of sharp blows, including the worst epidemic in modern history, labor violence, race riots, and public hysteria in the form of a government-promoted "red scare."[4]

Historians of the postwar period, however, have all but ignored the subject of society at war as a causal factor in the formation of public policy. World War I is our "forgotten war" in terms of social and intellectual history. For the most part, scholars have striven to discount and to explain away the upheaval in government and society as a temporary glitch, quickly passed over in the rush to return to "normalcy."[5] A failure to take account of the war and its battle of the home front in the lives of the postwar generation of planners is representative of this historiographical problem. While a fairly vast literature on city and regional planning has accumulated, it has been treated almost entirely as an intellectual enterprise, consisting of a logical and progressive evolution of ideas over time. In these accounts, the war and the 1920s are usually treated as a dull period of transition between the creativity of the Progressive Era and the excitement of the New Deal. Only a few suggestive essays have attempted to place the sources of the planners' thoughts within a context of their personal and professional lives.[6]

Equally important perhaps, this lack of attention to the social history of city planners has meant that the technology available to them has not been given the importance it deserves as a source of influence in the formation of public policy. As urban historian Blaine Brownell contends, "The impact of and responses to technology have all too often been considered apart from the larger intellectual and socio-economic setting, giving a much simpler and more linear process than is justified."[7] The end result of such a narrow intellectual focus is a distorted interpretation of historical causation. In the case of the origins of regional planning, a study that encompasses not only the life of the mind but also the social experience of the war managers and the influence of technology on their decision-making provides a better approach.[8]

Applying this type of inclusive conceptual framework to the post–World War I period, Brownell shows how the insecurities of the planning profession led to a narrowing of career goals. From the prewar authors of grand visions, such as Daniel Burnham's 1909 plan of Chicago, the planners of the 1920s tended to become technocrats with special skills in highway building, traffic management, and zoning regulation. Burnham's own son and other would-be regional planners sought to establish their occupational credentials by forswearing a role as social reformers and focusing instead on the practical mission of accommodating the automobile to the suburban sprawl of the metropolis. In their search for professional identity, these experts learned how to please their conservative clients, the "commercial-civic groups [that] endlessly repeated the necessity for efficient urban transportation."[9] In short, after the war the planners put technology to self-serving ends in order to gain professional recognition and personal profit. A reexamination of society at war using Brownell's broad interpretative framework helps explain this turn to technology and its crucial role in widening the scope of planning ideas from city to regional proportions.

Rather than an evolutionary process, World War I was pivotal in focusing attention on technology as a powerful tool in the realization of planning goals. To be sure, each war manager started with preconceived notions of how best to handle the tasks of raising an army and producing the munitions, supplies, and transport to get it to the battlefront in Europe. But the war at home soon became an incredibly intense learning experience that shattered existing beliefs and generated new perspectives. In spite of the sharp contrast in the wartime roles of the house builders and the power engineers, for example, both were especially influenced by the electric power grid as a graphic technological metaphor of regional integration and its social benefits. Electricity was already a well-established cultural icon of high technology; the war would make it the supreme symbol of the Machine Age.

Ever since Chicago's Columbian Exposition of 1893, Americans had associated this technology with notions of modernity, democratic values, class status, and conspicuous consumption. The war taught the practical lesson of how to translate these popular images of progress into the construction of an energy-intensive society. Keller, for example, came away from the emergency as an apostle of "interconnection," leading to the creation of "superpower" systems. For the engineer's counterparts in the housing department, the regional power grid also offered a technological model for planning the future.[10]

The policy implications of the two positions pointed in opposite directions, but, at the same time, both planning concepts rested upon a common base of assumptions and objectives. Both contained a mix of elitist and democratic impulses, realism and idealism, and both relied heavily on technology, especially automobiles and electricity, to achieve the goal of urban deconcentration. This common ground complicates the task of giving the two ideological camps neutral labels. For purposes here, members of the first camp will be called "physical planners" since they worked to facilitate the suburban thrust of the city to metropolitan proportions. This group corresponds closely to the technocrats identified by Brownell as career-oriented men in search of professional recognition. In a similar way, advocates of the second position will be called "community planners" since they sought to create a new type of human ecology, a harmonious balance between the natural environment and modern society. Forming the Regional Planning Association of America (RPAA) in 1923, these reformers would remain on the margins of public-policy formation during the Republican ascendancy of the postwar decade. With the election of Franklin D. Roosevelt in 1932, however, their lonely voices of protest would finally find a sympathetic audience.[11]

To understand how the war amplified the importance of technology in the formation of public policy during the 1920s, a brief review of the debate over urban planning on the eve of the conflict is necessary. Chicago provides a logical point to survey this hotly contested terrain because it was the preeminent national center of reform leadership and city building innovation. The fastest growing city in the world, Chicago had been forced to develop long-range plans just to keep pace with a population that had increased from three hundred thousand at the time of the Great Fire of 1871 to 1.7 million inhabitants at the turn of the century. Civic leaders learned to rely on the expert advice of engineers to build the necessary infrastructure of a modern "networked city." In 1889 the construction of a sanitation system on a metropolitan scale epitomized the emergence of the city engineers as key players in the formation of public policy.

Architects were a second group of urban planners to rise from the ashes of the fire. Daniel Burnham's role as the chief designer of the world's fair of 1893, a futuristic "Dream City," not only represented Chicago's coming of age but also established the profession's claim to influence in the decision-making process. Burnham's great 1909 plan of Chicago would strongly reinforce the authority of the architects as planners.[12]

By the time of the fair, social reformers too were becoming an important voice in the debate over the future of the city. Jane Addams and other settlement-house workers promoted social environmentalism, or the belief that improvements in the physical conditions of the city would ameliorate human suffering while promoting good citizenship. For example, Addams focused attention on the need for housing reform to alleviate the social problems of the immigrant working classes. Burnham shared her conviction that the "City Beautiful" would help restore a sense of community in the modern metropolis, and both engaged in a transatlantic conversation on planning policies to achieve this ideal. Most influential on the social reformers perhaps was the organicism of Ebenezer Howard and Patrick Geddes. The Englishmen's proposals for garden cities surrounded by green belts were compared with other planning initiatives, including public housing projects in several German cities.[13]

The ferment of reform in urban planning during the Progressive Era was fueled in part by a new mastery of city building. Recent breakthroughs in technology armed would-be planners with powerful new tools, especially structural steel and glass, electric light and power, trolley cars and automobiles, and telephones. Chicago made such an indelible impression on a generation of Americans at the time of the world's fair in large measure because it offered so much promise. The downtown skyscrapers and the dazzling displays of electricity at the fair suggested that planning and technology could create any type of built environment one desired. For Burnham, this promise was embodied in the neoclassical motifs of the "White City"; for many others, including Frank Lloyd Wright, it took the form of a suburban ideal. The new technologies encouraged these outlying areas to build their own modern infrastructure, encouraging governmental fragmentation and social segregation.[14]

By 1914 planners in Chicago had reached a consensus that their field encompassed a metropolitan expanse of territory, but they agreed on little else. After twenty-five years of intense debate, a large number of players still fought over the ideal vision of the city, as well as which professional group—the engineers, architects, or social reformers—should have priority in the formation of public policy.

In addition to leadership in planning theory before the Great War, Chicago offered a second type of initiative in the field of high technology. Under the direction of a businessman, Samuel Insull, the city became the location of the world's first prototype of a regional network of power. Covering more than 4,300 square miles, this early form of a superpower system had been taking shape for over a decade under the corporate banner of the Public Service Company of Northern Illinois (PSCNI). Whether or not the Chicago area was actually first was less important perhaps than the persistent claims by its creator to such a distinction.[15] And there is no question that Insull's leadership of the electric utility industry after the turn of the century helped this master of self-promotion to foster such a belief in the minds of contemporaries. A brief description of the system that Insull built deserves attention because it provided a practical demonstration of the technical feasibility of a regional power system as America entered the war. Together with Insull's exceptional success in fighting the battle of the home front and his tireless campaign against alternative, self-contained technological solutions to industry's demand for more energy, the example of the Chicago region exerted a persuasive influence on the physical and community planners alike.

In the decade leading up to American entry into the war, Insull had begun turning from earlier efforts to consolidate a monopoly of the electric supply within the city to securing a similar hold on the surrounding metropolitan area. The recent technical triumph of the large-scale turbogenerator at his innovative Fisk Street Station and the financial guarantees contained in lucrative street railway contracts had freed the

Table 1. Population Growth of Chicago and Its Suburbs, 1890–1930

Year	Chicago		Suburban Cook County		Lake County	
1890						
Population	1,099,850		92,072		24,235	
1900						
Population	1,698,575		140,160		34,504	
Increase	598,725		48,088		10,269	
Percent gain		54.4%		52.2%		42.4%
1910						
Population	2,185,283		219,950		55,058	
Increase	486,708		79,790		20,554	
Percent gain		28.6%		56.9%		59.6%
1920						
Population	2,701,705		351,312		74,285	
Increase	516,422		131,362		19,227	
Percent gain		23.6%		59.7%		34.9%
1930						
Population	3,376,438		605,685		104,387	
Increase	674,733		254,373		30,102	
Percent gain		25.0%		72.4%		40.5%

Sources: U.S. Census-Population, 1890, 1900, 1910, 1920, 1930.

chief of the Commonwealth Edison Company to focus on Chicago's fast-growing suburbs (see Table 1). In 1908 Insull had made the first interconnection between the city and the affluent North Shore, initiating a rapid process of building a sprawling metropolitan web of power (see Fig. 1). Three years later, moreover, he had built the nation's first working model of rural electrification. Although keeping pace with the rapid growth of the suburbs restricted this pioneering effort to an isolated experiment for another twenty years, its promise of profits fed Insull's virtually boundless ambition.[16]

In 1911 the utility czar formed the PSCNI in order bring the water-power resources of the Illinois River Valley under his control. To be sure, the flat topography that characterizes the Midwest did not offer much potential for hydroelectric development. Beginning in the 1890s, however, local entrepreneurs in river towns such as Joliet and Kankakee had great success in converting gristmills into power plants. Insull was quick to realize that this technology supplied a source of energy cheaper than even his biggest, most efficient coal-burning steam generators. He began to invest heavily in these water-power sites, eventually bringing them into his holding company, the PSCNI. Two other key aspects of this

Fig. 1. Power Grid of the Public Service Company of Northern Illinois, 1912.

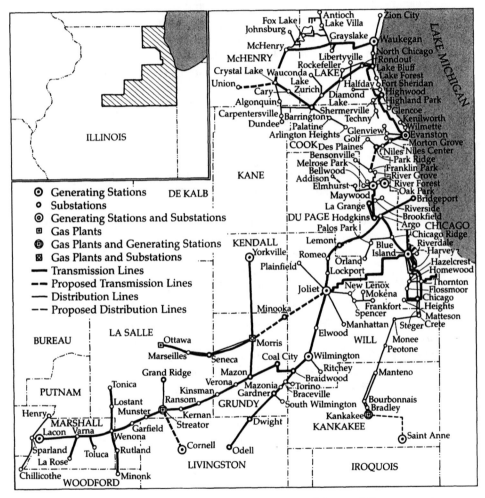

Source: Public Service Company of Northern Illinois, *Annual Report*, 1912, as reprinted in Harold L. Platt, *The Electric City: Energy and the Growth of the Chicago Area, 1880–1930* (Chicago, 1991), 185.

grand strategy were long-term cost-plus contracts with the Peabody Coal Company to purchase immense reserves of fuel in southern Illinois and Indiana, and ownership of a railroad to ensure against disruptions in supply. Through these now-classic maneuvers of horizontal and vertical integration applied to the utility industry, Insull assembled the pieces of a unified network of power on a regional scale.[17]

As the storm clouds of war gathered over Europe in 1914, Insull was well positioned to meet the coming crisis. During the nearly three-year interval between the outbreak of hostilities and U.S. entry into the conflict, his contacts abroad put the English immigrant in the forefront of the preparedness campaign. Insull mounted a publicity offensive to "buy and store" fuel in spite of fast-rising prices. But few coal dealers or factory managers heeded this prophetic advice until it was too late. No major industrial city seemed more able to supply energy consumers with as much fuel as they could possibly want. Chicago's geographic location made the central city of the Midwest not only the rail hub of the nation but also a thriving inland port with maritime shipping routes to eastern coal fields as well as to downstate mines. If past experience guided the city's captains of industry, it pointed clearly to an unbroken record of chronic glut and depressed prices in local fuel markets.[18]

Yet even Chicago's strategic site and unsurpassed transportation facilities did not exclude it from the energy crisis of World War I. The city consumed 30 million tons of coal a year. At least two thousand railroad cars a day full of the fuel were required to keep its factories running, buildings warm, and utilities operating. In addition to the city's electric stations, water works, and street railways, its gasworks used coal (and petroleum) to manufacture the lighting and cooking fuel. As the winter weather and the mismanagement of the railroads conspired to interrupt the city's energy supplies, only Insull and his massive stockpile of coal were ready to meet the emergency. His foresight would be rewarded by an appointment to the chairmanship of the prestigious Illinois State Council of Defense. But even Insull could not save the city. In mid-December the steel mills began to shut down for a lack of fuel, the schools were closed, and the city's lights were darkened in accord with orders from U.S. Fuel Administrator Harry Garfield. By the end of the year, the government had taken control of the railroads, but blizzards, called the "worst in the city's history," brought Chicago to a complete standstill. For the next two weeks the war at home became a grim struggle for survival. City and suburban residents suffered without any renewal of fuel and food supplies. While the death toll from exposure mounted daily, more and more workers were forced into idleness. On the eve of the president's Draconian order, 17 January 1918, to stop the war machine for five days, 150,000 factory hands, almost half of the total, had already been forced out of work by the coal famine.[19]

For factory managers in Chicago, this crisis was a convincing demonstration of the value of central station service. Their counterparts in other industrial centers had similar experiences, and they drew similar conclusions that collectively resulted in a second industrial revolution during the postwar decade. Shops using Insull's central station service to run their machinery escaped the energy crisis, but they accounted for less than 20 percent of the primary power used by Chicago industry. Most, especially the bigger plants, relied on their own coal-burning steam engines to drive machines and/or self-contained electric generators for light and motor power. The war forced industrial policymakers to give serious consideration to questions about the reliability of power supplies and the fuel efficiency of equipment for the first time. What a quarter century of agitation by Insull and other central station operators against the "isolated [power] plant" failed to accomplish, the unprecedented coal shortages of World War I achieved with remarkable speed. During the conflict, the abandonment of these self-contained systems became a patriotic duty to conserve fuel. Afterward, industry's conversion to central station service would become a stampede, whipped along by a cultural fascination with high technology, efficiency, scientific management, and the perfection of assembly-line methods of mass-production, popularly known as "Fordism."[20]

The war played a similar role in sharply reorienting policymakers in Washington toward technological approaches to problem solving. A closer look at the wartime efforts of Keller and his fellow power engineers illustrates how this turn to technology brought about the crystallization of regional concepts among the physical planners. Confessing that "we were taken by surprise by the [power] shortages," they suddenly faced mounting levels of stress on the networked infrastructure of an urban-industrial economy. Demand on the nation's transportation, energy, and food distribution systems soared far beyond any previously imaged. For them, the war became a cram course in learning how to reorganize the complex parts of a badly overloaded infrastructure in order to meet industry's skyrocketing need for more energy. In tracing the roots of the problem of increasing the supply of electricity, the engineers found that they had to start with natural resources—coal and flowing water—in the hinterland surrounding each industrial center. Pressing needs to coordinate the use of these ultimate sources of energy forced them to draw new links between technology, the environment, and long-term planning. Available hardware in the form of high-voltage transmission lines pointed unmistakably toward regional areas, or "natural power districts," as the most efficient geographical units for the reorganization of the electric supply.[21]

For the physical planners, the rapid shift of industry to mechanization and electrification added a special urgency to prepare realistic proposals to meet the swelling demand of the cities for more energy. Insull's sprawling, regional system of large-scale steam- and water-powered generating stations interconnected by high-voltage transmission lines offered an appealing model to emulate. Chicago, for example, was the only major industrial center conspicuously absent from the Army Corps' report on electric power shortages. In addition, the peculiar technological characteristics of the turbogenerator produced significant economies of scale in terms of fuel consumption, capitalization, and final costs to utility customers. An overloaded transportation system also pointed planners toward the development of hydroelectric sites and the construction of new power plants at the mouths of the coal mines as the best means of strengthening the technological relationship between natural resources and energy consumers. From the shop floors of the factories to the offices of the federal government, the battle of the home front became a formative experience, replacing older patterns of thought with new environmental perspectives on a regional scale. As one electrical engineer put it in the midst of the struggle, "The opportunity and necessity for doing things on a grand scale are upon us. This problem of power supply is a thing so big and important, not only for our war program but for the future economic life of the country, that no petty obstacles of inertia or personal prejudice or corporate caution should be permitted to stand in its way."[22]

The reorientation of the engineers' geographical perspectives toward regional concepts of planning had several major policy implications. Environmental considerations suggested the centralization of the nation's electric supply into ten huge integrated systems. To create these regional networks of power, the Army Corps engineers suggested, would require a complete overhaul of the laws governing the utility business as well as the administrative apparatus for regulating it. A federal system of state utility commissions was clearly incompatible with a technology based in the natural resources of the region. Calling for reforms to exempt utility companies from antitrust laws, Keller looked to the Fuel Administration and other wartime agencies as ideal models of government-business relations. In addition, he called for experts like himself to be put in central decision-making roles as planners in the proposed regulatory commissions: "They should include trained engineers and men experienced in the electric-power business," Keller quoted a subordinate with approval, "who will appreciate the saving that can be made by building up big power systems that will supplant wasteful and costly isolated plants with superior service and with powers to coordinate electric-power with river improvements, flood control, and irrigation works." It did not take Keller long to realize that such self-serving ends would not be forthcoming under the Republican administration of President Warren G. Harding. Two years after issuing his report, he resigned his commission, moved to Chicago, and joined the Byllesby Engineering and Management Corporation, where he became a consultant to electric utility companies.[23]

In 1919 the birth of regional concepts of planning was plainly evident at the annual meeting of the National Conference on City Planning (NCCP). For the first time in its ten-year existence, the organization devoted an entire session to the topic of regional planning. Perhaps holding the meeting at Niagara Falls helped to focus attention on the links between urban technology and the natural environment. In any case, this dramatic international site of hydroelectric development provided a platform for Thomas Adams, an English pioneer of suburban planning who had recently become an adviser to the Canadian government. "Recent events throughout the world," he stated,

> have shown the extent to which the town and the country are interdependent. Recent tendencies in industrial decentralization have also shown the importance of one of the modern aspects of town planning, namely, the direction and control of the growth taking place within the rural and semi-rural districts where new industries are being established. The artificial [political] boundaries of cities are becoming more and more meaningless. The real controlling factors are physical and natural to a greater extent than they are administrative and artificial.[24]

Adams reiterated his call for regional surveys or inventories of the natural, industrial, and demographic resources of large geographical areas. More important, the planner broke new ground by outlining the principal dimensions of policy-making that could control the direction of suburbanization. Setting the agenda of physical planning for a generation, Adams listed zoning and other land-use regulations, transportation, power supplies, water management, and "general amenities" such as parks and recreational facilities.[25]

Significantly, an engineer delivered a second complementary paper. Morris Knowles of Pittsburgh believed that regional planning had been recently "born in the efforts of neighboring towns to cooperate in the solution of their joint engineering and utility problems." He echoed Adams's appeal for a shift in the planning profession from the romantic idealism of the prewar, city-beautiful movement to a more technical focus on practical problem solving under the direction of experts like himself. Besides making self-serving statements, Knowles revealed how the war at home gave him a regional perspective. The wartime disaster of the railroads and coal famines, he asserted, could only be avoided in the future through the consideration of transportation and energy planning. Drawing new connections between technology and the environment, Knowles argued that "the study of electrification must be continued with the elimination of noise and dirt in our cities, and the general power program for the region in [which] the railroad is located," including a much more extensive development of electric-powered interurban transit lines.[26]

The secretary of the Niagara Falls Chamber of Commerce, W. J. Donald, rounded out the session in a third paper, devoted to setting an agenda of civic efforts on behalf of regional planning. Donald called upon fellow city boosters to appreciate the value of professional planners and engineers in fueling urban growth and in raising property values. He suggested that together, experts and boosters could mount irresistible propaganda campaigns to influence elected officials and the public at large.[27] Over the next few years, many localities followed his suggestion to institute planning commissions composed of businessmen, engineers, and professional planners. The formation of the Los Angeles Regional Planning Commission in 1922 became a model that was widely copied elsewhere. In Chicago, for instance, Graham Taylor of the City Club sponsored the creation of a similar body after attending the preliminary conference in Los Angeles that led to the creation of its innovative agency. The following year, Taylor helped establish the Chicago Regional Planning Association with Daniel Burnham, Jr., at its head. And in New York, Tom Adams would continue his national leadership of the physical planners by taking charge of the Russell Sage Foundation's well-financed regional planning project. Four years later in 1927, the NCCP could report with a great sense of self-satisfaction the existence of city and regional planning commissions in 390 American cities.[28]

In the immediate postwar period, the promotion of Insull-style "superpower" systems percolated from professional circles to the highest levels of the federal government. His sprawling network of power provided an appealing technological metaphor of urban deconcentration and regional integration. For would-be planners, utility industry leaders, and city boosters, "superpower" offered a ready-made model of the city of tomorrow, a modern metropolis of high technology and energy flowing smoothly throughout the region.

Engineers in and out of government took the lead in translating the lessons of the war into public policies that opened the way for investor-owned utilities to create regional power systems. Seeking to establish the legitimacy of these monopolistic schemes at the highest level, professional associations tied to the utility industry lobbied Washington to sponsor a "Superpower Survey" of the eastern seaboard. William S. Murray and Henry Flood, Jr., consulting engineers from New York City, represented the American Institute of Electrical Engineers and the American Institute of Mining and Metallurgical Engineers. In early 1920, they spearheaded the lobby drive, along with fellow association member George Otis Smith of the U.S. Geological Survey, who had been one of the earliest wartime advocates of the interconnection of hydroelectric and coal-burning stations into integrated power systems. Together, the engineers persuaded Secretary of Interior Franklin Lane to seek approval of a congressional appropriation to pay for the study and to appoint Murray to head it. A year and a half later, the report marshaled a mass of technical data in support of a regional plan. Representing an official endorsement of the superpower concept, the federal government gave sanction to permissive policies by state utility commissions.[29]

While jurisdiction over the consolidation movement of the utility companies rested with the states, related efforts to exploit hydroelectric sites demanded more direct federal action. Since the turn of the century, the battle over the nation's waterways had been locked in a stalemate between the utilities and the conservationists. The war, however, marked a turning point in this long-running controversy. The utilities used the imperatives of technological efficiency to hammer home the lessons of the war with telling effect. Less than a month after the Armistice was signed, Henry I. Harriman, president of New England Power Company, argued that

> the time is now more than ever ripe for the passage of legislation by Congress which will permit the development of water power on public land and on navigable streams. The importance of such legislation as a real conservation measure is not easily exaggerated. . . . Efficiency[,] engineering and research should be given the utmost support; fuel economy should be continued and increased and interconnection of electric systems favored wherever commercial considerations warrant this policy.[30]

When a water-power bill was introduced in 1918, the coal shortages allowed the friends of the utilities to strip the measure of its environmental protection features. The final Water Power Act of 1920, according to historian Samuel Hays, "marked the end of the conservation era." The resulting Federal Power Commission was a regulatory agency designed to fail. With a single employee, it quickly became a rubber stamp for the utility industry.[31]

Over the next few years, the electric industry used the logic of the large-scale technological system to promote the idea of regional planning with great success. In October 1923, for example, Secretary of Commerce Herbert Hoover endorsed this vision of the future by hosting a national superpower conference. This wartime hero of humanitarian aid and voluntary service as the U.S. Food Administrator called upon public officials, especially state utility regulators, to work out appropriate policy guidelines to encourage this type of development. The "Great Engineer" looked forward to the imminent dawning of

> a new era . . . of great areas of cheaper power . . . [by] the construction of great power highways traversing several states into which we should pour great streams [of electricity] at high voltages from great giant water-power or central steam stations to be distributed to the public utilities and other large users along the lines of these great power streams. This, indeed, serves perhaps to picture what is meant by superpower development.

At the same time, Hoover rejected proposals for any type of national or interstate "superregulation." On the contrary, he called for voluntary cooperation among states agencies that would group together into several regional areas as defined by their natural resources.[32]

The following year, Hoover helped popularize the policy implications of the superpower concept by addressing a national audience of five million people on the radio. The Insull-dominated National Electric Light Association (NELA), composed of central station operators, sponsored the Secretary of Commerce's speech. He drew a direct analogy between the interconnection of the power grid and the network of radio stations that carried his message to thirty states. Calling electricity "the greatest tool that has ever come into the hands of man," and evoking the deified image of Thomas Edison, Hoover promised that superpower would bring a "higher standard of living, [and] wider enjoyment and comfort to every fireside." To achieve this technological vision of progress, he reiterated his position in favor of public policies that gave private utility companies an open-ended opportunity to consolidate monopolistic control of regional areas. To the delight of the utility industry, the Secretary of Commerce went further, attacking those who proposed alternative plans for similar regional networks of power but under government ownership and control. Hoover rejected these critics' warnings that his policy proposals would encourage a "gigantic and grinding trust [to form] in the background." Instead, he told the American people to have faith in organizations like the NELA to put the public interest ahead of private gain.[33] With assurances from men like Hoover, most Americans put aside traditional anxieties about the growth of such huge and powerful monopolies and joined in the march toward the creation of a consumer-oriented, energy-intensive society.

In large part, the triumph of the physical planners in achieving professional legitimacy rested on their ability to master the technological underpinnings of America's deep-seated suburban ethos. While Brownell and other scholars have examined the role of the automobile in the realization of this cultural idea, the equally crucial part played by electricity has received much less attention. In the postwar period, the spread of metropolitan webs of power became a prerequisite to the outward thrust of people and modern, mechanized factories to the "crabgrass frontier." To lift suburban life to a level of amenity on a par with the city, central station service not only brought electricity directly into shops, homes, and factories, but it powered a wide range of other essential components of an urban infrastructure as well. For example, electricity was required to pump water, gas, and sewage in these areas of low density. Suburbanites also depended on interurban railroads, telephones, and telegraphs to connect their communities to the urban core. In short, a more intense use of energy in the form of electricity and gas-guzzling vehicles opened the suburbs to the American middle class at a price it could afford to pay.[34]

Hoover's reference to the policy option of public power on a regional scale—called "giant power" by its advocates—gave recognition to the attractive appeal of an alternative, suburban vision of progress through technology. In Washington, the fight for regional planning based on electrification revolved around the disposition of the federal government's power plant and nitrate factory at Muscle Shoals, Alabama. During the Twenties, this by-product of the war's power shortage became the cause célèbre of the champions of the public ownership of the country's hydroelectric facilities. Eventually, it would become the nucleus of the Tennessee Valley Authority (TVA) during the New Deal.[35] The noisy controversy over Muscle Shoals in the U.S. Congress gave hope to the members of the RPAA and other community planners. In 1925 the RPAA published a comprehensive report, a complete model of regionalism based on organic principles of ecology.[36] Like the physical planners, the wartime experiences of these community planners was also formative in giving birth to regional perspectives on the interplay of modern technology and the natural environment. And like their counterparts, the community planners looked to the automobile, highway, and electric power grid to bring about urban deconcentration. But for them, a technical mastery of technology never became an end in itself or the best way to achieve professional status. On the contrary, they envisioned modern technologies simply as tools, albeit extremely powerful ones, to achieve the goal of a dispersed pattern of human-scale settlements living in harmony with nature.

In the case of the community planners, the war brought a diverse group of reformers together to build housing, and out of that common enterprise came an enduring network of personal relationships. Other historians have discussed this extraordinary group of individuals, which included the forester and conservationist Benton MacKaye, developer Alexander M. Bing, economist Stuart Chase, editor Charles H. Whitaker of the *Journal of the American Institute of Architects,* and architects Robert D. Kohn, Clarence S. Stein, Frederick L. Ackerman, and Henry Wright. What is important here is to understand how the wartime experience of these men produced a new synergy of creative thought about technology and the environment. Most important was the successful demonstration of the garden city/green belt idea of Ebenezer Howard and Patrick Geddes. The success of the housing projects represented convincing proof of the Englishmen's theories of organicism and social environmentalism.[37]

The community builders emerged from the war transformed; they had gained confidence in themselves and their alternative vision of progress. As Whitaker would shortly exclaim, "It was the Whole Welfare which suddenly became illuminated in the red light of War! It must not be allowed to darken in the light of Peace." He called for a radical departure from the past because "city planning is only a bite at the cherry. . . . [I]t is useless to plan a certain territory or area such as a city, or rapidly growing town, unless there are corresponding plans for merging that territory with the surrounding areas." "Community planning," Whitaker explained, involved "planning on a larger scale," including extensive land-use controls to limit speculators' profits and environmental policies to achieve a balanced industrial economy.[38]

Waging the battle of the home front was pivotal not only in giving birth to novel concepts of planning but also in infusing Whitaker's group of friends with personal conviction in their cause. In 1919, for example,

Whitaker opened the pages of his architectural journal to Frederick Ackerman for the purpose of boldly denouncing the profession's drift toward self-serving definitions of the planner's job description. The contrast between Ackerman's fiery manifesto and the papers presented at the NCCP conference in Niagara Falls could not have been more complete. The architect urged his colleagues to turn away from the easy path of simply perpetuating the status quo, the "normal tendencies" of capitalism toward metropolitan sprawl. He accused the budding group of physical planners of reinforcing socially destructive principles that "represent the right of the individual to use the community as a machine for procuring individual profits and benefits, without regard to what happens to the community."[39]

Although the government liquidated the housing program after the armistice, the community planners remained in close touch as they moved back to New York City, including Whitaker and his important editorial office. In these early days of postwar adjustment, he played a key role in keeping them together, providing a platform for their opinions, and introducing new converts to the group. Most important, Whitaker brought Lewis Mumford into this circle of friends. The most prolific and reflective writer of the group, Mumford sheds light on the origins of the RPAA and its seminal report, the regional plan issue of the *Survey Graphic*. To avoid the draft, he had joined the Navy and served out the war at Harvard University, becoming a radio operator. Describing himself during this period as a "lonely" student of "cities and landscapes," his contact with journal editor Whitaker changed his life. "Gradually," Mumford, recalled, "I found myself drawn closer to a circle of professionally trained people who shared my interest in the entire human environment and sought not merely to conserve its visible beauties but to do justice to our fuller cultural potentialities in the planning and building of cities."[40]

Over the next few years, Mumford, Whitaker, and the others were especially impressed with the environmentalism of Benton MacKay and his plan for a national Appalachian trail. More than any other individual in the group, this conservationist and outdoorsman helped focus attention on the region as the natural geographical setting for the garden city. He also introduced the group to Robert W. Bruere, the final crucial intellectual ingredient in the making of the RPAA and its blueprint of regionalism. He added a technocratic point of view, although his background was in education, welfare reform, and industrial training. After the war, this experience won him a position as an associate editor of the social work magazine, *Survey Graphic*. An investigation of the problems in the coal fields led Bruere to become a strong champion of giant power and the conservation of natural resources. He and his wife, home economist Martha Bensley Bruere, believed that electric energy was a virtual "pandora's box" that would trigger a "second industrial revolution . . . [and permit] a healthier distribution of our people over the face of the country."[41] In Clarence Stein's Manhattan apartment and in MacKay-led expeditions to farm retreats in New Jersey, the RPAA collectively imaged a holistic vision of community life in a regional environmental setting. Mumford aptly described this creative process as "a kind of fusion that released energy and light."[42]

The resulting issue of *Survey Graphic* represents an incredibly rich and provocative anthology of essays on planning proposals to create a balance between technology and the environment. Reflecting on the massive dislocations caused by World War I, for example, Mumford argued that "in a period of flow, men have the opportunity to remold themselves and their institutions." Calling for a "fourth migration," he believed that a revolution in technology—automobile and highway, electric power and electronic communications—presented just such an opportunity to reverse settlement patterns from urban agglomeration to regional dispersal. To the RPAA, an alternative to the policy directions pursued by the physical planners was urgently needed to save the environment, the quality of modern life, and a sense of human community. "Even if there was no fourth migration on the horizon," Mumford exclaimed, "it would be necessary to invent one. It is at least a more fruitful hypothesis than any of those we are now blindly following!"[43]

While the community planners depended on modern machines to bring about their vision of regionalism, they were careful to warn policymakers to harness technology on behalf of social objectives. In "Giant Power-Region Builder," for instance, Bruere drew a sharp contrast between the use of Niagara Fall's cheap electricity on the two sides of the border. On the Canadian side, planners were successfully pursuing a coordinated social policy to disperse industry, revive small towns, and relieve rural life from its isolation and drudgery, especially for farm women. This use of technology, the social worker explained, was producing a new type of regional community that "combines within itself and its immediate rural environment the opportunities for a balanced city and country life, of diversified industry and indigenous culture." On the American side, the unchecked concentration of electrochemical industries was acting like "a huge suction pump . . . draw[ing] the life out of [the surrounding] communities and leav[ing] them gossip-rattling Main Street shells or mere suburban satellites." To Bruere and fellow members of the RPAA, modern technologies and planning techniques offered a tremendous potential to reshape the environment in ways beneficial to society. Ultimately, however, they were merely tools, dependent upon the political processes of policy formation that put them to use.[44]

In the mid- to late 1920s, the community planners remained on the fringes of American political power compared to the success of the physical planners, who moved into the mainstream of urban decision-making. Yet the RPAA and its alternative perspectives on regional planning maintained an influential presence at local, state, and national levels of government. With financial support from Alexander Bing, the community planners built a garden city at Radburn, New Jersey, as another demonstration of the practicality of their ideas. Its designers, Clarence Stein and Henry Wright, also received support from New York Governor Al Smith to prepare a comprehensive regional plan for the state. Published in 1926, the report's policy proposals represented a model study that placed top priority on environmental protection and community values. Smith's counterpart in the neighboring state of Pennsylvania, moreover, Benton MacKay's former mentor in the Forestry Service, Gifford Pinchot, was sponsoring a similar regional study, a "Giant Power Survey." And in the U.S. Senate, Frank Norris, Burton Wheeler, and other guardians of the Muscle Shoals hydroelectric station were shifting from a defensive posture to a more aggressive attack on the political and financial abuses of Sam Insull, the utility industry, and the "power trust." If nothing else, the community planners and their political allies made a decisive impression on Franklin D. Roosevelt, a country-life advocate, who would soon be handed an unparalleled political mandate to redirect public policy.

With a single exception, however, the return of the community planners to positions of power in Washington during another national emergency, the Great Depression, had a virtually negligible impact on American life. Nor were they able during their ascendancy to build a political constituency behind the creation of a national environmental policy. Major programs such as the TVA, the resettlement administration, the greenbelt/new towns, and the other regional planning proposals must be regarded as failures. Only the Rural Electrification Administration achieved a fair measure of immediate success in terms of improving the quality of life of a sizable number of people. And yet even this notable accomplishment proved ephemeral in the long run to stem the decline of the rural population and its economic base in family farming.[45]

Looking back on the missed opportunities of the New Deal, Mumford suggests that "regionalism must be made the cultural motive of regional planning, if it isn't to relapse into an arid technological scheme."[46] In the absence of a fundamental reorientation of American culture from consumer to community values, technology remained an end in itself rather than a means toward the achievement of social goals. The gap between the unprecedented political momentum behind FDR's campaign for social planning and its meager results gives some idea of just how difficult it will be to avoid an equally ineffectual, technological "fix" for our current environmental problems.

Loyola University of Chicago

Notes

1. Charles Keller, *The Power Situation During the War* (Washington, D.C., 1921), 19; see pp. 1–9 for an account of the problems at Buffalo. For biographical information, see "Charles Keller," *National Cyclopedia of American Biography* (New York, 1953), 38:99. See also James P. Johnson, "The Wilsonians as War Managers: Coal and the 1917–18 Winter Crisis," *Prologue* 9 (Winter 1977): 193–208.

2. Christian Topalov, "Scientific Urban Planning and the Ordering of Daily Life— The First 'War Housing' Experiment in the United States, 1917–1919," *Journal of Urban History* 17 (November 1990): 16; for a description of their work, see pp. 14–45. See also Roy Lubove, "Homes and 'A Few Well Placed Fruit Trees': An Object Lesson in Federal Housing," *Social Research* 27 (Winter 1960): 469–86; and Charles Harris Whitaker, *The Joke About Housing* (College Park, Md., 1969 [1920]), 17–25.

3. James P. Johnson, *The Politics of Soft Coal: The Bituminous Industry from World War I Through the New Deal* (Urbana, Ill., 1979), presents the most complete account of the Fuel Administration. Johnson's book is essential reading, full of insight on the policy implications of the war experience for the coal industry and the government's attempts to help it achieve stability. Cf. Robert C. Cuff, "Harry Garfield, the Fuel Administration, and the Search for a Cooperative Order During World War I," *American Quarterly* 30 (Spring 1978): 39–53, which is not particularly useful on the coal crisis but does provide good biographical information on Garfield.

4. For a general overview, see David M. Kennedy, *Over Here: The First World War and American Society* (New York, 1980). For special topics, see Alfred W. Crosby, Jr., *Epidemic and Peace, 1918* (Westport, Conn., 1976); William Tuttle, *Race Riot: Chicago in the Red Summer of 1919* (New York, 1970); and Robert K. Murray, *Red Scare: A Study in National Hysteria, 1919–1920* (Minneapolis, 1955).

5. I have attempted to examine this historiographical problem at length in Harold L. Pratt, *The Electric City: Energy and the Growth of the Chicago Area, 1880–1930* (Chicago, 1991), 201–8. For two standard interpretations, see Kennedy, *Over Here;* and Ellis Hawley, *The Great War and the Search for a Modern Order: A History of the American People and Their Institutions, 1917–1933* (New York, 1979). In the area of policy studies, the leading exponent of discounting the war's impact on society is Robert C. Cuff, *The War Industries Board: Business-Government Relations During World War I* (Baltimore, 1973). For a dissenting view, presented from a European perspective, see Neil A. Wynn, *From Progressivism to Prosperity: World War I and American Society* (New York, 1986). Cultural historians have also been sensitive to the pivotal nature of the war. See the brilliant essay by Modris Ekstein in *The Rites of Spring: The Great War and the Birth of the Modern Age* (Boston, 1989). Also consider Richard Guy Wilson, "America in the Machine Age," in *The Machine Age*, ed. Richard Guy Wilson, Dianne H. Pilgrim, and Dickran Tashjian (New York, 1968), 23–42.

6. Consult Anthony Sutcliffe, comp., *The History of Urban and Regional Planning: An Annotated Bibliography* (New York, 1981); and Eugenie Ladner Birch, "Design, Process, and Institutions: Planning in Urban History," in *American Urbanism: A Historiographical Review*, ed. Howard Gillette, Jr., and Zane Miller (Westport, Conn., 1987). For recent perspectives, see two review articles, Christopher Silver, "New Paths in City Planning History," *Journal of Urban History* 15 (May 1989): 337–51, and Patricia Burgess Stach, "Preparing for the Urban Future: The Theory and Practice of City Planning," *Journal of Urban History* 17 (February 1991): 207–13.

7. Blaine A. Brownell, "Urban Planning, the Planning Profession, and the Motor Vehicle in Early Twentieth-Century America," in *Shaping an Urban World: Planning in the Twentieth Century*, ed. Gordon E. Cherry (London, 1980), 60.

8. The argument here is not that historians have missed the connections between technology and the emergence of city planning. On the contrary, scholars have paid considerable attention to this topic. Recent studies that emphasize this relation include Eric H. Monkkonen, *America Becomes Urban* (Berkeley and Los Angeles, 1988); Stanley K. Schultz, *Constructing Urban Culture: American Cities and City Planning, 1800–1920* (Philadelphia, 1989); William H. Wilson, *The City Beautiful Movement* (Baltimore, 1989); and Joel A. Tarr and Gabriel Dupuy, eds., *Technology and the Rise of the Networked City in Europe and America* (Philadelphia, 1988). The point I emphasize in this article is the role of the war in broadening the planners' perspectives to regional proportions. The planners' wartime experiences with technology, especially the electric power grid and hydroelectric and water-related issues helped bring this environmental concept into focus.

9. Brownell, "Urban Planning," 67. Brownell relies heavily on Mark Foster, *From Streetcar to Superhighway: American City Planners and Urban Transportation, 1900–1940* (Philadelphia, 1981). See also Paul Barrett, *The Automobile and Urban Transit: The Formation of Public Policy in Chicago, 1900–1930* (Philadelphia, 1983); and Bruce E. Seely, *Building the American Highway System: Engineers as Policy Makers* (Philadelphia, 1987). For a useful overview of energy policy, see Martin V. Melosi, *Coping with Abundance: Energy and Environment in Industrial America* (New York, 1985).

10. Platt, *Electric City*; Wilson, Pilgrim, and Tashjian, *The Machine Age*; Gilman M. Ostrander, *American Civilization in the First Machine Age: 1890–1940* (New York, 1970); and Helen A. Harrison, ed., *Dawn of a New Day: The New York World's Fair, 1939/40* (New York, 1980). Thomas P. Hughes, *Networks of Power: Electrification in Western Society, 1880–1930* (Baltimore, 1983), 201–26, confirms that the war had radical impacts on the electric utility industry here and abroad.

11. For the best introduction to the RPAA, see Carl Sussman, ed., *Planning the Fourth Migration: The Neglected Vision of the Regional Planning Association of America* (Cambridge, 1976), 1–45. See also the still-valuable book of Roy Lubove, *Community Planning in the 1920s: The Contributions of the Regional Planning Association of America* (Pittsburgh, 1963).

12. On Chicago, see Ross Miller, *American Apocalyspe: The Great Fire and the Myth of Chicago* (Chicago, 1990); Thomas S. Hines, *Burnham of Chicago: Architect and Planner* (Chicago, 1979); and Louis P. Cain, "The Creation of Chicago's Sanitary District and Construction of the Sanitary and Ship Canal," *Chicago History* 8 (Summer 1979): 98–111. On engineers as planners, see note 8 above.

13. Gwendolyn Wright, *Moralism and the Model Home: Domestic Architecture and Cultural Conflict in Chicago, 1873–1913* (Chicago, 1980); Helen Miller, "Cities and Evolution: Patrick Geddes as an International Prophet of Town Planning before 1914," in *The Rise of Modern Urban Planning 1800–1914*, ed. Anthony Sutcliffe (New York, 1980), 199–223; John R. Mullen, "American Perceptions of German City Planning at the Turn of the Century," *Urbanism Past and Present* 3 (1976–77): 5–15.

14. See Mary Corbin Sies, "The City Transformed: Nature, Technology and the Suburban Ideal, 1877–1917," *Journal of Urban History* 14 (November 1987): 81–111; and Ann Durkin Keating, *Building Chicago: Suburban Developers and the Creation of a Divided Metropolis* (Columbus, Ohio, 1988).

15. Platt, *Electric City;* Forrest McDonald, *Insull* (Chicago, 1962). For a wartime affirmation of Insull's reputation as the creator of the first regional grid, see "Atlantic City Convention of the N.E.L.A.," *Electric World* 71 (15 June 1918): 1245. The trade reported that Insull was "gratified at . . . the belated recognition of the economy of concentrated power production from superstations. . . . Mr. Insull has been the leading exponent of the central-station industry in that cause and in the welding together of great distribution networks." Quoted in ibid. The phrase "superstation" in this article is the first use of the prefix "super" that I could find.

16. Hughes, *Networks of Power,* 201–26; Platt, *Electric City,* 163–97; Samuel Insull, "The Production and Distribution of Energy," a paper presented to the Franklin Institute, Philadelphia, in 1913, as reprinted in *Central Station Electric Service,* ed. William Eugene Kelly (Chicago, privately printed 1915), 357–91; U.S. Census Bureau, *Special Reports: Central Electric Light and Power Stations—1912,* pt. 2, 112–13.

17. Platt, *Electric City,* 163–97; Public Service Company of Northern Illinois (PSCNI), "Report of the PSCNI," 31 December 1912, in Commonwealth Edison Company Historical Archives, Box 4222; Imogene Whetstone, "Historical Factors in the Development of Northern Illinois and Its Utilities" (typescript, Chicago, PSCNI, 1928), in Commonwealth Edison Company Library.

18. For quantities and prices of coal in Chicago, see Chicago Board of Trade, *Annual Report* (1858–1902), passim. For the blight of coal dealers faced with glutted markets, see A. Alexander Bischoff, comp., *Coal Trade at Chicago* (Chicago, 1885). For the rise of Chicago as a regional transportation hub, see William J. Cronon, "To be the Central City, Chicago, 1848–1858," *Chicago History* 10 (Fall 1981): 130–40.

19. *Chicago Tribune,* 7 January 1918; for the crisis in Chicago, see 1 December 1917–27 January 1918, passim; Johnson, "Coal Crisis"; Platt, *Electric City,* 201–34.

20. John L'Brant, "Technological Change in American Manufacturing During the 1920s," *Journal of Economic History* 27 (June 1972): 234–43; Richard DuBoff, "The Introduction of Electric Power in American Manufacturing," *Journal of Economic History* 20 (December 1967): 508–18; Committee on Recent Economic Changes of President's Conference on Unemployment, *Recent Economic Changes in the United States,* 2 vols. (New York, 1929). For the concept of "Fordism," see James J. Flink, *The Car Culture* (Cambridge, Mass., 1975), 67–112; and David A. Hounshell, *From the American System to Mass Production: The Development of Manufacturing Technology in the United States* (Baltimore, 1984), 1–15.

21. Keller, *The Power Situation,* 28; the term "natural power districts" is Major Malcom MacLaren's, as quoted in ibid., 23. For similar regional perspectives resulting from the war-borne emergency, see the report of the Director of the U.S. Geological Survey, George Otis Smith, in "Problem of Energy Supply Under Conditions of War," *Electric World* 70 (14 July 1917): 75; "Electrical Interconnection to Conserve Fuel," *Electric World* 71 (5 January 1918): 12–14, on meetings among utility company representatives and state regulatory officials in New York and California; "Pacific Coast Companies Meet War Problems," ibid., 15–17; and detailed regional plan proposed for New England by R. J McClelland, "Electric Power Supply for War Industries," *Electric World* 72 (20 July 1918): 100–105. An analysis of the index of this important trade journal reveals that the word "interconnection" was not used in 1917 (vols. 69–70), although it appears in several articles. In contrast, the term became a subtopic under "Transmission Systems" the following year with seventy-three citations (vols. 71–72). However, the term "superpower" first appears in the index for 1919, where it is cited twice. Also see the presidential address of E. W. Rice of the American Institute of Electrical Engineers, as reported in "A Review and Forecast of the Electrical Industry," *General Electric Review* 21 (August 1918): 528–34.

22. McClelland, "Electric Power Supply," 105. See Hughes, *Networks of Power,* 285–362, for the construction of regional power systems in the United States and Europe after World War I. Hughes provides an especially valuable transatlantic perspective on the

engineers' reactions to power shortages during the war leading to the construction of regional systems. On the economies of scale of the steam turbogenerator, see Richard Hirsh, *Technology and Transformation in the American Electric Utility Industry* (New York, 1989).

23. MacLaren as quoted in Keller, *The Power Situation*, 25; see ibid., 29, for similar statements by Keller. For Keller's career, see *National Cyclopedia*, 38:99. For similar conclusions from the wartime experience, see the remarks of Keller's successor on the Power Section of the War Industries Board, Frederick Darling, "Vision of Power Development," *Electric World* 74 (15 and 22 November 1919): 930–32. Darling was an engineer at the Westinghouse Electric and Manufacturing Company.

24. Thomas Adams, "Regional and Town Planning," *Proceedings of the Eleventh National Conference on City Planning* (Niagara Falls and Buffalo, 1919), 77 [hereafter cited as NCCP *Proceedings*].

25. Ibid., 77–89. Considering the divergent paths of Adams and the community planners, it is ironic that Adams's notions of the regional survey probably came from his countryman Patrick Geddes, who would be one of the community planners' major inspirations. See Helen Miller, "Cities and Evolution," 199–223.

26. Morris Knowles, "Engineering Problems of Regional Planning," in NCCP *Proceedings* (1919), 115, 116.

27. W. J. Donald, "Regional Planning in Motion," NCCP *Proceedings* (1919), 103–13. Also see the followup paper, B. Antrim Haldeman, "Report on Regional Planning," NCCP *Proceedings* (1920), 118–28; and discussion by Tom Adams, ibid., 128–30.

28. Mel Scott, *American City Planning Since 1890* (Berkeley and Los Angeles, 1969), 204–13, 248–51; and the list compiled by John Nolen, "Twenty Years of City Planning Progress in the United States," *Planning Problems of Town, City, and Region: Papers and Discussions of the Nineteenth National Conference on City Planning*.

29. For the origins of the study, see "Super-Power Zones Urged by Mining Engineers' Committee," *Electric World* 75 (24 April 1920): 968; Lieutenant Colonel C. F. Lacombe, "Urgent Need of Super-Power Development," *Electric World* 75 (15 May 1920): 1128–31; "Superpower Report Reveals Electrical Opportunities," *Electric World* 78 (5 November 1921): 910; and Henry Flood, Jr., "The Superpower System-I," *Journal of the American Institute of Electrical Engineers* 41 (April 1922): 287–91. For a summary of the report, see L. E. Imlay, "The Superpower System-II," ibid., 292–97; H. Goodwin, Jr. (a committee member), "What the Superpower Survey Means to the United States," *General Electric Review* 25 (February 1922): 77–87; and "Advantages of Superpower System," *Electric World* 78 (5 November 1921): 916–21. For Smith's early call for regional coordination of energy systems, see Smith, "Problem."

30. Henry I. Harriman, as quoted in "Meeting the Problems of the Reconstruction Era," *Electric World* 72 (November 1918): 1021.

31. Samuel P. Hays, *Conservation and the Gospel of Efficiency: The Progressive Conservation Movement, 1890–1920* (Cambridge, Mass., 1959), 240. See Nancy Farm Mannikko, "Regulating the Water Wheels: Hydroelectricity and the Federal Power Commission in the 1920s," a paper presented at the meeting of American Society for Environmental History (Houston, 1991), for an analysis of the legislation and its enforcement during the postwar decade.

32. Herbert Hoover, "For Superpower Development and Control," Superpower Conference (New York City, October 1923), as quoted in *American City* 29 (November 1923): 525. Of course, the electric industry was elated at Hoover's endorsement. See the trade journal editorial, "Support Action with Action," *Electric World* 82 (20 October 1923): 793. See also the extensive bibliography of contemporary discussion in professional and popular publication in Lemar T. Beman, comp., *Superpower*, The Reference Shelf, vol. 2, no. 9 (New York, 1924). For perspectives on Hoover, see Joan Hoff Wilson, *Herbert Hoover: Forgotten Progressive* (Boston, 1975).

33. Herbert Hoover, "Public Relationship to Power Development," radio address to the annual meeting of the National Electric Light Association (Atlanta City, May 1924), reprinted in Beman, *Superpower*, 15, 17, 25, 15–27, and passim. Hoover's use of the term "interconnection" in reference to the radio is an accurate description of early radio broadcasts. Signals from the source of the sound would be transmitted over long-distance telephone lines to local stations, where they would be broadcast electronically to listeners.

34. Platt, *Electric City*, 235–67, on the 1920s; Sies, "The City Transformed," 81–111, for an admirable summary of the origins of a suburban ideal in the prewar period; Keating, *Building Chicago*, on the influence of the real estate industry in the formation of public policy. For two important overviews, see Ken Jackson, *Crabgrass Frontier: The Suburbanization of the United States* (New York, 1985); and Marc Weiss, *The Rise of the Community Builders: The American Real Estate Industry and Urban Land Planning* (New York, 1987).

35. See Preston J. Hubbard, *Origins of the TVA: The Muscle Shoals Controversy, 1920–1932* (Nashville, 1961); Thomas K. McCraw, *The TVA and the Power Fight, 1933–1939* (Philadelphia, 1971); Philip J. Funigillo, *Toward A National Power Policy: The New Deal and the Electric Utility Industry, 1933–1941* (Pittsburgh, 1973).

36. *Survey Graphic*, no. 54 [The Regional Plan Number] (May 1925), as reprinted in Sussman, *Planning the Fourth Migration*, 51–140.

37. See notes 2 and 13 above.

38. Charles Whitaker, *The Joke About Housing*, 14 and 132–33.

39. Frederick L. Ackerman, "Where Goes the City-Planning Movement?" *Journal of the American Institute of Architects* 7 (December 1919); 520 and 519–21.

40. Lewis Mumford, *Sketches of Life: The Autobiography of Lewis Mumford: the Early Years* (New York, 1982), 333. See Donald L. Miller, *Lewis Mumford: A Life* (New York, 1989), 100–107, 170–71, for his wartime experience and introduction to Whitaker. For insight on Mumford's early views, see Lewis Mumford, "The City," in *Civilization in the United States: An Inquiry by Thirty Americans*, ed. Harold E. Stearns (New York, 1922), 3–20.

41. See Lewis Mumford, "Introduction," in Benton MacKay, *The New Exploration: A Philosophy of Regional Planning* (reprint ed.; Urbana, Ill., 1962 [1928]), 34–43; Robert W. Bruere, "Pandora's Box," *Survey Graphic*, no. 51 (March 1925): 557, for the term; Robert W. Bruere, "Giant Power," *Survey Graphic*, no. 53 (October 1924): 84, for the quotation. See also Martha Bensley Bruere, "What Is Giant Power For?" American Academy of Political and Social Science, *Annals* 117 (March 1925): 120–23. For biographical information on the Brueres, see *Who's Who in America* (Chicago, 1918–19), 10:3, and (1924–25), 13:556.

42. Mumford, *Sketches from Life*, 338.

43. Lewis Mumford, "The Fourth Migration," *Survey Graphic*, no. 54 (May 1925): 130–33, as reprinted in Sussman, *Planning the Fourth Migration*, 55 and 64.

44. Robert W. Bruere, "Giant Power-Region Builder," *Survey Graphic*, no. 54 (May 1925): 161–64, 188, as reprinted in Sussman, *Planning the Fourth Migration*, 114 and 111–20.

45. Clarence Stein, *Toward New Towns for America* (Cambridge, Mass., 1966 [1957]); Lubove, *Community Planning*, 63–67; Joseph L. Arnold, *The New Deal in the Suburbs: A History of the Greenbelt Town Program, 1935–1954* (Columbus, Ohio, 1971); State of New York, *Report of the Commission of Housing and Regional Planning to Governor Alfred E. Smith* (Albany, 1926), as reprinted in Sussman, *Planning the Fourth Migration*, 141–98; D. Clayton Brown, *Electricity for Rural America: The Fight for the REA* (Westport, Conn., 1980); Richard A. Pence, *The Next Greatest Thing* (Washington, D.C., 1984). On the TVA, see note 28 above and Jane Jacobs, *Cities and the Wealth of Nations* (New York, 1984), 105–23.

46. Lewis Mumford, *My Work and Days: A Personal Chronicle* (New York, 1979), 107.

ALAN MAYNE

City as Artifact: Heritage Preservation in Comparative Perspective

Let me take you on a Cook's tour of urban historic preservation outcomes in the United States.[1] The undertaking is doubly complicated. First, I am an outsider from Australia, a nation that is known more for its sheep farms than for its cities—or, indeed, for a significant national history or a non-Aboriginal cultural heritage that is worth preserving. Second, the dislocation between subject matter and observer is further compounded because I am writing from the ancient Italian city of Parma. Here, in contrast both to the United States and Australia, a multiplicity of structures and artifacts dating back to Etruscan times makes manifest the depth and richness of the surrounding historical texture.

In Australia, even more so than in North America, the chronological thinness of European settlement and of the matching material culture long inhibited interest in historic preservation. The ethos of the place, as in America, was steeped in a settler tradition of felling trees and blasting rock rather than in conservation. Indeed, the maverick frontier state of Queensland, in Australia's northeast, delayed effective heritage legislation until 1990.[2] This utilitarian modernizing spirit has especially characterized Australian and American attitudes to cities, the prodigious growth of which in Australia during the nineteenth century turned that new European settler society into one of the most highly urbanized nations in the world. A key feature of this city-building process was the dearth of local traditions and associations that, in an established society like Italy, bound people in pride with place. Australian cityscapes reflected the raw unmitigated logic of commerce and entrepreneurial ambitions for future growth. Indeed, this obsessive "eye for the future" and disregard for the past was one of the most disorienting features of Australian urbanization

that struck an Italian visitor late in the nineteenth century.[3] It was
axiomatic in such societies—future gazing, and governed by capitalist
elites—that buildings and neighborhoods as they aged were regarded, in
the absence of a strong sense of tradition, as simply outmoded and as ripe
for replacement. A century later, the same mentality continues. In the
early 1980s the Italian-born owner of a major construction company
asserted, when endeavoring to demolish the handsome late nineteenth-
century Rialto buildings in Melbourne's chic Collins Street, that the
country had no historic structures worth preserving. For history, he said,
one traveled to Europe.[4]

The Melbourne developer's crude temporal and artifactual parochialism
was discounted by government historic-conservation arbiters. The significance of the Parmesan perspective does not lie in the different character
of Italian material culture from that of Australia or North America, but in
the attitudes adopted by Italians toward it. Two spans of a Roman bridge
stand in Parma within a pedestrian subway to the local produce market.
They were uncovered and preserved in situ when the subway was exca-
vated. Parmesans do not stop to gape each time they do their shopping,
but the bridge is nonetheless embedded in their mental maps of local
space, and in their prideful self-identifications with place. Their sense of
history is pervasive, cloaking with public meaning the streets, buildings,
and public spaces of the city. It is, moreover, low key and idiomatic,
combining a matter-of-fact appreciation of the past with present-day activities and associations.

Citizens of the New World have also read history lessons from their
cities. The meanings they recognized or inscribed have been, like those in
Parma, vernacular and present-centered. A century ago, Australian colonists designed grandiose city halls and stock exchanges with architectural
flourishes in the style of Renaissance Italy, in order to assert both the
historical depth of their transplanted European culture and its potential
for future greatness in its antipodean setting. The writers and illustrators
of promotional tracts and tourist guidebooks in the last quarter of the
nineteenth century characterized the flimsier relics of early colonial times
as historical relics, whose clearance to make way for modern structures
underscored the march of material progress. Commentators saw in the
inner city's perpetually recycled housing stock the rippled effects of successive waves of immigrant settlement. Families of the working and middle
classes read in the domestic artifacts and neat streetscapes of their suburban housing estates countless histories of achievement by kin and friends.

In these cities' physical fabrics, as in Parma, are thus located the roots
of an all-encompassing and vernacular cultural milieu. Notwithstanding

the preponderance of ruling-class and masculinist influences that fashion the physical forms and intended purposes of city places and spaces,[5] their translation from what sociologist Herbert Gans called "potential" into "effective" living, working, and recreational spaces has historically always been mediated by autonomous, and often divergent, popular activities and interpretations.[6] Indeed, it is precisely through this process of cultural adjustment that city people, in their places of work, "in the secrecy of their homes, in the complicity of neighbourhoods, in the communication of taverns, in the joy of street gatherings . . . find values, ideas, projects and, finally, demands that do not conform to the dominant social interests."[7] Local custom translates the diverse and changing forms and functions of the urban landscape into coherent blocks of inherited knowledge about social place, and with it, personal identity. The built environments of all these cities are thus artifices embedded with meanings. Some of their parts are public and their meanings widely shared; others are private spaces with coded meanings. Like a palimpsest, the physical forms are constantly reworked and their meanings lost or reinterpreted. But in the vernacular consciousness of everyday living, associations of place and history are accumulating and enduring.

It is beyond the scope of this article to explore how these associations have so decisively shaped spatial outcomes in the historic cores of Italian cities. These outcomes contrast with Australia and the United States, where the historic preservation movement has struggled to address the material basis of local identification and public knowledge, and to harness such idiomatic historical consciousness in urban policy-making. In consequence we confront an incipient crisis: lacking coherent, cohesive, and compelling arguments to put either to policymakers or to the general community against the ongoing degradation of the historic environments of our cities. This is the case especially of the decaying infrastructure of late nineteenth- and early twentieth-century urban living that formed the foundations of the metropolitan era. A rigorous requestioning of the basis for determining historic significance, and for conserving and interpreting historic structures in the present is urgently needed.

Much of the blame for this state of affairs attaches to the history profession, which has remained ambivalent about involvement with either preservation practice or with history-making as a public activity. It is an astonishing irony that the history profession as a whole has for so long ignored the artifacts thus fashioned out of a popular sense of history, and that a profession so steeped in reading texts has neglected to read the built environments of cities.[8] It is debatable whether historians collectively have either the will or the insight to change this. Historians in institutions of higher education have by and large ignored the activities of historical societies and of freelance and government-employed historians. They have also collectively remained aloof from other professionals—archaeologists, architects, curators, engineers—who have played a more significant role in protecting and publicizing the cultural heritage riches of our cities. Historical scholarship exhibits an across-the-board ignorance concerning the interpretation of material culture and spatial forms. Tellingly, the National Trust for Historic Preservation employs no historians in its Washington, D.C., headquarters, and J. Jackson Walter, its president since 1984, characterizes as "sloppy" much of the historical input in the cultural heritage field to date. Other experts in cultural resources management have for long lampooned the shallow outlook and technical incompetence of historians who have sought to enter the preservation field.[9]

Preserving the Past

Today it is superficially easy to conclude that protection for cultural heritage preservation has become an established component of United States urban policy making. It is underpinned by federal statute and grants-in-aid, and finds expression in the National Register of Historic Places. Preservation offices are located within major federal agencies. The National Park Service has administered historic sites since the 1930s. State and local government historic preservation offices, historical societies, and historical commissions administer archaeological and historic preservation programs. There is a grassroots network of thousands of local history societies and, in collaboration with it, there stands the National Trust for Historic Preservation, with a membership of approximately a quarter of a million people. Yet in America, as in Australia, a sensitivity to history is not consistently evident in urban policy making and design. Preservationists have signally failed to synthesize the loose strands of vernacular memory about particular structures and places into rigorous explications of cities in history. In order to understand why this should be so it is necessary to review the case that has hitherto been made for cultural heritage conservation, and—set against this—to consider what has been preserved and who have been the preservationists.

Why preserve at all? In the United States and Australia today the temptation is to assume that although there are many fierce battles still in course or yet to be fought over particular issues, the overall campaign to establish

the legitimacy of cultural-heritage conservation has been successfully concluded. What in fact has happened is that during the 1960s, 1970s, and
early 1980s the legitimacy of preservation was identified by its advocates,
and conceded by policymakers, with oases of nostalgia for an irrelevant
and often imaginary past. Such historical fragments were sufficiently disen-
gaged from present-day urban actualities as not significantly to impinge
upon public planning and private redevelopment activities. The pyrrhic
nature of this victory was rammed home during the latter 1980s and early
1990s.

There is now general agreement concerning the preservation of individual structures whose grandiose proportions, or associations with famous
personages and events, seemingly give them special historical significance. This consensus extends also to include elite enclaves whose architectural grace and early-colonial origins are recognized in the designations
"historic district," or "historic conservation area." There is, however,
little about such disconnected structures and neighborhood pockets that
sufficiently gel with vernacular associations of history and place to be at
all illustrative for most people of the social history of overall city growth
and urban living. Yet it is precisely in relation to the broader social history
of our cities—the material forms of which are constantly undergoing
piecemeal and insufficiently regulated change—that the question is repeatedly and impatiently being urged by developers, policymakers, and by
many local community groups in pursuit of enhanced and extended amenities like shops and medical care: why this urge to preserve these old forms?
The question has more substance than preservationists admit, and is one
to which they have still to give credible answers. It is not simply a ploy
used by developers and politicians who see history as standing in way of a
fast buck or local votes. It is asked often by reasonable people whose own
sense of place seems unconnected to the history-making and policy agen-
das pursued by cultural-heritage activists.

A civil and humane society needs folk traditions, which in turn feed
into concepts of history that are accessible, respected, and hence mediat-
ing with the present. Urban material culture, and especially the fixed and
movable artifacts of everyday living, are potent vehicles of individual and
public memory because they trigger cross-generational associations about
people and place through time. The historic fabric of our cities—in all
their untidiness, diversity, and ugliness—constitutes a profoundly democratic basis for public knowledge because viewers are not totally dependent
upon the special pleading of written texts but are themselves active interpreters of historical meaning and significance. The built environment, by
thus encouraging exchanges and comparisons between diverse social

groups as they explore differences and build on similarities, has the potential to break down barriers and parochialism. By thus facilitating public history making, the built environment functions as a catalyst for community associational life. An informed sense of place in history is therefore a necessary precondition for wise decision making in the present.

Such a sensitivity to history has not been applied generally in the interpretation and preservation of the historical environments of our cities. Public memory and official designations of significance in history have not sufficiently meshed. This is not because Americans or Australians are uninterested in their local history, but because the case for historic preservation that has been put to them has not seemed sufficiently relevant to their local knowledge of place through time. Notwithstanding the huge numbers of visitors to historic places and museums, the case for historic preservation has seemingly reached a threshold of influence beyond which it has been unable to develop.

Closely tied up with the question "Why preserve?" is the rider, "What should be preserved?" Criteria for determining historical significance have traditionally emphasized monumentalism rather than the mundane objects and places associated with everyday urban social life. Preservation outcomes have consequently stood distant from vernacular modes of historical consciousness. It has also meant that the professional groups whose decisions tend most to shape the built environment—engineers, architects, and urban planners—see history as having limited relevance to their work because so much of their training and job experience lie in areas that fall outside what have been traditionally considered as having historic significance.

The narrowness of traditional tests of historical significance result, in part, because an indigenous sense of history and appreciation of historical structures originally relied on imported traditions. In Australia, even after school children ceased to be taught as much about the monarchs of early modern Europe as they were about the history of their own country, it was still felt that a full appreciation of real history required a pilgrimage to Europe. Australians were socialized into believing that to think historically was not a normal part of daily living, and that visits to historical places were formal and stilted affairs that were to be reserved for special occasions. Historic places were defined for them, as for Americans, in terms of inappropriate reference points to architectural styles in premodern, precapitalist Europe. This Eurocentric conservation philosophy was formalized in the Athens Charter of 1933 and is perpetuated today in the 1964 Venice Charter, which was adopted as the bible of the International

Council on Monuments and Sites (ICOMOS). The charter's focus on "historic monuments" and "age-old traditions" is singularly inappropriate to the New World. As Miles Lewis, one of Australia's leading conservationists has pointed out, the document was framed with an eye to classical temples and Gothic cathedrals, and is consequently "not well suited to dealing with vernacular or primitive buildings, urban conservation areas, industrial archaeological sites, or 20th century buildings."[10]

The selective nature of assessments of historical significance has also been greatly influenced by historiographical preoccupation with nation building and with propagating the myths that sustain national identity. This has resulted in the present-day relevance of historic places being acknowledged by government policymakers mainly in terms of celebratory lore of nationhood. According to the National Register of Historic Places in the United States, historic places "are tangible links with the Nation's past that help provide a sense of identity and stability."[11] The National Trust for Historic preservation trumpets its "deep roots in the patriotism and community pride that provided the original impetus for American historic preservation."[12] An early leader of the National Trust in New South Wales said of Sydney's grand historic buildings that it was "only by the cherishing of such treasure that we can hope to evolve a National Soul."[13]

One consequence of this emphasis has been to interpret historical significance largely in terms of the public figures involved in politics, intellectual life, diplomacy, and war. This has been the central preoccupation of the criteria for evaluation used by the United States' National Register of Historic Places. Preservation outcomes have consequently emphasized the public and home lives of wealthy white men and have marginalized the historical experiences of women, the working classes, African Americans, immigrants, and other minority groups. Another consequence has been that in celebrating the building blocks of national unity and asserting the core values that underpin national consensus, aspects of the past that seem unhelpful to such a reading of the past are neglected. In supporting the National Trust, President George Bush said that "to the extent that America's traditional cultural values have helped make America uniquely strong, it is important that these values be preserved—in order that they may be built upon as America continues to advance."[14] Historic preservation has consequently skirted poverty, bigotry, protest, and repression and has disdained viewpoints that contradict or challenge elite readings of the past.

Cities, historically centers of diversity, conflict, and nastiness rather than of heroic deeds, have not fitted comfortably into his prevailing framework for determining historical significance. In both Australia and the United States, national myths have tended to be strongly anti-urban, and such early experiments in historic preservation as Colonial Williamsburg in Virginia reinforced this bias. Cities have tended to figure only incidentally and in fragments in preservation outcomes: state legislatures, churches, and the birth- or death-places of the rich and famous. The preoccupation with contrived turning points and dramatic episodes in national history has of course produced some fine urban historic landmarks, such as the Ford Theater in Washington, D.C., where Abraham Lincoln was assassinated. The seemingly unheroic commercial and industrial activities, however, and the public works and technological innovations that underpinned city growth and national prosperity, have until recently been neglected. Also obscured has been the web of apparently mundane neighborhood social activities—family formation, work, shopping, medical care, education, recreation—that comprised the day-to-day experiences and hence the predominating horizons of people in the past.

The Valentine Museum in Richmond, Virginia, is a notable exception to this neglect of urban history. In 1985 the museum embarked upon a long-range plan to reinterpret the city's history. It deliberately sought to draw upon recent scholarship in urban and social history, and by providing a synthesizing and dynamic historical perspective, to tap other publics than its hitherto "primarily . . . white, elite audience."[15] The museum's strategy has been to utilize historic places throughout the city as museum sites. It has sponsored a series of temporary exhibitions as works in progress toward the achievement of that goal: "In Bondage and in Freedom: Antebellum Black Life in Richmond, Virginia, 1790–1860" in 1988; "Jim Crow: Racism and Reaction Within the New South" in 1989; "2 Street" in 1990, which examined twentieth-century neighborhood life in Richmond's Second Street; and "The Working People of Richmond: Life and Labor in an Industrial City, 1865–1920" in 1991. The Valentine also unveiled plans in 1991 for a $22.5 million additional museum site, the Valentine Riverside, in the nineteenth-century Tredegar Iron Works, which is to open in 1993. As Michael McGrann, director of public relations, explained, the museum sought "to present the whole history of the city, not just bits and pieces. We want to tell the story of the average person, the slaves, women, . . . immigrants, so that everyone can find something to identify with."[16]

The prevailing preservation inadequacies that the Valentine addressed are clearly bound up with the nature of the participants in the cultural heritage movement. The National Trust, blamed by academic critics in both countries for having skewed heritage outcomes by elitist preoccupation with the villa lifestyles of the colonial gentry, is really something of a straw man. The Trusts certainly were major vehicles for these views, but the criticism obscures the broadening range of Trust activities over time. The allegation moreover endorses uncritically the Trusts' claim to leadership of and formative influence upon preservation policy, and ignores the extent of grassroots activity since the 1960s.

Historic preservation originated in conservative nostalgia for a less tumultuous world. In the United States during the 1920s the monied classes, relying upon sentimentality and empathy rather than upon rigorous historical interpretation, constructed romanticized visions of harmonious small-town communities in the past. These emphases received federal government backing in 1935 with the passage of the Historic Sites Act, which authorized the National Park Service to acquire historic and archaeological sites. The same emphases were also reflected in an additional private initiative, launched with seeding finance from the Mellon family, which led to the creation by Congress of the National Trust for Historic Preservation in 1949. The Trust in turn stamped its mark upon the 1966 National Historic Preservation Act, which is still the basis of cultural resources management today. The statute set up guidelines to be followed by federal agencies and required each state to establish historic preservation offices and programs. The law also established the National Register of Historic Places as a definitive list of all historically significant places, structures, and artifacts. Thereafter the Trust and the new state and city agencies concentrated upon listing in the National Register and its local equivalents all those places the earlier preservation movement had identified as having historical significance. They simultaneously sought to protect these places from destruction, and to display them to the public as formal showcases of a vanished world.[17]

In Australia, sustained interest in historic places began with the celebration of grand architecture by the well-to-do. The heritage movement was launched early in the twentieth century by bourgeois artists and antiquarians. They recoiled from what they regarded as the vulgar mediocrity of modern cities, and publicized instead the charm of colonial architecture and the elite lifestyles it expressed. These activities were formalized in 1947 with the establishment of the National Trust of New South Wales, which was closely modeled upon the English National Trust. Complementary organizations were subsequently formed in the other states: in South Australia in 1955, Victoria in 1956, Western Australia in 1959, Tasmania in 1960, and Queensland in 1963. A Council of National Trusts was established in 1965. The Trusts' organizers, who were still predominantly drawn from the intellectual wing of the Australian establishment, sought to save and restore the grand mansions of the colonial elite, such as Old Government House near Sydney and Como and Ripponlea in Melbourne. These historic places formed the "jewels in the crown" of the register of classified historic buildings that each state organization built up and campaigned to save.[18]

Legislative endorsement of such activities came considerably later in Australia than in the United States. In 1974 Victoria, because of the close links between the conservation state government and the Victorian National Trust, became the first Australian state to enact historic-building legislation. The Historic Buildings Act established a state register that used the National Trust's list of classified buildings as its blueprint. In the same year the federal government launched a Commission of Inquiry into the National Estate, and in response to its report established the Australian Heritage Commission in 1975 to compile a national register of places of "aesthetic, historic, scientific or social significance,"[19] and to coordinate national planning, research, and education.

It is of course misleading to picture the origins of cultural-heritage conservation as being so skewed in emphasis as to have been without merit. The homes of the early-colonial gentry in New South Wales are architectural gems that are rich in the social history of both the owning and the working classes.[20] Lobbying in the early 1930s by society women in Charleston was responsible for a city ordinance that established the first "historic district" in the United States and initiated a fruitful working relationship between the local community and local government that was still evident in the city in the aftermath of hurricane Hugo in 1989. In 1933 a National Park Service scheme using unemployed architects to survey and record historic buildings led to the establishment of the Historic American Building Survey (HABS), which recorded thousands of historical structures during the 1930s, many of which had no connection whatever to famous men but were rooted instead in local memories and traditions. Nonetheless, by the 1960s the heritage movement as a whole in both countries remained as it had begun, an elite activity that sifted the material culture of the urban past for artifacts that could be presented as majestic statements of an orderly and rational world.

It is frequently said that earlier urban-policy preoccupations were discarded during the 1960s and 1970s as historic preservation came of age, building up a momentum that successfully carried it into the 1980s and 1990s. Although there were certainly major developments in the heritage field, the most exciting possibility to be generated in these decades—the prospect of union between the historic preservation movement and vernacular identifications of place in history—went ultimately unrealized.

The changing focus of preservation activity in the United States and Australia since the 1960s was in part the result of crystalizing interest by architects, engineers, archaeologists, and historians, who increasingly undertook voluntary, consultancy, and regular employment in culturalheritage assessment and management. New associations and professional journals appeared, the effect of which was to broaden both the ranks and the interests of preservationists. In the United States, architects and some historians formed a network of local societies for architectural history. In 1969, the work of HABS in recording places of architectural significance was augmented when the American Society of Civil Engineers joined the National Park Service and the Library of Congress in establishing the Historic American Engineering Record (HAER) to document the nation's engineering and industrial heritage. Four other engineering societies subsequently backed the program. The history and heritage committees of the American Society for Civil Engineers, the American Society for Mechanical Engineers, and the Institute of Electrical and Electronics Engineers became active identifying and publicizing sites and artifacts of historical significance. Civil engineers and historians employed by publicworks agencies, museums, and state and local historical societies in 1975 founded the Public Works Historical Society in order to encourage research on water resources, transportation, waste management, municipal engineering, parks, and planning, and to seek the preservation of historically significant public works. In 1980 professional and scholarly exchanges among the architects, archaeologists, and historians employed in State Historic Preservation Offices was formalized with the establishment of the Vernacular Architecture Forum.[21]

Growing professional engagement in conservation issues in Australia since the 1960s culminated in 1980, when the Australian branch of ICOMOS, meeting in the South Australian town of Burra, adopted the Burra Charter, which effectively superseded the Venice Charter and remains today the theoretical basis for all conservation work in Australia. The Burra Charter substituted the previous Eurocentric stress upon grand monuments with a new focus on "places," which was designed to encompass archaeological sites, ruins, buildings, engineering structures, groups of buildings, and whole urban areas. In another major departure from the Venice Charter, Australia ICOMOS introduced the concept of "cultural significance"—defined by the Burra Charter as "aesthetic, historic, scientific or social value for past, present and future generations"—as the key measuring stick in heritage assessments. Heritage professionals were now

able to break away from the older preoccupation with individual structures in order to study buildings as elements in historic environments that
changed through time, to include "humbler" sites and structures in these
broader frameworks and to address competing versions of significance.[22]

The changing parameters of preservation activity were also influenced
in both countries by innovations in institutions of higher education since
the 1960s, taken in response to new openings in the job market and
demands by the professions they serviced. Cross-disciplinary exchanges
resulted in universities offering degrees and diplomas in new professional
areas such as conservation and archives management. Established disciplines introduced cultural heritage studies. This was most evident in
schools of architecture, where coursework in the history of architecture
and historic preservation proliferated from the mid-1960s. A handful of
educators in engineering also began to include the history of engineering
in their coursework. Departments of art history forged new programs in
applied skills for conservators and curators. Formal new subdisciplines
arose, notably historical archaeology in the 1960s, with specialized
coursework and new periodicals. In some college and university history
departments, as a consequence of the epistemological revolution we call
social history and of interest in the subdiscipline of urban history, a few
innovative faculty began to introduce their students to material culture
and to historic preservation as an urban-policy tool.

Community interest in heritage issues, however, was awakened less by
initiatives among the professions and in institutions of higher education
than by grassroots mobilization to protect endangered inner-city neighborhoods from encroaching development. It has been customary to interpret
the groundswell of grassroots mobilization that began during the 1960s
and 1970s in defense of the historic built environment as the result of
middle-class intervention and leadership. It has also been customary to
interpret the consequence of this mobilization as catapulting heritage
conservation into the middle of the public policy arena and into the
essential toolbox of politicians, planners, and developers. The reality was
more complex and less certain in its outcomes.

First, most city dwellers did not discover heritage preservation in the
1960s as the result of bulldozers rumbling into their own neighborhoods.
Demographically, the most significant features of postwar urban change
were not occurring in the inner city at all, but in the proliferating suburbs.
This is not to say that the shift of population away from historic city cores
unraveled vernacular interest in the past. The development of historic
towns and villages into satellite communities and suburban estate development into historic rural areas in fact stimulated the growth of local historic

societies and museums. Moreover, the decline in heavy manufacturing led by the 1970s to an across-the-board curiosity in the hitherto-ignored industrial history of cities. Robert J. Kapsch, chief of HABS/HAER, commented that as the factories closed down "all of a sudden, the industry that sustained the community is no longer there, and they want to know what happened." In addition, he said, the transition to a postindustrial economy fueled general interest "in other people that actually make things and produce things."[23] This "nostalgia boom" was equally evident in Australia during the prosperous 1970s.[24]

Second, notwithstanding the stirrings of concern about the cultural-heritage vandalism caused since the late 1940s by highway construction, slum clearance, urban renewal, and ongoing commercial redevelopments, the main suburban preoccupations that fed into urban policy-making during the 1960s and 1970s had to do less with protecting historic precincts than with efficient fiscal management and the fuller provision of urban services. In Australia, widespread concerns were voiced about environmental pollution and the uneven quality of life that resulted from unequal access to urban services and amenities, and from the looseness of regulatory controls over the private marketplace. These concerns were responsible for the landslide victory in the 1972 federal elections of the social democratic Australian Labor Party on the platform—aimed in large measure at new suburban constituencies—of social equity, environmental protection, and controlled economic development.

Third, bourgeois intervention was neither totally innovative nor wholly positive. In both Australia and the United States "gentrification"—the colonization and renovation of historic inner-city districts—undeniably saw middle-class activists forcing politicians and urban planners to add historic preservation to the list of quality-of-life issues that were being addressed as a result of the altering frameworks of political discourse during the 1960s. In the United States, this mobilization of inner-city middle-class constituencies was pioneered by Jane Jacobs in Greenwich Village during the early 1960s. Their mood was well expressed in the fiery first newsletter of the D.C. Historic Preservation League in 1971: "Don't Tear It Down."[25] In Australian inner cities, middle-class residents' associations blocked bulldozers and picketed development sites until politicians and bureaucrats included them in the decision-making process. Among the first of these groups was the Parkville Association in Melbourne, which was formed in 1967 to fight the proposed expansion of the Royal Melbourne Hospital into this charming inner-city pocket of late Victorian and Edwardian terrace houses. The association's leaders also assisted on forming the neighboring Carlton Association, which was established in 1969 to fight the Victorian Housing Commission's "slum reclamation" plans in the district. The new association embarked on an effective lobbying and publicity campaign that asserted that the residents "are not 'slum dwellers,' " and that explored the suburb's history in order to demonstrate its architectural and historical significance.[26] Both neighborhoods are now historic-conservation areas. In Sydney similar mobilization occurred during the late 1960s and early 1970s to protect emerging high-income enclaves in Paddington and Balmain from main-road and chemical-storage proposals.[27]

Gentrification and the restoration of historic homes, however, exacerbated social problems as rental accommodation and rooming houses were converted to single-family-owner occupancy.[28] Local politics sometimes became a battleground between the new arrivals and the close-knit working-class communities they were displacing.[29] The high-profile and successful campaigns conducted by residents' associations overshadowed a longer tradition of resistance to urban renewal by working-class neighborhoods. In Australia this resistance at last received national publicity during the early 1970s as the result of intervention by the communist-led Builders' Labourers' Federation. The BLF supported protesting working-class residents in Sydney by placing "Green Bans" on massive redevelopment schemes in the inner-city neighborhoods of the Rocks and Woolloomooloo.[30] In the United States the Carter administration responded to the spread of similar neighborhood resistance groups among working- and lower-middle-class ethics since the 1950s by creating the National Commission on Neighborhoods in 1977.

Perhaps the greatest significance of middle-class neighborhood activism was its bridging function between public policy-making and popular interest in the histories of local communities. The National Trusts, swayed by the residents' associations' sophisticated arguments about the heritage significance of domestic architecture, neighborhoods, and the elaborate public infrastructure that serviced them, belatedly came to recognize during the 1970s that the long-standing popular interest in vernacular structures and mundane activities had cultural and historical merit. This recognition was assisted by the influx of professionals into cultural-heritage assessment and management, and by the need for the Trusts to address the local preservation interests of the proliferating local historical societies and museums if they were still to claim to represent the preservation movement to governments. In Australia, this alliance emerged in popular campaigns like the one in Brisbane, Queensland's state capital, to save the 1880s Bellevue Hotel. The building was eventually demolished overnight in 1979, while the police held back many hundreds of demonstrators.[31]

One result of this accommodation between preservation traditionlists, heritage professionals, and grassroots activists was government recognition for a startlingly different range of historic city structures and places. Victoria's new Science and Technology Museum, for example, is housed in the technologically remarkable Spotswood Pumping Station, which pumped Melbourne's sewage from 1897 until 1964. Spotswood exemplifies the technological and administrative innovations, and the massive public capital investment, that supported the low-density metropolitan lifestyles that had emerged in many New World cities by the turn of the century.[32] Spotswood also highlights a remarkable recent trend in cultural resources management: a transition away from the long-standing preoccupation with isolated structures in social, spatial, and historical vacuum. This transition represented more than a broadening of attention from grand public structures to domestic architecture; from civic monuments to the humble and utilitarian places and artifacts of work; from individual structures to the broader communities of which they were a part. It represented as well a trend away from conceptualizations of history as essentially static, and of preservation as an activity akin to the arranging of dried flowers. It represented a trend toward history-making as an explication of process and the rhythms of daily life; and toward heritage conservation as an exploration of the roots of family, neighborhood, city, and region. This new thinking was underscored in the United States by the Valentine Museum's renaissance in the mid-1980s. In Australia it was exemplified by the creation of Melbourne's Living Museum of the West. The museum, launched in 1984 in loose imitation of French ecomuseums, was intended to be a catalyst for people in Melbourne's immigrant and working-class western region to examine and present their own histories.[33]

The museum ultimately faltered because of its tenuous links with the communities it claimed to represent. Its uneasy relationship with the western region is symptomatic of the broader preservation movement's reluctance wholeheartedly to collaborate with its grassroots constituencies. Democratization of the National Trust in Australia did not extend much beyond addressing middle-class gentrifiers' preoccupations with Victorian and Edwardian domestic architecture.[34] Trust administrators in both countries placed more emphasis upon building links with governments and business than with consolidating their links with local activists. The decade of the 1980s consequently saw the disintegration of immediate prospects for a broader and more effective coalition of groups working to preserve and interpret historic city environments. Paradoxically, at the same time, the decade represented perhaps the greatest achievements for historic preservation principles in terms of public policy commitments. In the Australian state of Victoria, for example, these policy advances culminated in the 1987 Victorian Planning and Environment Act, which explicitly included conservation of heritage assets as an integral responsibility of routine government planning. In neither Australia nor the United States, however, was historic preservation adopted as an urban planning tool because of any intrinsic interest in history, but because of pragmatic calculations based upon economic development considerations.

This weakness in preservationist strategies was highlighted in the United States, beset by the decaying physical infrastructure and fiscal problems of many of its inner cities. During the 1980s, swayed by National Trust lobbying, government agencies adopted heritage preservation as a vehicle for the revitalization of downtown business districts and neighborhoods. The first federal tax incentives for investors in historic preservation were authorized in 1976, but preservation activity did not take off in large measure until the introduction of the 1981 Historic Rehabilitation Tax Credit Scheme. Thereafter, collaboration between developers, preservation advocates, and city officials funneled billions of private-sector investment into urban revitalization. However, this brave new world of fast-track preservation activity collapsed following the gutting of the tax incentive scheme in 1986. Since then the volume of undertakings under the scheme has dropped by more than two-thirds, and a National Trust survey in June 1990 indicated a rise in the pace of demolitions.[35] Between one-third and one-half of the HABS and HAER collections relate to buildings and sites that no longer exist.[36] The physical fabric of many of the surviving historic buildings continues to deteriorate. In Australia the skin-deep commitment by governments to cultural-heritage preservation was highlighted during Heritage Week in 1990 by the demolition of the 1910 Dennys, Lascelles, Austin and Company (Bow String Truss) Wool Stores in the Victorian city of Geelong. The building, a reinforced-concrete structure that had been a candidate for World Heritage listing, was demolished after the state government intervened to override the state's expert heritage body, the Historic Buildings Council. That disaster is likely to be repeated in Sydney, where the New South Wales Government is considering the fate of the 1913 Woolloomooloo Bay finger wharf, the largest covered wooden wharf in the world.[37]

The disappointments experienced in the public policy field during the 1980s and early 1990s were paralleled in institutions of higher education. In both American and Australian universities, the efforts that had been made since the 1960s to include the study of material culture in coursework were inhibited by a lack of qualified staff, the skepticism of colleagues, tough accreditation requirements, and the squeeze of technical curriculum requirements that reduced the scope of elective coursework. In particular, social history failed to develop sustained interest by academics in innovative applications of the new historical thinking and of outreach work within local communities. The tenure-track dictates of monograph publication rather than teaching innovation and community activism defined the role of academic historians, constraining their engagement in policy work relating to historic preservation. In October 1990, at the landmark Chicago conference, "Modes of Inquiry for American City History," the American urban history profession reacted with impatience and derision to suggestions that historians might engage on equal terms with museum curators and other heritage professionals in applied cultural-heritage work at historic sites, structures, and in exhibitions.

Presenting the Past

The key failure of cultural-heritage planning in 1980s was the inability of preservationists to communicate effectively with the public as they read the urban past in new and more comprehensive ways. In particular, historians failed to interact sufficiently with and consolidate the vernacular identifications of historic significance that had been seeking policy recognition since the 1960s. Notwithstanding the proliferating membership of preservation societies, and of visitors to museums and historic parks, the full participation of the new members and the sustained interest of visitors to historic places were missed. With this missed opportunity was lost the chance to harness the intellectual and grassroots innovations of the 1960s and 1970s in order to shift decisively the traditional frameworks of historic preservation. This failure forces the question how best to communicate and justify the case for historic preservation in the 1990s. The question challenges prevailing calculations of historical significance and the complacent cosiness of academic historians about participation in history making.

A major phenomenon of the 1960s and 1970s was the upsurge in urban protest movements. Newly organized groups, rooted not only in neighborhood resistance to urban redevelopment but also in opposition to the Vietnam War, and in assertions of feminist, racial, and ethnic identities, pushed forward to tell their own histories in opposition to the entrenched readings of the past, which had marginalized them in official history and perpetuated their unequal status in contemporary society. It was partially in response to and partially in tandem with this grassroots ferment of inquiry and criticism that social history emerged during the 1960s and

1970s to become the dominant epistemological method of historical inquiry. Social history looked to everyday activities and objects from the past for evidence of the social processes shaping society. It spurred the development of historical archaeology to study the material culture of everyday living, the accumulating findings of which in turn enriched historical inquiry in the 1980s. As academic interest in one early application of social history endeavor—urban history—waned during the 1980s, it was augmented by the material basis of social-history interest in family, immigrant, labor, public works, urban planning, industrial, transportation, and public history. As Kapsch now notes of the test for historical significance at HABS/HAER, "Our starting point is material culture: we start with the object."[38]

It is a paradox that communication of these professional developments to the general public has faltered. This is, in part, because of the mixed signals coming from preservation admininstrators and government agencies about the priority areas to be highlighted in communicating the new social history. It results also from confusion among and between preservationists, urban policymakers, and the business community about the appropriate forms and parameters of preservation outcomes. It flows, too, from the tenuousness of the professional collaboration necessary in order to interpret and communicate fully the significance of complex sites, and also from the timidity or insincerity of professionals' commitment to concept of history as a public resource. I will briefly review these four areas in turn.

To a significant degree, communicating history by reference to the built environment still sustains a contrived and elitist vision of the past. This is notwithstanding the impact of grassroots mobilization and of social-history methodology on historical inquiry since the 1960s, and of experimentation with alternative approaches by professionals working in the preservation field. Registers of the National Estate and of the National Trusts still mirror the skewed focus of past preservation interest in the mansions of public figures. Moreover, the protection and administration of places of historic significance all too often entrench warped conceptualizations of time and human agency by explaining the significance of historic places in terms of particular persons and favored activities and time periods. In so doing, evidence of the lives and activities of other people associated with such places over time is marginalized or obliterated.

These weaknesses are perhaps clearest in the communication of the histories of the grand houses, but they are also evident in the field of industrial heritage, an area of preservation activity that blossomed with the growing interest since the 1960s in vernacular architecture and activities. Government officials and heritage administrators worried that industrial heritage was "plain ugly."[39] They responded by emphasizing features of industrial heritage that were quaint, memorable, and picturesque.[40] The Footscray Arts and Community Centre in Melbourne's western region is a good example. It is housed in an attractive 1870s bluestone structure called Henderson House. Nothing to do with its restoration suggests that the building was originally associated with a vile-smelling fellmongery. There is also nothing to show that Samuel Henderson, the building's first owner, occupied it for only one year. The restoration gives no sense of the building's diverse occupants and activities between Henderson's departure in 1874 and its purchase by the City of Footscray in 1981. The same selectivity is evident at the site of the Living Museum of the West, which is located in an industrial-history park. The industrial structures that state planners chose for preservation were pretty nineteenth-century bluestone buildings associated with colonial meat preserving, rather than the technologically exciting but visually unremarkable structures nearby, which had been associated with the development of concrete pipe technology in the twentieth century.

It is only partially true to say that such inadequacies in communicating history result from a long-standing fetish among preservationists with architectural aesthetics. This fetish is in turn based upon a fixation with shallow commemoration of prevailing historical myths. Commemorationism has been encouraged by sensitivity to the expectations of governments and private benefactors in providing financial support for heritage conservation, and thus timidity to embrace sites or interpretations that challenge the prevailing historical stereotypes that underpin national identity and regional or civic loyalties. It has been facilitated as well by the indifference of most historians to influencing preservation principles so as to ensure that they incorporate the latest academic research. Historic preservation as a whole has consequently remained an instrument for mythologizing rather than for unraveling the past.

One consequence of this has been the reluctance of historic-preservation planners to address structures and artifacts from the recent past, whose significance in folk memory—whether contentious or mundane—is still too entrenched to make them appear suitable candidates for myth making. Another consequence has been to disengage time and place. The historical significance of the physical environment has been communicated in large part by a profoundly ahistorical snapshot approach that seeks to commemorate celebrated epochs or celebrated personages at key points in their lives. In so doing, the unfolding quality of historical

change is obscured. Moreover, material settings are represented unprob-
lematically as an incidental stage, or as a neutral container for frozen
moments in time, not as the main text telling the story of ongoing
change. A third consequence of commemorationism is to privilege certain
visions of the past over all others. The renovations to Victorian terrace
houses in Melbourne that were made by southern European migrant
home-buyers during the 1950s and 1960s are still in the main deplored by
preservationists and gentrifiers, who see the houses' historic significance
only in terms of the years when they were built and first occupied. To
commemorate is to discount all alternative viewpoints and experiences of
the past. Its effect is to endorse the histories of powerful groups over those
of minorities and the oppressed. In United States, unlike Australia,
whose historiography—perhaps because of the convict origins of European settlement—has always addressed the underdog, historic preservation still exhibits a reluctance to address conflict and injustice. It shies
away from presenting the past in the eyes of others than dominant elites,
or, when other experiences are presented, from doing so without contrived heroic flourishes. At Colonial Williamsburg, where historic preservation sought to commemorate the Virginian planter elite, the lives of
African-Americans were ignored until the 1970s, and thereafter were
presented as though disconnected from the lifestyles of the planter elite. It
was not until 1988 that the Valentine Museum's exhibition, "In Bondage
and Freedom: Antebellum Black Life in Richmond, Virginia, 1790–
1860," first explored African-American community life and race relations
in the capital city of the confederacy.[41]

A significant break from commemoration orthodoxy was achieved with
the launching of the Maryland State Outdoor Museum at St. Mary's City
in 1969. St. Mary's City was founded by English catholic colonists in
1634, becoming the fourth permanent settlement in British North America. It was the capital of Maryland until 1695, after which the settlement
was gradually abandoned and given over to the fields of local plantations.
The State Commission, which administers the site, began by rejecting the
then-current preservationist viewpoint of Colonial Williamsburg, which
still saw only small periods of time and selected structures as significant.
The commission aimed instead to show the site evolving layer upon layer
through time, thereby exploring the dynamics of social life in each: Native
American society, the early capital, the late seventeenth-century village,
eighteenth-century farms, and nineteenth-century plantation society.

Another major advance in communicating credible history was achieved
in September 1990, with the National Park Service's reopening of the
main immigrant reception hall at Ellis Island in New York City. The

privately funded $156 million restoration project, begun early in the 1980s, is the largest in American history. The hall's interpretive displays, eschewing the usual preoccupation with narrow slices of time in a chronological and social vacuum, address not only the site's evolution throughout the whole period of its operation as an immigrant reception station, from 1892 to 1954, but also the closing of the immigrant station, its transformation from ruin into national museum, and a three hundred-year overview of the island's history. Equally important, Ellis Island is used as a vehicle to communicate the experiences of the immigrants who passed through it—the hopes, traumas, setbacks, and personal triumphs of credible individuals at the ports of embarkation, on board ship, and arriving and settling in America. Yet even at Ellis Island communication of history continues to be clouded by commemorationism. The site is frequently represented as a "shrine," whose historical significance lies in illuminating the "sage" of "the great traditions of freedom and opportunity in America."[42]

Communicating the city in history has also been inhibited by disagreement about the most appropriate applications for preserving cultural heritage. The principal form of heritage endeavor to date has not been preservation or conservation, but documentation. The 1970s and 1980s saw a boom in Australia in heritage studies commissioned by government agencies, and which was paralleled in the United States by the commissioning of environmental site assessments. The most significant application in the United States of this genre of preservation by documentation is to be found in the work of HABS and HAER, which together form a division in the National Park Service. This small unit of architects, engineers, historians, and photographers does not itself conserve material objects or even nominate them for listing on the National Register. Rather, it surveys endangered sites and objects, assesses their historic significance, and documents their social history by text, measured and interpretive drawings, and photographs. Most of the work is undertaken by hired field teams of professional and student historians, architects, engineers, illustrators, and photographers, who work under the supervision of the division's permanent staff. Additional documentation is provided by preservation contractors working for other federal agencies, which have been required by federal legislation since 1980 to commission recording projects on all federally owned historic properties that are to be altered or demolished. Other donations are received from interested professionals and from class projects by university students. Approximately one thousand historic structures are documented annually and are added to the Library of Congress.

Two problems characterize such preservation activity. First, the tenuousness of the achievement: Is preservation through documentation an
adequate or sufficient form of preserving the past? Second, is documentation an adequate means of incorporating popular history and of communicating a sense of the past to a general audience?

"Preservation through documentation," says Robert Kapsch, is "the
minimum preservation which all of our historic buildings and structures
should receive."[43] Many preservation activists worry, however, that to
adopt documentation as a minimum standard in the urban planning process would simply be to rubber stamp rather than to influence the redevelopment process. Once the history is documented, it is feared, city planning
authorities would see their way clear to allow unfettered redevelopment of
the physical sites. In the United States, many of the structures surveyed by
HABS/HAER teams have been lost to redevelopment. In Australia, concerns about the adequacy of documentation were strengthened by the
demolition of the ICOMOS-nominated Bow String Truss Wool Stores in
Geelong. Accumulating experiences of bad faith and missed opportunities
during the 1980s have demonstrated that the implementation of effective
urban-planning controls do not automatically flow from the commissioning of heritage-conservation studies by state and local governments.

In Australia, the question of the adequacy of historic heritage documentation flared in the mid-1980s and continues to polarize heritage professionals. Critics of Melbourne's Living Museum of the West charged it
with devising a deliberately commemorationist approach in heritage-
assessment consultancy projects. The museum was accused of placating
developers and government planners by concentrating on documenting
the social history of endangered industrial sites while marginalizing the
present significance of the physical structures themselves. The issue first
came to a head before the Historic Buildings Council in 1987, when the
director of the museum gave evidence in support of a multi-million-dollar
shopping development on the site of the former "Sunshine" harvester
works, which had been begun by the pioneer agricultural implement
manufacturer, H. V. McKay. The museum director argued that the industrial complex should not be listed on the Register. The museum, which
had been commissioned to assess the historical significance of the site,
prepared two volumes of oral history and photographic evidence but paid
only superficial attention to the factory's material fabric and to the possibility of preservation. Notwithstanding this fiasco, in 1987 the museum
was commissioned by the Ministry for Planning and Environment, against
the advice of the ministry's own Heritage Branch, to undertake a heritage
assessment of a historically-rich site in Footscray that had been designated

as part of another major redevelopment project. The museum's study so signally failed to address the heritage-preservation issues raised by the proposed development that the local historical society condemned the report and secured the commissioning of another study by historians at the University of Melbourne.[44]

Critics of the Living Museum acknowledged that the museum was attempting to build cultural-heritage assessment into the planning process, but they objected to the museum's slant toward commemoration in lieu of conservation. Heritage activists in Australia and the United States have long sought means of retaining historic structures and neighborhoods without strangling economic development. In both countries, this consideration led to the concept of adaptation or "adaptive reuse." Ada Louise Huxtable has argued that preservation "is the job of finding ways to keep those original buildings that provide the city's character and continuity and of incorporating them into its living mainstream."[45] It follows from this line of thinking that historic buildings "cannot be saved unless there are uses for them. There are very few properties that the country can afford to 'mothball,' hoping that someone, someday, will come up with a use."[46] American critics of adaptive reuse countered that the practice simply legitimated the overdevelopment process in American cities against which neighborhoods had mobilized since the 1960s. Adaptation and its frequent consequence, "facadism," have been accused in both countries of draining structures and places of historic meaning by obliterating their associations with the past.

The second problem with heritage documentation concerns accessibility. Documentation is not a public process, either in its recording and assessment stage or in the communication of completed findings and recommendations. Perhaps the nearest approximation to public history are the records of the HABS/HAER. These are the most widely used of all the special collections in the Library of Congress, and are also available on microfilm in more than one hundred other institutions. Nonetheless, selection of sites and objects for survey and the actual work of documentation are clearly not public processes. Likewise in Australia, it is clear that commissioned heritage studies and citation reports by the National Trust are neither generated in public nor serve to inform the public. In theory they are available to all. Access and use are constrained, however, by the often limited budgets that produced them and by the specific and technical purposes of commissioning agencies. The majority of reports do not get to public libraries. The very nature of the consultancy process—the frequent vested interests in particular manipulations of history by both client and consultant, constraints of timetable and budget, the minimal opportunities for input by interested individuals and groups—is producing a new kind of history, a streamlined commodification and privatization of what ought to be a public resource.

How can heritage professionals overcome these problems? Plainly, the communication of history needs to be democratized. Whereas academic historians procrastinate, other professionals are addressing this challenge. The National Trusts in both countries are now very much alive to the need for education programs and outreach work. National Historic Preservation Week in the United States and Heritage Week in Australia are examples of the Trusts' efforts to encourage public participation. The HAER, alive to limitations of documentation, is helping the National Park Service to identify interesting industrial-history sites that can be turned into national parks along the lines of the popular industrial-history park established in Lowell, Massachusetts, in the early 1980s. Preliminary planning has been undertaken since the mid-1980s for America's Industrial Heritage Project, which is designed to span the iron and steel, coal, and transportation industries in nine counties of the Allegheny highlands in southwestern Pennsylvania. National Park Service planners aim to use the historic sites as focal points for tourist routes that link the natural and historic environments.

Museum professionals are likewise rethinking the communication of history. At the successful Chicago conference "Venues of Inquiry into the American City," which followed the disappointing "Modes" conference for academic historians, museum professionals debated the challenge thrown to them by Frank Jewell, director of Richmond's Valentine Museum: to find means for "interpreting the American city to a broad, popular audience."[47] The State Outdoor Museum at St. Mary's City may be taken to illustrate some of the new thinking about communicating the past. The museum has developed an upbeat promotional program, with the jaunty promise that "Maryland's rich heritage comes to life in St. Mary's City."[48] The museum is gradually realizing a master plan prepared in the early 1970s, which envisions a major tourist attraction spread over eight hundred acres, including archaeological displays, reconstructions of seventeenth-century buildings, fortifications, ships and river craft, a tobacco plantation, an Indian settlement, and a scenic hiking trail through woodlands and along the Potomac shoreline.

Popularizing the past of course brings with it the danger that the imperatives of the tourist industry will overwhelm the communication of history. I was first urged to visit Williamsburg because of its amusement park, not its past. In Australia, there are encouraging signs that the general public is "tired of being served up plastic history. Many of them would rather visit a place which is scruffy and incomplete, but authentic, than one which has been built up with modern materials into a misleading romantic stereo-type."[49] In order to consolidate this trend, it is essential that communication of the past be overseen by heritage professionals with the will to build upon grassroots enthusiasm for history. As Jewell emphasized at the "Venues" conference, they must be prepared to interact with the multiplicity of opinions represented in the community, rather than arrogantly assuming an unchallenged right to lead. They must also, as Cary Carson, director at Colonial Williamsburg, argued at the same conference, strive to communicate the city "as a contested environment."[50] These difficult tasks are beyond the competence of any one professional grouping. They can be successfully addressed only by crossdisciplinary collaboration.

Early in 1989, considerable community and professional interest was generated in Australia by a collaborative historical and archaeological project in Melbourne to study the layered spatial forms and social history of an important industrial-history site in suburban Footscray. Volunteers flocked to help at the dig. In the United States, similar excitement was sparked in December 1990, when archaeologists and historians at St. Mary's City discovered the possible burial place of founding governor Philip Calvert. The two projects highlight a trend toward multidisciplinary professional research that is significantly enhancing not only academic knowledge of past but also community participation in interpreting history through the material culture of the past.

The St. Mary's City Commission has pioneered such collaborative work since the early 1970s. St. Mary's City, because of its abandonment after Annapolis was made colonial capital in 1695, is the best-preserved archaeological site of a seventeenth-century city in North America. The settlement is, however, poorly documented. No map of the settlement survives, no detailed written descriptions are known, and most of the land records have been destroyed. This has necessitated close collaboration— "a shotgun marriage," says Executive Director Burton K. Kummerow[51]— between historians and archaeologists in order to determine the nature of settlement on the site and to communicate it intelligibly to the general public.

Professionals in both disciplines acknowledge that this collaboration has greatly facilitated research at St. Mary's City. A major archaeological project was begun in 1981 to test historical knowledge of the settlement's spatial layout. The archaeologists, guided by historical reconstructions based upon the surviving land records, revealed a previously unsuspected town plan of two symmetrical triangles, which was apparently based on

European baroque principles of urban design. This is the earliest-known use of such sophisticated urban layouts in North America, and has necessitated modification of scholarly knowledge about colonial township formation, which had assumed the unsophistication of such frontier settlements.[52] The findings also expanded historical knowledge of religion and society. The town plan was found to give spatial expression to the pioneering efforts at St. Mary's City to achieve religious toleration and the separation of church and state, with the Church and State House standing at the axes of each of the triangles. In 1990 a combined archaeological and historical investigation was launched to find the site of the first chapel and its subsequent brick replacement—one of the largest structures in colonial America—and to explore the social, political, and physical contexts in which policies of religious freedom and separation of church and state were initiated in North America. It was this project, in December 1990, that located the chapel's seventeenth-century crypt and the three sealed lead coffins inside.

The multidisciplinary approach at St. Mary's City extends from research to experimentation with ways of exhibiting archaeological remains and historical documentation. As a first step to public interpretation of the site, the surviving footings of buildings were weather-proofed and the outlines of vanished structures marked out and displayed with explanatory texts. The commission, recognizing that foundations were unlikely to enable laypeople to picture accurately the vanished townscape, juggles historical and archaeological data in order to reconstruct selected structures. Sensitive to criticism of the principle of reconstruction, Dr. Henry M. Miller, archaeologist and director of research, contends that reconstructions are necessary, provided they are sufficiently based on documentation, to enable fuller—albeit more conjectural—interpretation of the material culture of daily life in this early colonial town to lay audiences today.[53] Complete reconstructions are avoided. Not only are these expensive but they deny visitors a chance to make intelligent interpretations on their own.[54] As Miles Lewis has argued in Australia, "We should assume that the visitor has got a mind, and not just a Nikon camera. We should present the place to him not as a fully finished and wrapped-up product, but the way it really is, with its imperfections and uncertainties. If it is possible to let him see investigation or restoration work actually under way, better still. . . . We should do this not merely because it interests the tourist or educates the school child, but because it is a pledge of our good faith, rather like listing the ingredients on a package of food for sale in a shop."[55]

Whereas the imprint of archaeology is most immediately visible in the collaborative research findings and exhibition materials at St. Mary's City, historians have played the most obvious role in the multidisciplinary effort that has gone into the restoration of Ellis Island. The eleven-member Statue of Liberty–Ellis Island history advisory committee played a key role since the early 1980s in cooperation with architects and archaeologists, in overseeing restoration work, and in planning how best to communicate the historical significance of the site through the Ellis Island Immigration Museum. The results of this collaborative oversight of the restoration project are seen in the interpretive re-creation of the entrance canopy and of the reception-hall staircase. The history committee convinced the National Park Service to change its plans and reinstall a staircase because the original—a physical fitness test that was monitored by medical examiners as the immigrants climbed to the Registry room—figured so prominently in the medical records and the recorded recollections of people who passed through.

The committee also persuaded the National Park Service to expand the scope of the museum beyond the peak period of the station's operations, from 1892 to 1924, in order to include a wider temporal perspective on immigration up to the present day, and to place American immigration in perspective of global movement of peoples. In collaboration with historians at the New York company Metaform, which conceptualized, researched, and designed the museum exhibits, the committee also succeeded in feeding the latest historical research findings into the displays. The result has been to communicate to the public the rich social history of immigration that had been concealed by the romantic myths of Emma Lazarus's "huddled masses" and of Oscar Handlin's "uprooted." The impressive displays, which draw upon the physical structures of the station, movable artifacts, photographic displays and film, sound, text, and interactive devices, show that migrants were not a cowed peasant herd that was "pushed" and "pulled" by impersonal and inexorable historical forces, but astute individuals whose decisions to emigrate were part of strategies designed to turn to personal advantage the complex processes of social change in their homelands and in the New World.

Professor Alan Kraut, consultant historian for the Ellis Island restoration, explained his enthusiasm for the project by saying: "History belongs to the people. It's their heritage."[56] As devices for harnessing grassroots interest in history, he applauds populist initiatives at Ellis Island such as the American Immigrant Wall of Honor, on which families can have the names of their migrant ancestors recorded, and America's Family Album, in which contributors can include a favorite family photo on video discs at the Ellis Island Immigration Museum. Kraut's innovative proselytizing approach to making and communicating history is sadly disregarded by most academic historians, as are the multidisciplinary achievements of historians and archaeologists at St. Mary's City. As Kummerow pointed out concerning this collaborative undertaking, "So far we haven't been able to convince many that this marriage of disciplines is necessary or even possible in other areas of American history."[57] The majority of historians are either indifferent about, or openly contemptuous toward, the principle—which runs through both Ellis Island and St. Mary's City—of history as a public domain. Others feel threatened by the concept. Moreover, even among those historians who have sought careers as public historians, some display hesitation and insensitivity when confronted by the insistent demands of people to tell their own stories about households, neighborhoods, and workplaces and to construct their own frameworks of historical significance.[58]

Increasing numbers of historians and other professionals are, of course, working closely and unpretentiously with local community groups to help them read the histories of their neighborhoods. In Australia, this is especially the case concerning the settlement experiences of post–World War II immigrants. In the United States likewise, community history projects have multiplied since 1982, when "Philadelphia Moving Past," a traveling history exhibition that was devised as part of the city's tricentennial celebrations, tapped enormous neighborhood interest.[59] Such projects unabashedly pursue places, themes, and activities that hitherto had been discounted as without historical significance. Thus, in New York City, the Lower East Side Tenement Museum was begun in 1988 in order to preserve an 1863 tenement building. The museum is run by a small permanent staff and a larger group of consultant architects, archaeologists, and historians. Their aim is not simply to preserve the tenement as an artifact in a glass case, frozen in a particular moment in time, but to use it as an instrument by which people can explore immigrant and tenement life over the generations, from the perspectives of women and children, the African-American community, the Jewish Lower East Side, Chinatown, and Little Italy. Tenement life is interpreted variously by exhibitions of photographs, multimedia presentations, drama, and working tours with community activists and interested professionals from city universities. Whereas the history profession as a whole has done little systematically to introduce history to school-age children, the museum has already built up a heavily used educational program for children.

The Past in the Present

Late in 1990 the president of the American National Trust for Historic Preservation issued a public appeal for the planned redevelopment of the historic McMillan Reservoir in Washington, D.C., to be considered "in the context of our city's heritage." Jackson Walter requested a stay on proceedings and described the site's historical significance as part of the capital city's elaborate nineteenth-century water-purification system. He argued that preserving the reservoir would be a means of "enhancing the 'quality of life' that is vanishing in our urban environment."[60] Walter's plea was answered by the president of the local civic association, who retorted that the district had more urgent priorities than the retention of "ivy-covered towers and . . . vaults." Redevelopment of the site, he said, would enable expansion of the local children's hospital and would provide a library, a community center, a police station, and housing for the elderly and for low-income families. The project would generate jobs and boost tax revenues for the District of Columbia. Although freely conceding that "there is merit in historic preservation," he concluded that "preserving the past cannot take priority over preserving the present and future."[61] This exchange, representing two reasonable but seemingly irreconcilable viewpoints, encapsulates the crisis confronting the historic fabric of American cities today. Yet Walter and his opponent did share some common ground: a commitment to achieving more-livable cities. Preservationists need to build upon this common ground if they are to achieve success in the 1990s.

Many critics of present-day urban policy-making assert that development decisions are consistently taken without sensitivity to history and hence without cognizance of the replicated social networks, memories, and customs that fashion physical forms into familiar and usable social spaces. History, Jackson Walter believes, has been taken out of the present. Many historians agree. Sam Bass Warner, Jr., argued that the result of this historical amnesia is that Americans have been left with no overall framework for comprehending their urban surroundings. Americans, he contended, "have no urban history. They live in one of the world's most urbanized countries as if it were a wilderness in both time and space. Beyond some civic and ethnic myths and a few family neighborhood memories, Americans are not conscious that they have a past and that by their actions they participate in making the future. As they tackle today's problems . . . they have no sense of where cities came from, how they grew, or even what direction the large forces of history are taking them."[62]

The opportunity exists for historic-preservation programs, enervated by public-history making that addresses vernacular identifications with city environs, to insert a sense of human scale and social justice in urban policy-making. Already, influenced by advances in academic interpretation of urban material culture, advocates of historic preservation argue for policy recognition on the grounds that historic environments function as a medium reflecting the social life of the past for the edification of present generations. Others go further, interpreting cities' built forms as catalysts that prompt recognition of the connections between past and present, and in so doing promote social mobilization and action to redress historic wrongs and inequalities. Decrying the detachment from history and the denial of memory in American cities, Michael Frisch has called for community projects "that will involve people in exploring what it means to remember, and what to do with memories to make them active and alive, as opposed to mere objects of collection."[63]

This casting of cultural heritage as a potent means of addressing the past in the present is as essential for humane city planning as it is profoundly problematic for traditionalists in the heritage field and the academy. Notwithstanding the broader range of urban activities, artifacts, and structures that are now officially recognized as having historical significance, and notwithstanding also a quarter-century's progress in presenting and interpreting their historical significance in more convincing ways, preservation activism remains largely as it always has been: an elite activity with marginal relevance to urban policy, labor, and recreation. Its ability to communicate a compelling sense of the past to decision-making in the present is uncertain. In order for historic preservation to help produce more-livable cities, its advocates must first communicate rigorously the historical interconnectedness of the material fabric of our cities, and in so doing accommodate these physical forms of the past with present-day activities. Second, they must engage wholeheartedly with the multiple viewpoints of the local knowledge contained within our cities.

Preserving the forms of the past in the absence of reciprocal public meanings and present-day functional relevance is pointless. An essential first step for avoiding these problems is the adopting by heritage professionals in the New World of a code of principles that is methodologically credible and uniform, and yet practical in its application to cultural resources management. The Burra Charter provides a basis for such a code. Its concept of cultural significance deliberately eschewed the selective attention on historic activities, structures, epochs, and districts that characterized the assessment and communication of historical significance in the past. The focus of historic-preservation programs must become, as was intended by the Burra Charter, the explication of material culture in ways that focus upon the social context in which historic places, cultures, and artifacts were embedded and from which they derive meaning. This necessitates communication of history as process: not predetermined, impersonal, and inexorable, but contingent upon the multiple individual and group decisions, calculations, and confrontations of everyday living. To attempt this difficult task necessitates a change in focus away from spatially and socially disconnected structures in cities, to cities as totalities embracing a complex web of social relations between rich and poor, men and women, host and immigrant.

The policies of the Valentine Museum since its revitalization in 1985 under Jewell's direction provide a partial example of the scholarly preoccupations and communication strategies these tasks require. However, the sensitivity to local history that the Valentine has promoted in museum settings needs to be pursued in preservation programs that can be applied throughout our cities. The outcomes of such cultural heritage assessment will range, depending upon the heritage significance of the structures and places under review, from documentation to preservation, restoration, and reconstruction. Regardless of outcomes, however, it is necessary that heritage assessment and supervision be uniformly public processes. There is nothing intrinsically worthy of preservation about material forms if the social significance that once derived from their place in past social life is lost. It is crucial therefore that cultural heritage programs be public in order to accommodate multiple readings of the urban past. We are thereby well placed to combine the tangible—albeit competing—memories of local knowledge with the hypothesizing and synthesizing strengths of heritage professionals.

It is also crucial, in order that cultural-heritage assessment—and where appropriate, conservation and reuse—be adopted on a large scale that they be so managed as to avoid becoming impediments to careful urban development. If preservation is to occupy a significant and lasting place in city planning, it must not be misconstrued as serving to drain modern-day utility from historic built environments by turning them into empty halls of memory to a remote past. We need to cultivate a sense of history that is unabashedly worldly and mundane. There is no need to apologize for devising new functions and renewed relevance for buildings and places whose historic character was, after all, shaped by their intimacy with, and not remoteness from, everyday living. It is a triumph for heritage conservation if a sense of history can be brought to bear in recycling yesterday's buildings to provide affordable housing, offices, shops, and places of popular entertainment. The Valentine's restoration of the Tredegar Iron Works is strongly supported by business and city managers, who see the

new museum as a spur to revitalizing downtown Richmond. More ambi-
tiously, the Burra Charter provides a general model for such carefully
managed adaptation, reasoning that "finding a viable use for a place is an
important aid to its conservation."[64] We cannot afford to allow heritage
planning to remain a fetish that provides entertainment to a pretentious
few. Cultural-heritage conservation must be grounded in a sense of history
that is doubly public: not only should it present the people's history, but it
should do so in public and relevant ways.

This accumulating public knowledge of our historic environments must
be constantly applied to activities that are not thought of as being for-
mally historic in nature. For example, such knowledge needs to be widely
applied in professional training. More than half the workplace applications for engineering skills today take place within existing structures.[65] A
notable model for the application of historical knowledge to professional
skills is afforded by the Public Works Historical Society. Of its 1,800
members, some 1,500 are active public-works professionals and 300 are
academic historians. The association's newsletter, research projects, and
annual book award attempt to bring the latest scholarship in public-works
history to the attention of the engineers and public-works administrators
who form the bulk of its membership. The hard work of applying history
also needs to be systematically extended in the planning process. Historical research must be shown to be usable in the public and private corporations where hard-nosed policymakers determine options.[66] In Melbourne,
the heritage studies commissioned during the 1980s constitute such an
important body of information that it is now crucial that planners and
developers must be encouraged to address it as part of the normal planning
process, rather than allow the reports to be dismissed as an abrasive but
containable forward push by conservationist extremists.[67]

In view of the continuing skepticism and ambivalence by state and
local authorities toward heritage conservation, mass electoral pressure is
needed to consolidate and extend the uneven achievements of the
1980s. It is here that historians could provide a lead, where preservationists have traditionally faltered, by communicating cultural-heritage studies and mobilizing participation and support. In so doing they must
accommodate multiple viewpoints about historic significance and cultural resources management: encouraging "members of various publics
[to] come together to interact and perhaps to understand better a shared
culture and past."[68] The challenge for historians is to assist folk memory
rather than clouding it with fuzzy nostalgia and sentimentality. Moreover, the recovery of memory must be coupled with civic activism to
apply those memories to policy-making in the present. Without such

activism, the study of material culture is shallow antiquarianism, or worse, commemorationism that consciously or unwittingly provides an ideological justification for injustice and a green light for the overdevelopment of our cities. Historians must become advocates for social equity as they address the present-day policy arena. In so doing, they are particularly well placed "to try to create space in the public's historical memory for those who are too often pushed toward the margins. Public history can uncritically offer accounts that allow elites to use history to protect and legitimize themselves, or it can view history as a potential means of empowering those who lack power."[69]

Empowerment is not an intellectual exercise for armchair socialists. It requires historians to participate fully in the public-policy arena: not just conducting historical research, but sitting on committees, collecting signatures, and raising donations. In order to earn community respect, they need to demonstrate that history making is grounded in the quest for livable and human-scaled cities. Their responsibility, as citizens as well as professionals, requires them to engage in social programs such as those pioneered in Charleston under Mayor Daly in 1987, in Philadelphia's Diamond Street Historic District, and in the Springfield neighborhood in Jackson, Florida, to rehabilitate historic housing for low- and moderate-income earners. By thus engaging historians in public service, the opportunity exists to nurture "a broad-based, powerful coalition to promote history" in the interests of fashioning humane city environments akin to those in historic northern Italian cities such as Parma.[70]

University of Melbourne

Notes

1. This expression, widely and loosely used in the United States, is applied more narrowly in Australia. The Australian Heritage Commission defines *conservation* as "the process undertaken to retain and protect the national estate significance of a particular place" in either the natural or cultural environment. *Preservation*, which it defines as "maintaining the fabric of a place in its existing state and retarding its deterioration," is but one component of this process, along with restoration, reconstruction, and adaptation. Australian Heritage Commission, *The National Estates Grants Program* (Canberra, 1991), 7–9.

2. Rod Fisher, " 'Nocturnal Demolitions': The Long March Toward Heritage Legislation In Queensland," in John Rickard and Peter Spearritt, eds., *Packaging the Past? Public Histories*, a special issue of *Australian Historical Studies* 24 (April 1991): 55–69.

3. Giovanni Battista Balangero, *Australia e Ceylan: Studi e memorie di tredici anni di missione* (Turin, 1897).

4. See Graeme Davison, "Marrying History with the Future: The Rialto Story," *Victo-*

rian Historical Journal 58 (March 1987): 6–19. In 1963 the distinguished British social historian Asa Briggs had included Melbourne as the only non-English case study in his pioneering urban history, *Victorian Cities* (New York, 1965 edition).

5. See Donald J. Olsen, *The City as a Work of Art* (New Haven, 1986).

6. See Herbert J. Gans, "The Potential Environment and the Effective Environment," in *People and Plans: Essays on Urban Problems and Solutions* (New York, 1968), 4–11.

7. Manuel Castells, *The City and the Grassroots: A Cross-Cultural Theory of Urban Social Movements* (London, 1983), 70.

8. See Graeme Davison, *What Makes a Building Historic?* (Melbourne, 1986).

9. Larry E. Tise, "The Practice of Public History in State Government," in Barbara J. Howe and Emory Kemp, eds., *Public History: An Introduction* (Malabar, Fla., 1986), 333. Miles Lewis, "The Ugly Historian," *Historic Environment* 5, no. 4 (1986): 4–7.

10. Miles Lewis, "Conservation: A Regional Point of View," in Max Bourke, Miles Lewis, and Bal Saini eds., *Protecting the Past for the Future. Proceedings of the Unesco Regional Conference on Historic Places* (Canberra, 1983), 6. Miles Lewis, "Philosophy of Restoration," paper delivered at the conference "Heritage and Conservation: The Challenges in the Asian/Pacific Basin," Darwin, May 1990, 3.

11. U.S. Department of the Interior, National Park Service, *The National Register of Historic Places.*

12. National Trust for Historic Preservation, *Annual Report* (Washington, D.C., 1989), 4.

13. Quoted by Davison in "A Brief History of the Australian Heritage Movement," in Graeme Davison and Chris McConville, eds., *A Heritage Handbook* (Sydney, 1991), 16.

14. Quoted in National Trust for Historic Preservation, *1979 Annual Report,* 3.

15. "Valentine Museum Mission and Recent History," undated publicity release by The Valentine: The Museum of the Life and History of Richmond.

16. Mike Lake, "Valentine Museum Expanding Development to the Riverfront," *Oh Magazine,* 31 January–6 February 1991.

17. See Michael Wallace, "Reflections on the History of Historic Preservation," in Susan P. Benson, Stephen Brier, and Roy Rosenweig, eds., *Presenting the Past: Essays on History and the Public* (Philadelphia, 1986), 165–99.

18. See Davison in "A Brief History of the Australian Heritage Movement," 14–19.

19. Australian Heritage Commission Act 1975, subsection 4(1).

20. Barrie Dyster, *Servant and Master: Building and Running the Grand Houses of Sydney, 1788–1850* (Kensington, New South Wales, 1989).

21. Sarah Brown, "Making Common Building Knowledge," *Public Historian* 12 (Fall 1990): 79–92.

22. Lewis, "Conservation: A Regional Point of View," 6; Lewis, "Philosophy of Restoration," 4–19.

23. Robert J. Kapsch, "HABS/HAER: A User's Guide," *Association for Preservation Technology Bulletin* 22, no. 1/2 (1990): 22–23.

24. Helen Proudfoot, "The Concept of Historical Significance in Relation to Heritage," typescript prepared for the Australian Heritage Commission, September 1988, 34.

25. Benjamin Forgey, "Preservation Perseverance," *Washington Post,* 11 May 1991.

26. Carlton Association, *Housing Survival in Carlton* (North Carlton, 1969).

27. Zula Nittim, "The Coalition of Resident Action Groups," in Jill Roe, ed., *Twentieth-Century Sydney: Studies in Urban and Social History* (Sydney, 1980), 231–47.

28. See "Gentrification in Melbourne's Inner City," in Paul Madden, Andrew Burbidge, and Renate Howe, *The Displaced: A Study of Housing Conflict in Melbourne's Inner City* (Melbourne, 1977).

29. Stever Harris, "Residents in Policy Planning: A Sydney Case Study," *Polis* 7, no. 2 (1980): 29–34.

30. George Morgan, "History on the Rocks," in Rickard and Spearritt, *Packaging the Past,* 78–87. Jack Mundy, *Green Bans and Beyond* (Sydney, 1981).

31. Fisher, "Nocturnal Demolitions," 55–57.

32. See Lionel Frost, *The New Urban Frontier: Urbanisation and City-Building in Austral-asia and the American West Before 1910* (Sydney, 1991).

33. For a cynical review of the museum's development, see David Dunstan, "Heritage Conservation and Museum Development in Melbourne's Western Suburbs in the 1980s," *Victorian Historical Journal* 61 (August 1990): 214–16; and Chris Healy, "Working for the Living Museum of the West," in Rickard and Spearritt, *Packaging the Past,* 153–67.

34. See Chris McConville, " 'In Trust'? Heritage and History," *Melbourne Historical Journal* 16 (1984): 60–74.

35. Donovan Rypkema and Ian D. Spatz, "Rehab Takes a Fall" (Washington, D.C., 1990).

36. Kapsch, "HABS/HAER: A User's Guide," 22–23.

37. Peter Spearritt, "Money, Taste, and Industrial Heritage," in Rickard and Spearritt, *Packaging the Past,* 33–45.

38. David Brittan, "Saving U.S. Industry in Words and Pictures," *Technology Review* (July 1990): 57.

39. Simon R. Molesworth, "The Challenge of Our Industrial Heritage," *Victorian Historical Journal* 61 (August 1990): 93.

40. Spearritt, "Money, Taste, and Industrial Heritage," 35–36.

41. Gregg D. Kimball and Marie Tyler-McGraw, "Integrating the Interpretation of the Southern City: An Exhibition Case Study," *Public Historian* 12 (Spring 1990): 31–43.

42. "Once the Final Hurdle for Immigrants, Ellis Will Bear Witness to Their Legacy," *Washington Post,* 2 September 1991. The Statue of Liberty–Ellis Island Foundation, Inc., "If You Don't Keep Their Names Alive . . . Who Will?" (New York, 1991).

43. Kapsch, "HABS/HAER: A User's Guide," 23.

44. Dunstan, "Heritage Conservation and Museum Development in Melbourne," 218–20. Andrew May and Alan Mayne, "Consulting the Past: The Footscray City Link Heritage Study," *Victorian Historical Journal* 61 (August 1990): 193–94.

45. Quoted by Wallace, "Reflections on the History of Historic Preservation," 177.

46. Barbara J. Howe, "Historic Preservation: An Interdisciplinary Field," in Howe and Kemp, *Public History,* 159.

47. Quoted by Philip Scranton, "From Modes to Venues," in the Urban History Association's *Urban History Newsletter* 5 (March 1991): 5.

48. Promotional tract, "Historic St. Mary's City: Where Maryland Began."

49. Lewis, "Conservation: A Regional Point of View," 7.

50. Scranton, "From Modes to Venues," 5.

51. Letter from Kummerow To Mayne, 19 April 1991.

52. Henry Miller, "Baroque Cities in the Wilderness: Archaeology and Urban Development in the Colonial Chesapeake," *Historical Archaeology* 22.2 (1988): 57–73.

53. Interview with Henry Miller, 8 April 1991.

54. St. Mary's City Commission, "St. Mary's City: A Plan for the Outdoor Museum, Part 2," April 1974.

55. Lewis, "Conservation: A Regional Point of View," 9.

56. Mary Jo Binker, "Creating America's Gateway: Alan Kraut and the Restoration of Ellis Island," *American* 42 (Winter 1991): 3.

57. Letter from Kummerow to Mayne, 19 April 1991.

58. Linda Shopes, "Oral History and Community Involvement: The Baltimore Neighborhood Heritage Project," in Benson, Brier, and Rosenzweig, *Presenting the Past,* 249–63.

59. See Cynthia Jeffress Little, "Celebrating Three Hundred Years in a City of Neighbourhoods: Philadelphia Moving Past," in Howe and Kemp, *Public History,* 265–76.

60. J. Jackson Walter, "At Stake, Not Only Open Land, But a Landmark," *Washington Post,* 16 December 1990.

61. George W. Crawford, "Making a Case for Progress," *Washington Post,* 23 December 1990.

62. Sam Bass Warner, Jr., *The Urban Wilderness: A History of the American City* (New York, 1972), 4.

63. Michael H. Frisch, "The Memory of History," in Benson, Brier, and Rosenweig, *Presenting the Past*, 11, 17.

64. Lewis, "Philosophy of Restoration," 13.

65. Kathleen A. McCarthy, "Bringing History Up to Date: An Engineering Perspective of the Past," reprinted from *Engineering Education*, ASEE, 1988 by HAER.

66. Michael C. Scardaville, "Looking Backward Toward the Future: An Assessment of the Public History Movement," *Public Historian* 9 (Fall 1987): 35–43.

67. Dunstan, "Heritage Conservation and Museum Development in Melbourne," 214.

68. Fath Davis Ruffins, "Exhibition Reviews," *Journal of American History* (June 1991): 268.

69. Jerrold Hirsch, "Cherished Values: The New Deal, Cultural Policy, and Public History," *Public Historian* 12 (Fall 1990): 78.

70. Theodore J. Karamanski, "Making History Whole: Public Service, Public History, and the Profession," *Public Historian* 12 (Summer 1990): 93.

SEYMOUR J. MANDELBAUM

Reading Old Plans

Citizens and Strangers

My initial decision to explicate how I read formal planning texts was provoked by the 1988 publication of a scheme for the CBD of Philadelphia and the adjacent residential neighborhoods. I thought initially that I might be able to help people directly read *The Plan for Center City.*[1] Ultimately, however, I settled on a more modest goal: encouraging a conversation among planners about both reading and writing plans. My contribution to that conversation, an essay entitled "Reading Plans," started with the notion that a plan, like any other text, creates images of an "ideal" and a "real" author and reader. I went on to explore the ways in which I located myself within and against those images. Once I'd fixed my location, I suggested, I read the core of a plan—whether it was a budget, a simple plat of streets and lots, a formal set of legal rules controlling land use, or an elaborately argued hybrid like *The Plan for Center City*—in three complementary ways: as a complex set of policy arguments, as an elaboration of a decision opportunity, and as a story.

A year passed between the revision of the essay in 1989 and its publication.[2] Only with the distance of that year did I appreciate that I had not paused to reflect on the context in which I had written about reading: I assumed throughout my essay that I was both a contemporary of the plan I was interpreting and, in one way or another a party to it. I described ways

An earlier version of this article was presented at the joint Fourth National Conference on American Planning History and the Fifth International Conference of the Planning History Group, Richmond, Virginia, 7–10 November 1991.

of reading that were informed by the engagements and expectations of a citizen who was ready to assent to a plan only after interpreting the identity, intentions, and capabilities of its authors, judging the wisdom and the feasibility of their construction of the future, and assessing the likely response of other readers. Reading as a citizen, I complained when I thought that authors set their vision in a world I did not recognize or in which I was disempowered; when they wrote as if their words barely mattered because, after all, "no one reads." "Reading Plans" asks planners and citizens alike to recognize reading as a strenuous public activity practiced on present and pressing but very recalcitrant texts.

Rereading my own essay after it too had aged, I began to wonder: How do I read "old" plans? Are "old" plans different? Are the historian's glasses different from those of the contemporary?

Even before I had clarified the meaning of those questions or sketched tentative answers in my mind, I had a title that pleased me—"Reading Old Plans"—and had promised to append an essay to it. As soon as I began to think seriously about fulfilling that promise, however, the title gave me pause. The situation of the reader of an old and of a contemporary but politically remote plan are not, after all, so very different. Except in my dreams, I cannot offer Thomas Holme and William Penn advice on the planning of Philadelphia; nor is my opinion of their labors likely to alter the history of the last three hundred years. Reading a freshly minted vision of the future of London, Mexico City, Tokyo, or even of a nearby Philadelphia suburb, I sometimes have a similar sense: I am observing shadows I cannot touch in a space in which I have no effective voice. My reading is detached rather than engaged and prosthetic. Alarmed by these reflections, I thought that I would, perhaps, be on safer though less euphonious grounds if I called the essay, "Reading Plans I Cannot Influence."

While I was still mulling over this issue, I had occasion to scan a set of quite disparate planning documents, including a Japanese-encouraged scheme to construct a "multifunction polis" in Australia, the next phases of the London Docklands program, rezoning requests that would allow a dramatic shift in the conventional suburban pattern on a large tract in Chester County outside Philadelphia, proposals to engage the European Community more broadly in regional planning, and the ambitious reconstruction plans of the Port of Yokohama. In each case, I came to see that distance in political space and distance in historical time are not fully equivalent. "Old" plans are not addressed to me: they don't require my assent and I cannot effectively challenge their authors. In contrast, while none of the plans I had scanned treated me directly as a citizen—they were not plans for "my community"—neither they did ignore me.

Stakeholders who are not citizens are an important—perhaps even a dominant—part of the audience of contemporary planning texts. Strangers cast as prospective investors are lured by exaggerated expressions of a shared commitment to a civic purpose, the dampening of conflict, and a heroic gloss on the capabilities of the *dramatis personnae*; cast as competitive strategists playing against the plan, they are challenged by a rhetoric devised to mystify, intimidate, impress, or confuse.

While I wrote "Reading Plans" from the perspective of a citizen-reader, it also speaks, I hope, to the interpretive difficulties confronting external stakeholders. When I assume the role of prospective investor or competitor, I do not seek either to understand a community or to repair it: I want only to allocate my capital wisely or to prepare my response in the next round of a continuing struggle. My purposes are, however, broad enough to force me to penetrate the same rhetoric of estrangement that engages the citizen in an elaborate confidence game.[3] As citizen or stranger, I struggle within the toils of that game and its rhetorical forms. I am forced to supply missing elements of the policy argument, to infer constraints of will in what often appears as unlimited devotion to the commonweal, and to wonder whether the cast can complete the scripted story.

The title remains, but so does its essential ambiguity. Starting at the beginning: When do we—when should we—represent a plan as "old"?

"Old" Is "Obsolete"

Among the several sensible answers to that question, one particularly seems to me to be deeply embedded in the conception of professional planning as a progressive craft. A plan is "old" in this usage when it is obsolete. While some plans, therefore, are stigmatized as old at birth, in the more interesting cases, each had a day when it was new and (perhaps) fitting. That day, however, has passed even if the plan continues to guide the design of sites, policies, or programs. So the modernists condemned the Beaux Arts tradition only to suffer the same fate at postmodern hands; so each of the downtown renewal strategies described by Carl Abbott in this issue of the *Journal of Policy History* created a present for itself by framing its predecessor as out of date.

As in many things, Frederick Law Olmsted provides a wonderful example of this professional construction of obsolescence. His 1876 report on the design of the recently annexed Westchester wards of New York City (written with J. J. R. Croes) attempted to block the simple extension of the Manhattan grid to the hills of Riverdale.[4] He recognized, however, that his critique of the "regular" street pattern was not widely shared. In old districts and new, every effort to change the street design, he lamented, had been blocked by the pervasive assumption that the system was nearly "perfect" and that it could be extended unaltered across the city with only minor variations in the hilliest sections.

Confronting this ubiquitous prejudice in favor of the current system, Olmsted attempted to distance his readers from their own present by representing current practices as the expression of a primitive time and an obsolete plan. The grid, he insisted, had been adopted early in the century "very nearly in the position which a small, poor, remote provincial village would now be expected to take."

> Under these circumstances, it was not to be expected that, if the utmost human wisdom had been used in the preparation of the plan, means would be aptly devised for all such ends as a commission charged with a similar duty at the present day must necessarily have before it.[5]

Olmsted's (mainly) failed challenge to the grid is illuminated by considering abstractly the difficulties in representing current practices as the expression of a prior and now obsolete plan.

The first step in the symbolic construction of old plans is to link text and practice. That seems simple enough when the plan is a plat and the practice is a map of street and property lines. If plat and practice are isomorphic, the causal link is tightly drawn: the city, we reasonably assume, has been built to the plan.

Olmsted's brief history of the early nineteenth-century Manhattan grid reveals the dangers of this assumption even in a relatively uncomplicated case where the convergence was strong. Some plans (particularly for individual buildings) are realized in what appears in retrospect to be a single moment. The commitment to act carries forward through the process of implementation ineluctably. More complex plans that seek to shape the flow of resources and decisions over protracted time must, necessarily, re-create themselves: recruiting supporters, sustaining coalitions, eliciting maintenance expenditures, and adapting to environmental shifts. The re-created plan cannot be grasped by simply reading the original specifications: like the U.S. Constitution, it must be understood politically as a text living in history. A plan—not as symbols on a page but as a dominant coalition or an institution creating transaction costs—cannot be read and it cannot by replaced by merely revising a text or substituting a new one in its place. While the practices that emerge from re-creation may appear to be identical with those prefigured in the original text, their meaning, their scope, and their place in a complex social system may all be new. In the most familiar cases, the "old city" that continues to be controlled by the original plan is reduced to a limited zone in a metropolitan region; even within its borders, surface appearances mask a dramatic transformation in use, infrastructure, communication, and accessibility. The old plan of "historic" Charleston or of the Paris beloved of tourists may indeed be obsolete. Despite appearances, it may not, however, be the plan on the ground.

There is a way around these difficulties. A reader may sensibly designate a text as old without regard to its practical influence if it meets three subjective tests: (1) even if it is new, it appears to fit a prior period; (2) it does not fit current or wisely anticipated conditions; and, finally, (3) other plans fit better. The first test prevents treating every bad plan as obsolete; the second captures the core meaning of the label; the third avoids the trap of arrogantly dismissing the best possible plan as inappropriate to its time.

These tests are imprinted on every argument for changes in the technology of planning—including Olmsted's. The rhetoric is familiar: the current plan or method is obsolete; we must transform the culture that lags behind our technology; we must drop the expectation of stability in order to cope with a turbulent world.[6]

Explicating these tests suggests why the construction of old plans is so often controversial. Even when participants in public debate agree upon the needs of the future and speak with a strong and consensual voice about the first two tests, they often cannot agree upon what fits better and settle, reluctantly, for the evils they understand. Negotiations on the construction of old plans are even more difficult when protagonists cannot agree whether they value or even recognize the world of the plan; whether the differences in urban technologies or rhetoric critically mark a temporal shift or are mere appearances cloaking the continuity of essential social forms. Participants in religious, cultural, and now environmental debates argue: Is the past or the present inappropriate? Ought we abandon old plans or bring our current practice under their regime? Should we, for example, treat the high densities characteristic of pre-1920 urban plans as obsolete or as tomorrow's remedy for a failed suburban dream? Political economists and policymakers surveying a succession of budgets and fiscal policies wonder whether a misfit is a sign of a temporary (though recurrent) phase in the fluctuations of a structurally stable system or an indication of secular change. If a plan is simply out of phase, patience will restore its contemporaneity; if it builds upon a structure that no longer exists, then it is old and intractably flawed. We are not, however, graced with eyes that can certainly distinguish secular and cyclic changes as we create them. We are forced to locate ourselves in a present that we have crafted from a remembered past and a forecasted future.[7]

Misfits, Fits, and Meanings

There is a familiar complement to the image of readers busily constructing old plans by locating elements in texts that do not fit the present and future: many of us, with equal passion look at chronologically old or conceptually obsolete plans with an eye for surprising fits. We don't want to reconstruct a seventeenth-century village in the midst of a contemporary metropolis, but, we say, "Here's a neat old device that might do very nicely today." We read plans in order to maintain a repertoire of discrete physical forms and social arrangements from which we may pick and choose without being bound to restore (or even to understand) old contexts.

Professional historians are likely to sneer at this ersatz historicism and the decomposition of old plans into useful tricks. They also, however, read old plans with an eye to discrete elements that allow them to engage in retrospective assessments or to impute a sense of direction to the flow of events. I am particularly jealous of the confidence with which Whiggish British planning historians write of sanitary and town planning legislation in the nineteenth and early twentieth century. Each parliamentary act is interpreted as a landmark along a progressive developmental path: one step following upon the other. The repeated invocation of the canonical history of that path creates and sustains a tradition for professional planners that allows obsolete plans to speak to the present: the fight is long and the victories never perfect, but be of good cheer, the game can be won by those who persist.[8]

"There is more to reading old plans," I hear the historians in my head protesting, "than the decomposition of texts into fits and misfits, the specification of obsolescence, the construction of traditions, and the maintenance of a repetoire of physical and social devices." True enough, though I suspect that these forms are both ubiquitous and terribly important. As a practical matter, they leave only a little room for other intentions or readings.

That little room does, however, have a very large view: it occupies a treasured place in our image of the historian's craft. Occasionally, we are uncertain about the measures of obsolescence, the wisdom of copying a discrete feature, the character of the plan whose impact we choose to assess or of the tradition we choose to design. Troubled by these uncertainties, we designate a plan as belonging to a different time but pause to engage it deeply, attempting to interpret it within its own world as if we were, indeed, contemporaries of its authors. We attempt to respond to the text without the bias of our location in time; without knowing "what comes next" or allowing our hindsight to correct the mistaken forecasts of the past.

The difficulties of such a deep reading are ordinarily framed by contrasting them with the competence of actual contemporaries. We assume, for example, that those who read and listened to Roman town plans and participated in the rituals of site selection understood one another;[9] that Olmsted and his immediate clients shared a common conception of urban technologies and dynamics even if they disagreed about particular policies or designs. Contemporaries sometimes confuse one another, but the range of misunderstanding is narrowed by a shared present, a discursive formation, and a common culture. Confusion—when it appears—is obvious and (in principle) tractable. "Say that another way," we suggest: "Write clearly!" "Let's read that passage together." "Please tell the story again."

In contrast, the reader who engages an old plan deeply is sensibly alive to his or her incompetence. Explicit allusions in an old text fall easily before the skill of the historical detective, but the shared texts and experiences that endow figurative terms with meaning are often virtually impenetrable. We barely pause over the word "water" in a nineteenth-century aqueduct or sanitation plan until we are taken aback by the fervor with which a new, gushing stream of living urban water is greeted. What is it that we have missed in the "intertext" that pervades the plan?[10] Similarly, do we understand, at the end of the twentieth century, the emotional power and the political meaning of the mid-nineteenth-century image of an urban promenade?[11] We cannot be the ideal reader created by the text or fully assume the role or experiences of any of its real contemporary interpreters. We cannot demand that the author respond to our confusion by speaking to us directly or providing a commentary on the original wording. There is no test of comprehension through which original authors and readers may affirm to us that we "have it right" and ritually acknowledge that we belong at least temporarily in their world.[12]

This familiar contrast between the competence of contemporary readers and the ignorance of later readers is, I suspect, overdrawn. Contemporaries communicate within and across a complex network of overlapping communities in which shared meanings are difficult to achieve even when there is no explicit attempt to confuse or to coerce one another. A great many sins are justified in the name of clarity: voices and stories suppressed, complex practices turned into vacuous goals and priorities, contingencies transformed into certainties. Under even the best circumstances, authors must necessarily give up control of their texts to readers who reshape them so that one becomes many. Contemporaries and neighbors surround themselves in quite different worlds. The discursive formations or the negotiated public orders that allow them to affiliate or to join in collective action are partial and tenuous. The opportunities to "read in public" are stratified: for many readers and (even more strikingly) for nonreaders, plans appear from a distant world that cannot be interrogated.[13]

The major difference between reading contemporary plans and reading old plans as if we were their contemporaries lies in the sequence and the difficulty, not in the substance of interpretive tasks. In the present, we are socialized into worlds and the ways we talk within them. If we read deeply, we must render opaque what we know "naturally" as transparent. We must force ourselves to stumble over familiar words and concepts until we make a working sense of them. We may start with a defiant expectation that we can understand a plan without reference to any other text and without depending on a tutor. (If we can't, the author is chastised for a lack of clarity.) Only slowly do we acknowledge the density of overlapping plans and the value of a guide.

If we choose to live temporarily in the past, the task is the same, but the emotional burden is different. Like travelers in a foreign country, we must suspend some of our adult identity, to be born again as children and then to allow ourselves to "grow up" within a new language and imagery. Old plans may sensibly be read in isolation—like artifacts torn from their culture and displayed in the gallery of a museum as works of art—when we seek only to label them as obsolete, to array them in a tradition, or to borrow from them. (To repeat myself: that is the way we read them most of the time.) When we occasionally choose to act as their contemporaries, then we are bound to read an ensemble of texts in order to complete our reeducation. Treated in isolation, we have no sense of the force of convention or the repertoire within which the authors planned. Only a multiplicity of texts allows us to suspend our memories and to recognize (as appropriate) that there are no telephones in the world of the plan, that there have been no world wars, that the New Deal coalition is triumphant, that people believe that they can dilute their wastes in rivers, that children die in great numbers, or that the entrails speak to them meaningfully. Reading old plans in context allows us to cultivate appropriate anticipations but to strip ourselves of foreknowledge.

When I read a current plan, I instantly recognize that the text is trying to cast me in a role. I may be educated, intrigued, angered, or intimidated by that image of an ideal reader, but I never adopt it wholly. As a contemporary and as a party to the plan, I have no reason to forget who I am even when I try to interpret a text through another's eyes; I cannot literally put myself behind a veil of ignorance.

Reading an old plan deeply, I must suspend my identity and am, therefore, vulnerable to the idealized self created by the text. It is contemporary and it is often definitive. It is also, of course, specious: no contemporary (not even the author of a plan) would have read with those eyes. To enter imaginatively into the community of readers that once endowed an old plan with meaning, I must discipline that idealization by inventing a possible identity. I cannot allow Alexander Hamilton to control fully my reading of the *Report on Manufactures* or John Wesley Powell his *Report on the Arid Region of the United States*. The identity I invent need not capture exactly the perspective of any particular reader—as if that were even possible—but it must be embedded in authentic practices and prejudices, in knowledge and passion, in flesh and in blood.

University of Pennsylvania

Notes

1. Philadelphia City Planning Commission, *The Plan for Center City* (Philadelphia, January 1988).

2. "Reading Plans," *Journal of the American Planning Association* 56 (Summer 1990): 350–56. For a sense of the conversation in which the essay is embedded, see Marco Frascari, "The Angelic Paradox of Reading Plans," and my reply, *Penn In Ink* (Spring 1990): 16–18, a comparable exchange with Tim McGinty in the Spring 1991 issue, p. 7, and the comments elicited by "Reading Plans," in the *Journal of the American Planning Association* 56 (Summer 1990): 356–58, and 57 (Winter 1991), 93. Recent essays on the same theme include: Beth Moore Milroy, "Constructing and Deconstructing Plausibility," *Society and Space* 7 (1980): 313–26; Alison Tett and Jeanne M. Wolfe, "Discourse Analysis and City Plans," *Journal of Planning Education and Research* 10 (1991): 195–200, and Patsy Healy, "The Communicative Work of Development Plans," a paper presented at the joint conference of the Association of the Collegiate Schools of Planning and the Association of European Schools of Planning, Oxford, July 1991.

3. The imagery is borrowed from Gerald D. Suttles, *The Man-Made City: The Land-Use Confidence Game in Chicago* (Chicago, 1990).

4. "Document No. 72 of the Board of the Department of Public Parks" (1876), reprinted in Albert Fein, ed., *Landscape into Cityscape: Frederick Law Olmsted's Plans for a Greater New York City* (Ithaca, N.Y., 1967), 349–73.

5. Ibid., 351–1.

6. Compare the rhetoric of the innovative judges described in Morton J. Horowitz, *The Transformation of American Law, 1780–1860* (Cambridge, Mass., 1977), the analysts of cultural lag in the President's Research Committee on Social Trends, *Recent Social Trends*

in the United States (New York, 1933), and Donald A. Schon, *Beyond the Stable State* (New York, 1971).

7. I have elaborated on these issues in "Temporal Conventions in Planning Discourse," *Environment and Planning B: Planning and Design* 11 (1984): 5–13.

8. See, for example, Gordon E. Cherry, *Cities and Plans: The Shaping of Urban Britain in the Nineteenth and Twentieth Centuries* (London, 1988).

9. Joseph Rykwert, *The Idea of a Town: The Anthropology of Urban Form in Rome, Italy, and the Ancient World* (Princeton, 1976; Cambridge, Mass., 1988).

10. Michael Riffatere, *Fictional Truth* (Baltimore, 1991), 84–111.

11. Donald J. Olsen, *The City as a Work of Art: London, Paris, Vienna* (New Haven, 1986), 219–34.

12. This paragraph cryptically sketches issues that have dominated many discussions of the methods and uses of intellectual history. See, for example, J. G. A. Pocock, *Politics, Language, and Time: Essays on Political Thought and History* (New York, 1973); Dominick LaCapra, *Rethinking Intellectual History: Texts, Contexts, Language* (Ithaca, N.Y., 1983); and John Dunn, *Interpreting Political Responsibility: Essays, 1981–1989* (Princeton, 1989).

13. I have elaborated on these issues in "Open Moral Communities," *Society* 26 (November–December 1988): 20–27.

MARTIN V. MELOSI

Bibliographic Essay

In the last decade, urban historians—and other urban scholars interested in history—have begun to identify urban public policy as an emerging theme in the literature of the history of American cities. Michael H. Ebner, in "Urban History: Retrospect and Prospect," *Journal of American History* 68 (June 1981): 69–84, stated that one of three priorities facing urban historians in the future was the "contribution to the formulation of public policy" (82). Mark H. Rose, in "Machine Politics: The Historiography of Technology and Public Policy," *Public Historian* 10 (Spring 1988): 27–47, noted that "during the past several years, the study of politics and public policy appears to have begun a mild renaissance among historians" (35). And speaking more specifically about the theme of technology and the city, Josef W. Konvitz, Mark H. Rose, and Joel A. Tarr stated in "Technology and the City," *Technology and Culture* 31 (April 1990): 284–94, that, beginning as early as 1970, technology, public policy and politics constituted an important area of study for those interested in urban technology.

For some historians, urban public policy has come to mean—more narrowly—federal-city relations as suggested in Raymond A. Mohl, "New Perspectives on American Urban History," *International Journal of Social Education* 1 (Spring 1986): 69–97, and Jon C. Teaford, "Finis for Tweed and Steffens: Rewriting the History of Urban Rule," *Reviews in American History* (December 1982): 133–49.

While several scholars have demonstrated interest in urban policy history, the lion's share of the resulting books and articles are directed at the academic community and the general reading public, but rarely at policymakers themselves. Nevertheless, the following studies provide access to some useful bibliographic information and to some important themes relevant to urban policy history.

For general information about recent trends in urban history, see Howard Gillette, Jr., and Zane L. Miller, *American Urbanism: A Historiographical Review* (New York, 1987). See also John D. Buenker, et al., *Urban History: A Guide to Information Sources* (Detroit, 1981); Allen F. Davis, "The American Historian vs. the City," *Social Studies* 56 (March 1965): 91–96; Michael Frisch, "American Urban History as an Example of Recent Historiography," *History and Theory* 18 (1979); Theodore Hershberg, "The New Urban History: Toward an Interdisciplinary History of the City," *Journal of Urban History* 5 (November 1978): 3–40; Duncan R. Jamieson, "The City in American History," *Choice* 16 (March 1979): 25–42; Eric Lampard, "American Historians and the Study of Urbanization," *American Historical Review* 67 (October 1961): 49–61; Roy Lubove, "The Urbanization Process: An Approach to Historical Research," *Journal of the American Institute of Planners* 33 (January 1967): 33–39; Zane L. Miller, "Scarcity, Abundance, and American Urban History," *Journal of Urban History* 4 (February 1978): 131–56; Raymond A. Mohl, "The New Urban History and Its Alternatives: Some Reflections on Recent U.S. Scholarship on the Twentieth-Century City," *Urban History Yearbook* (1983): 19–28; Leo F. Schnore, "Problems in the Quantitative Study of Urban History," in H. J. Dyos, ed., *The Study of Urban History* (New York, 1968), 189–208; John Sharpless and Sam Bass Warner, Jr., "Urban History," *American Behavioral Scientist* 21 (November–December 1977): 221–44; Stephen Thernstrom, "The New Urban History," in Charles F. Delzell, ed., *The Future of History* (Nashville, 1977); and Sam Bass Warner, Jr., "If All the World Were Philadelphia: A Scaffolding for Urban History, 1774–1930," *American Historical Review* 74 (October 1978): 26–43.

Social scientists have produced an extensive literature on urban public policy. A recent general overview is Lawrence J. R. Herson and John M. Bolland, *The Urban Web: Politics, Policy, and Theory* (Chicago, 1990). Other useful studies since 1970 include John C. Bollens and Henry J. Schmandt, *The Metropolis: Its People, Politics, and Economic Life,* 4th ed. (New York, 1982); Terry Nichols Clark, ed., *Urban Policy Analysis: Directions for Future Research* (Beverly Hills, Calif., 1981); Douglas M. Fox, *The New Urban Politics: Cities and the Federal Government* (Pacific Palisades, Calif., 1972); John Harrigan, *Political Change in the Metropolis,* 4th ed. (Boston, 1989); Chester W. Hartman, *Housing and Social Policy* (Englewood Cliffs, N.J., 1975); James Heilbrun, *Urban Economics and Public Policy,* 2d ed. (New York, 1981); Jeffrey R. Henig, *Public Policy and*

Federalism: Issues in State and Local Politics (New York, 1985); Bryan D. Jones, *Service Delivery in the City: Citizen Demand and Bureaucratic Rules* (New York, 1980); Bryan D. Jones, *Governing Urban America: A Policy Focus* (Boston, 1983); Charles O. Jones, *An Introduction to the Study of Public Policy* (Monterey, Calif., 1983); Dennis R. Judd, *The Politics of American Cities: Private Power and Public Policy*, 3d ed. (Boston, 1988); Paul Kantor, *The Dependent City: The Changing Political Economy of American Urban Politics Since 1789* (New York, 1988); Robert L. Lineberry, *Equality and Urban Policy: The Distribution of Municipal Public Services* (Beverly Hills, Calif., 1977); Robert L. Lineberry and Ira Sharkansky, *Urban Politics and Public Policy* (New York, 1971); Marian Lief Palley and Howard A. Palley, *Urban America and Public Policies* (Lexington, Mass., 1981); Dennis J. Palumbo and George A. Taylor, *Urban Policy: A Guide to Information Sources* (Detroit, 1979); Bernard H. Ross and Murray S. Stedman, Jr., *Urban Politics*, 3d ed. (Itasca, Ill., 1985); Clarence N. Stone, Robert K. Whelen, and William J. Murin, *Urban Policy and Politics in a Bureaucratic Age*, 2d ed. (Englewood Cliffs, N.J., 1986); Douglas Yates, *The Ungovernable City: The Politics of Urban Problems and Policy Making* (Cambridge, Mass., 1977).

Central to policy themes is the acquisition and use of political power in American cities. David C. Hammack's *Power and Society: Greater New York at the Turn of the Century* (New York, 1982) is a model study of interest-group dynamics in policy formation. See also Alan D. Anderson, *The Origin and Resolution of an Urban Crisis: Baltimore, 1890–1930* (Baltimore, 1977); Robert A. Caro, *The Power Broker: Robert Moses and the Fall of New York* (New York, 1974); Joe R. Feagin, *Free Enterprise City: Houston in Political and Economic Perspective* (New Brunswick, N.J., 1988); Carl V. Harris, *Political Power in Birmingham, 1871–1921* (Knoxville, Tenn., 1977); Floyd Hunter, *Community Power Structure: A Study of Decision Makers* (Chapel Hill, N.C., 1953); and Clarence Stone and H. Sanders, eds., *The Politics of Urban Development* (Cambridge, Mass., 1987). For more traditional attention to the "bosses and reformers" theme in American urban history, see several of the bibliographic essays listed above.

In the last five or six years, a few historians have turned to the important, if not eye-catching, issue of urban fiscal policy. Terrence J. McDonald has produced some of the most impressive work in this area. See *The Parameters of Urban Fiscal Policy: Socioeconomic Change and Political Culture in San Francisco* (Berkeley and Los Angeles, 1987) and McDonald and Sally K. Ward, eds., *The Politics of Urban Fiscal Policy* (Beverly Hills, Calif., 1984). On economic planning, see Carl Abbott, "Perspectives on

Urban Economic Planning: The Case of Washington, D.C., Since 1880,"
Public Historian 11 (Spring 1989): 5–21; and "Planning and Financing
Public Works: Three Historical Cases," in *Essays in Public Works History*,
15 (Chicago, 1987).

Planning history has a long tradition among urban historians. For in-
sights about the relationship between urban planning and public policy,
see M. Christine Boyer, *Dreaming the Rational City: The Myth of American
City Planning* (Cambridge, Mass., 1983); Laurence C. Gerckens, "Histori-
cal Development of American City Planning," in Frank S. So, et al., *The
Practice of Local Government Planning* (Washington, D.C., 1979), 21–57;
Stephen W. Grable, "Applying Urban History to City Planning: A Case
Study in Atlanta," *Public Historian* 1 (Summer 1979): 45–63; Charles M.
Haar and Michael Allan Wolf, *Land-use Planning: A Casebook on the Use,
Misuse, and Re-use of Urban Land* (Boston, 1989); Donald A. Krueckeberg,
ed., *Introduction to Planning History in the United States* (New Brunswick,
N.J., 1983); Roy H. Lopata, "Historians in City Planning: A Personal
View," *Public Historian* 1 (Summer 1979): 40–44; Roy H. Lopata, "Small
Cities Planning from a Historic Perspective," *Public Historian* 4 (Winter
1982): 53–64; Raymond A. Mohl and Neil Betten, "The Failure of Indus-
trial City Planning: Gary, Indiana, 1906–1910," *Journal of the American
Institute of Planners* 38 (1972): 202–15; Christine M. Rosen, *The Limits of
Power: Great Fires and the Process of City Growth in America* (New York,
1986); and Sam Bass Warner, Jr., ed., *Planning for a Nation of Cities*
(Cambridge, Mass., 1966).

While few studies attempt to deal in any depth with the broad topic of
social policy, several studies are suggestive. Kenneth T. Jackson in *Crabgrass Frontier: The Suburbanization of the United States* (New York, 1985)
raises several important themes, especially with respect to inner city versus suburban development. See also Steven J. Diner, *A City and Its
Universities: Public Policy in Chicago, 1882–1919* (Chapel Hill, N.C.,
1980); Hugh Davis Graham and Ted Robert Gurr, eds., *Violence in America* (Beverly Hills, Calif., 1979); Stephanie W. Greenberg, "Neighborhood Change, Racial Transition, and Work Location: A Case Study in an
Industrial City, Philadelphia, 1880–1930," *Journal of Urban History* 7
(May 1981): 267–314; Robert Fisher, *Let the People Decide: Neighborhood
Organizing in America* (Boston, 1984); Robert Fisher and Peter Ro-
manofsky, eds., *Community Organizations for Urban Social Change: A Historical Perspective* (Westport, Conn., 1981); Robert W. Fogelson, *Violence
as Protest: A Study of Riots and Ghettos* (Garden City, N.Y., 1971); and
William J. Wilson, *The Truly Disadvantaged: The Inner City, the Un-
derclass, and Public Policy* (Chicago, 1987).

The literature on housing is extensive and includes a variety of themes affecting all social and economic classes. See Martin Anderson, *The Federal Bulldozer: A Critical Analysis of Urban Renewal, 1949–1962* (Cambridge, Mass., 1964); William R. Barnes, "A National Controversy in Miniature: The District of Columbia Struggle over Public Housing and Redevelopment, 1943–46," *Prologue* 9 (1977): 91–104; John F. Bauman, *Public Housing, Race, and Renewal: Urban Planning in Philadelphia, 1920–1974* (Philadelphia, 1987); Ronald H. Bayor, "Urban Renewal, Public Housing, and the Racial Shaping of Atlanta," *Journal of Policy History* 1 (1989): 419–39; Tridib Banerjee and William C. Baer, *Beyond the Neighborhood Unit: Residential Environments and Public Policy* (New York, 1984); Robert B. Fairbanks, *Making Better Citizens: Housing Reform and Community Development Strategy in Cincinnati, 1890–1960* (Urbana, Ill., 1988); Howard Gillette, Jr., "The Evolution of Neighborhood Planning: From the Progressive Era to the 1949 Housing Act," *Journal of Urban History* 9 (August 1983): 421–44; Arnold R. Hirsch, *Making the Second Ghetto: Race and Housing in Chicago, 1940–1960* (New York, 1983); Mark B. Lapping, "The Emergence of Federal Public Housing: Atlanta's Techwood Project," *American Journal of Economics and Sociology* 32 (Summer 1973): 379–85; Frederick Lazin, "Policy Perception of Program Failure: The Politics of Public Housing in Chicago and New York City," *Urbanism Past and Present* 9 (Winter 1979–80): 1–12; Peter Marcuse, "Housing Policy and City Planning: The Puzzling Split in the United States, 1893–1931," in Gordon E. Cherry, ed., *Shaping an Urban World* (New York, 1980), 23–58; Roger Montgomery, ed., "Pruitt-Igoe: Policy Failure or Societal System," in Barry Checkoway and Carl V. Patton, eds., *The Metropolitan Midwest, Policy Problems and Prospects for Change* (Urbana, Ill., 1985), 229–43; Roger D. Simon, *The City-Building Process: Housing and Services in the New Milwaukee Neighborhoods, 1880–1910* (Philadelphia, 1978); Robert A. Slayton, *Back of the Yards: The Making of a Local Democracy* (Chicago, 1986); Robert A. Slayton, "The Flophouse: Housing and Public Policy for the Single Poor," *Journal of Policy History* 1 (1989): 373–90; and Marc A. Weiss, *The Rise of the Community Builders: The American Real Estate Industry and Urban Land Planning* (New York, 1987).

Transportation policy is a central issue in urban development. The literature on automobiles and mass transit is well developed. Of particular value on establishing transportation policy is Joel A. Tarr's "Transportation Innovation and Changing Spatial Patterns in Pittsburgh, 1859–1934," *Essays in Public Works History*, no. 6 (Chicago, 1978). See also Sy Adler, "Infrastructure Politics: The Dynamics of Crossing San Francisco

Bay," *Public Historian* 10 (Fall 1988): 19–41; Alan Altshuler with James P. Womack and John R. Pucher, *The Urban Transportation System: Politics and Policy Innovation* (Cambridge, Mass., 1979); Paul Barrett, *The Automobile and Urban Transit: The Formation of Public Policy in Chicago, 1900–1930* (Philadelphia, 1983); Charles W. Cheape, *Moving the Masses: Urban Public Transit in New York, Boston, and Philadelphia, 1880–1912* (Philadelphia, 1980); Michael Chernoff, "The Effects of Superhighways in Urban Areas," *Urban Affairs Quarterly* 16 (March 1981): 317–36; Mark S. Foster, "The Automobile in the Urban Environment: Planning for an Energy-Short Future," *Public Historian* 3 (Fall 1981): 23–31; Mark S. Foster, *From Streetcar to Superhighway: American City Planners and Urban Transportation* (Philadelphia, 1981); Charles N. Glaab, *Kansas City and the Railroads: Community Policy in the Growth of a Regional Metropolis* (Madison, Wis., 1962); Clay McShane, *Technology and Reform: Street Railways and the Growth of Milwaukee, 1887–1900* (Madison, Wis., 1974); Mark N. Rose, *Interstate: Express Highway Politics, 1941–1956* (Lawrence, Kan., 1979); Glenn Yago, *The Decline of Transit: Urban Transportation in German and U.S. Cities, 1900–1970* (New York, 1984); and Olivier Zunz, "Technology and Society in an Urban Environment: The Case of the Third Avenue Elevated Railway," *Journal of Interdisciplinary History* 3 (Summer 1972): 89–101. More recently, a few studies on air travel and airports have begun to appear and promise to broaden our understanding of how cities are connected to the outside world and how they deal with this specialized land-use problem. See Paul Barrett, "Cities and Their Airports: Policy Formation, 1926–1952," *Journal of Urban History* 14 (November 1987): 112–37; Paul David Friedman, "Fear of Flying: Airport Noise, Airport Neighbors," *Public Historian* 1 (Summer 1979): 63–66; and Dorothy Nelkin, *Jetport: The Boston Airport Controversy* (New Brunswick, N.J., 1974).

Public works history, including transportation, has become a rich area of inquiry in recent years for studying the physical development of cities and the implications for growth. Studies of infrastructure, city services, and technical systems, once an idiosyncratic research area for historians, has become more central to urban history. A good starting point is Eugene P. Moehring, "Public Works and Urban History: Recent Trends and New Directions," in *Essays in Public Works History*, no. 13 (Chicago, 1982). Sam Bass Warner, Jr.'s, *Streetcar Suburbs: The Process of Growth in Boston, 1870–1900* (Cambridge, Mass., 1978) helped to set the standard for studying the impact of technology on urban growth. Joel A. Tarr and Gabriel Dupuy, eds., *Technology and the Rise of the Networked City in Europe and America* (Philadelphia, 1988), articulate many of the major themes in dealing with urban systems. See also David T. Beito with Bruce Smith, "The Formation of Urban Infrastructure Through Nongovernmental Planning: The Private Places of St. Louis, 1869–1920," *Journal of Urban History* 16 (May 1990): 263–303; Shelley Bookspan, "Potentially Responsible Party Searches: Finding the Cause of Urban Grime," *Public Historian* 13 (Spring 1991): 25–34; Louis P. Cain, *Sanitation Strategy for the Lakefront Metropolis: The Case of Chicago* (De Kalb, Ill., 1978); Carl W. Condit, *Chicago, 1910–1929: Building, Planning, and Urban Technology* (Chicago, 1974); Carl W. Condit, *Chicago, 1930–1970: Building, Planning and Urban Technology* (Chicago, 1974); Suellen M. Hoy and Michael C. Robinson, "Historical Analysis: A New Management Tool for Public Works Administrators," *Public Works* 108 (June 1977): 88–89; "Infrastructure and Urban Growth in the Nineteenth Century," in *Essays in Public Works History*, no. 14 (Chicago, 1985); Rita C. Lynch, "Experiencing a City: Public Works and Public History—Kansas City, Missouri, and Beyond," *Public Historian* 1 (Spring 1979): 77–82; Martin V. Melosi, *Garbage in the Cities: Refuse, Reform, and the Environment, 1880–1980* (College Station, Tex., 1981); Martin V. Melosi, ed., *Pollution and Reform in American Cities, 1870–1930* (Austin, Tex., 1980); Eugene P. Moehring, *Public Works and the Patterns of Real Estate Growth in Manhattan, 1835–1894* (New York, 1981); David L. Nass, "Public Policy and Public Works: Niagara Falls Redevelopment as a Case Study," in *Essays in Public Works History*, no. 7 (Chicago, 1979); Jon Peterson, "The Impact of Sanitary Reform upon American Urban Planning, 1840–1890," *Journal of Social History* 13 (Fall 1979): 83–103; Harold L. Platt, *City Building in the New South: The Growth of Public Services in Houston, 1830–1915* (Philadelphia, 1983); Harold L. Platt, *The Electric City: Energy and the Growth of the Chicago Area, 1880–1930* (Chicago, 1991); and "Public-Private Partnerships in Historical Perspective," in *Essays in Public Works History*, no. 16 (Chicago, 1989). A new journal, *Flux*, published in France, treats several of the urban technical systems from an international perspective.

On the general topic of federal-city relations, see Mark I. Gelfand, *A Nation of Cities: The Federal Government and Urban America, 1933–1965* (New York, 1975); Kenneth Fox, *Metropolitan America: Urban Life and Urban Policy in the United States, 1940–1980* (Jackson, Miss., 1986); and John H. Mollenkopf, *The Contested City* (Princeton, 1983). See also Joseph L. Arnold, *The New Deal in the Suburbs: A History of the Greenbelt Town Program, 1935–1954* (Columbus, Ohio, 1971); Philip J. Funigiello, *The Challenge of Urban Liberalism: Federal-City Relations During World War II* (Knoxville, Tenn., 1978); and Roger W. Lotchin, ed., *The Martial*

Metropolis: U.S. Cities in War and Peace (New York, 1984). On cities and regionalism see also Roberta Balstad Miller, *City and Hinterland: A Case Study of Urban Growth and Regional Development* (Westport, Conn., 1979).

Some useful studies that do not fit easily into the above categories include Hans Blumenfeld, "Continuity and Change in Urban Form: The City's Identity Problem," *Journal of Urban History* 1 (February 1975): 131–48; Steven J. Diner, "Writing History for Urban Policymakers," *AHA Perspectives* 20 (November 1982): 11–14; Howard Gillette, Jr., "A National Workshop for Urban Policy: The Metropolitanization of Washington, 1946–1968," *Public Historian* 7 (Winter 1985): 7–27; and Seymour J. Mandelbaum, "Urban Pasts and Urban Policies," *Journal of Urban History* 6 (August 1980): 453–83.

Contributors

MARTIN V. MELOSI is Professor of History and Director of the Institute for Public Policy at the University of Houston. His areas of research include urban, environmental, and energy history. Among his publications are *Garbage in the Cities* (1981), *Coping with Abundance* (1985), and *Thomas A. Edison and the Modernization of America* (1990). He is currently working on a study of the impact of technical systems on urban growth.

CARL ABBOTT is Professor of Urban Studies and Planning at Portland State University. He has special interests in regional differences in American urbanization and in the evolution of urban policy since 1940.

PAUL GEORGE LEWIS is a Ph.D. candidate at Princeton University. His interests include urban politics, political economy, and local and national policy-making. His dissertation examines how political forces are shaping contemporary suburban development.

NOEL A. CAZENAVE is Associate Professor of Sociology at The University of Connecticut. His teaching and research interests include poverty and equality, racism and public policy, social-and economic-justice movements, and political sociology. He is currently conducting a study of social science experts and community participation in precursors to the U.S. "War on Poverty."

SY ADLER is Associate Professor of Urban Studies and Planning at Portland State University. He teaches and does research in the areas of urban transportation policy, planning theory and practice, urban politics, and policy analysis.

HAROLD L. PLATT is Professor of History at Loyola University of Chicago. He is author of *The Electric City: Energy and the Growth of the Chicago Area, 1880–1930* (1991) and is writing a book on the environmental history of the city's energy system.

ALAN MAYNE is a graduate of the Australian National University and currently teaches comparative urban and immigration history at the University of Melbourne. He is coordinator of an interdisciplinary undergraduate program in heritage studies.

SEYMORE J. MANDELBAUM is Professor of Urban History in the Department of City and Regional Planning at the University of Pennsylvania. His current work deals with the poetics of policy and planning arguments.

Printed in the United States
64084LVS00003B/128